THE COSMIC VISION
OF TEILHARD DE CHARDIN

THE COSMIC VISION OF
TEILHARD DE CHARDIN

John F. Haught

ORBIS BOOKS

Maryknoll, New York 10545

Founded in 1970, Orbis Books endeavors to publish works that enlighten the mind, nourish the spirit, and challenge the conscience. The publishing arm of the Maryknoll Fathers and Brothers, Orbis seeks to explore the global dimensions of the Christian faith and mission, to invite dialogue with diverse cultures and religious traditions, and to serve the cause of reconciliation and peace. The books published reflect the views of their authors and do not represent the official position of the Maryknoll Society. To learn more about Orbis Books, please visit our website at www.orbisbooks.com.

Copyright © 2021 by John F. Haught

Published by Orbis Books, P.O. Box 302, Maryknoll, NY 10545-0302.

Manufactured in the United States of America

Manuscript editing and typesetting by Joan Weber Laflamme.

Library of Congress Cataloging-in-Publication Data

Names: Haught, John F., author.
Title: The cosmic vision of Teilhard de Chardin / John F. Haught.
Description: Maryknoll, New York : Orbis Books, [2021] | Includes bibliographical references and index. | Summary: "Brings the thought and theology of Teilhard de Chardin into conversation with other significant religious thinkers, philosophers, and scientists"— Provided by publisher.
Identifiers: LCCN 2021020061 (print) | LCCN 2021020062 (ebook) | ISBN 9781626984493 (trade paperback) | ISBN 9781608339129 (epub)
Subjects: LCSH: Teilhard de Chardin, Pierre. | Catholic Church—Clergy—Biography. | Cosmology. | Evolution—Religious aspects—Catholic Church. | Religion and science. | Religion—Philosophy. | Philosophers—France—Biography. | Theologians—France—Biography. | Paleontologists—France—Biography.
Classification: LCC B2430.T374 H29 2021 (print) | LCC B2430.T374 (ebook) | DDC 194—dc23
LC record available at https://lccn.loc.gov/2021020061
LC ebook record available at https://lccn.loc.gov/202102006

*I dedicate this book to friends of
Teilhard de Chardin everywhere,
both here on earth now,
and anywhere else in the universe
where they will be gathering
in the future*

CONTENTS

INTRODUCTION

When I was in my early twenties, I began reading the works of the Jesuit geologist and paleontologist Pierre Teilhard de Chardin (1881–1955), prompting my lifelong interest in science and religion. From 1966 to 1970, I studied theology at the Catholic University of America in Washington, DC, and while working on my doctoral thesis, I began teaching part time at Georgetown University across town. After getting my degree in 1970, I joined the regular faculty at Georgetown. In the early 1970s, I developed a course for undergraduates on science and religion and taught it almost every year until I retired from teaching. I was not trained as a scientist, so I had to do a lot of reading in physics, cosmology, biology, and other disciplines for which most theologians do not usually have the time.

Connecting a scientifically informed cosmic awareness to our spiritual lives was Teilhard's main preoccupation throughout his adult life, and it has become my own as well. Had it not been for Teilhard's influence, my own theological and academic life could have gone in other directions. I first encountered Teilhard's cosmic vision soon after graduating from college in 1964 and was immediately swept away by the power and freshness of his thought. I did not realize fully at the time that my excitement was due also to the fact that I was becoming dissatisfied intellectually and spiritually with the medieval theological worldview presupposed by my religious education up to that point. Before encountering Teilhard, I had been studying in a Catholic seminary where I had been schooled in Scholastic philosophy, much of which I was required to read and memorize in the original Latin. I am grateful for having had the opportunity to study medieval thought, including that of Thomas Aquinas. I began to realize long ago, however, that Thomas's prescientific philosophy, ingenious and adventurous as it was in the thirteenth century, cannot fully contextualize contemporary science—although some Catholic philosophers and theologians are still attempting to forge such a synthesis. I appreciate the effort and good will behind these attempts, but I believe they are intellectually and spiritually inadequate given what we now know about the universe in the age of science, especially after Darwin and Einstein.

In any case, I left the seminary soon after the Second Vatican Council and began immediately to pursue a career in academic theology as a layperson. My decision to take up theological studies was a consequence not only of my reading of Teilhard but also of my earlier exposure to the writings of Karl Rahner and contemporary biblical scholarship, including especially that of my teacher, the Johannine scholar Raymond Brown. To this day I am grateful for the historical-critical understanding of scripture since it liberates theology from the anachronistic impulse to seek scientific information in the Bible. This is a lesson that countless Christians and most anti-Christian evolutionists have yet to learn.

As I recall, however, it was mostly due to the excitement I had felt in my growing acquaintance at that time with Teilhard's Christian vision of nature and evolution that I found myself drawn to a life in systematic theology. From the start, Teilhard has been an inspiration to me both intellectually and spiritually. I am not as uncritical of his thought today as I may have been when I was younger, but I still draw upon the audacity of his cosmic vision.

When I first explored his writings, Teilhard's bold ideas had already influenced some of the theological reflection that would make the Second Vatican Council such an important event in the history of the church as well as in my personal life. Teilhard had begun developing his ideas on God, cosmology, and evolution in *The Human Phenomenon* and *The Divine Milieu* while he was living in China—where he became one of the most highly esteemed geologists of the Asian continent. Because of church censorship, however, Teilhard was never given the opportunity to expose his work to the critique of other experts. No doubt, then, there are deficiencies in his writings that could easily have been avoided and corrected had his beloved church allowed for the circulation of his ideas.

After Teilhard's death in 1955, at any rate, his lay friends fed his manuscripts to hungry publishers who marketed them widely. Some of these were immediately devoured by theologians who helped shape the documents of the Second Vatican Council. Teilhard's hope for the future of humanity and of our need to take responsibility for "building the earth" greatly influenced one of modern Catholicism's main documents, *Gaudium et Spes.* This is ironic because, in 1962, the same year the council met for its first session, the Holy Office of the Vatican issued an admonition advising seminary professors and heads of Catholic colleges and universities to "protect the minds, particularly of the youth, against the dangers presented by the works of Fr. Teilhard de Chardin and his followers." Fortunately, I was one of those who escaped the efforts to protect the tender minds of young Catholics.

Because of the theological ferment fostered by Vatican II, my own theological understanding began to evolve during my time at Catholic University. It was then that a developing sense of the cosmic future started to become the main preoccupation of my theology. With Teilhard, I maintain that, in the light of geology, evolutionary biology, and contemporary post-Einsteinian cosmology, theology needs to begin with the observation that the cosmos remains a work in progress. For if the cosmos is still coming into being, we may entertain the thought that something of great importance may be starting to form, at least vaguely, up ahead, and that human technology and morally chastened engineering will be increasingly essential to the shaping of the terrestrial future, perhaps in ways that we cannot yet imagine.

Concern for the cosmic future and for what is going on in the physical universe has not yet become a major theme in Western theology. Classical Christianity and its theologies first came to expression at a time when people took for granted that the universe is fundamentally fixed and unchanging. Today, however, especially because of developments in the natural sciences, theologians can no longer plausibly ignore the fact that the whole universe, not just life and human history, is still in the process of becoming. A sense of the universe as a still unfinished drama of awakening has yet to settle deeply into Christian spiritual and theological sensibilities. Theology and religious instruction still tend, for the most part, to nurture nostalgia for a lost Eden, or else they look skyward toward a final heavenly communion with a God who is thought to exist timelessly, apart from natural history and the cosmic future. Meanwhile, intellectual life, philosophy of science, and journalistic culture remain tied to a deadening materialist pessimism that undermines any hope that the cosmos can somehow be rescued from the jaws of meaninglessness.

With Teilhard, I believe that Christian hope needs to be channeled into a common human concern for a cosmic and not just human salvation. In other words, religious expectation may look forward not only to everlasting communion of human persons with God but also to the fulfillment of an entire universe, as Pope Francis affirms in his 2015 encyclical, *Laudato Si'*.[1] The God of Abraham who arrives from out of the future when it seems that everything has reached a dead end may now be sought by looking in the direction of a new future not only for individual souls but also for the cosmos. Abrahamic faith in the age of science anticipates not only human and personal redemption but also the transfiguration of the whole universe into wondrous beauty saved everlastingly in the heart of God. Science's fresh picture of the cosmos as an unfinished drama rather than a fixed design gives new significance and wider scope than ever to the ancient Abrahamic expectations.

Both as a scientist and as a religious thinker, Teilhard sought to make sense of evolution. Evolution, as he understood it broadly, is a process in which the natural world is becoming more, giving rise to fuller being over the course of time. But at each stage of its journey, the cosmos becomes *more* only by organizing itself around successively new and higher centers. Teilhard called this recurrent cosmic trend "centration." Centration occurred very early in cosmic history when subatomic elements organized themselves around an atomic nucleus. Centration happened later when large molecules clustered around nuclear DNA in the eukaryotic cell, and still later when the "central" nervous system took shape in vertebrate evolution.

At present, the latest dominant units in terrestrial evolution are human persons, and they too can be centrated—brought together socially into higher organic syntheses—only if there exists a powerfully attractive unifying center that is also personal. Human persons cannot be fully alive or moved to "become more" except by surrender in faith to the reality of a magnetic, transcendent, promising personal Center to which the whole universe may still be in the early stages of awakening. In the following chapters I ask what this cosmic awakening means by looking with Teilhard at a variety of topics: the cosmos, the future, hope, humanity, morality, spirituality, God, life, suffering, religion, thought, and transhumanism. In a final chapter I respond to several criticisms of Teilhard's thought.

Ordained a priest in 1911, Teilhard became a stretcher-bearer during World War I and received awards for his courage in battle. It was especially during his life in the trenches that his cosmic spiritual vision began to take shape. After the war and the completion of his studies in Paris, he journeyed to China, where he became one of the most respected geologists in the Far East. It was there that he began to compose his great synthesis of science and faith, *The Human Phenomenon*. Both the Vatican and Teilhard's religious superiors, however, forbade its publication. It appeared in print only after his death in New York in 1955.

Snubbed by his own church during his lifetime, this great scientist and visionary has arguably turned out to be the most important Christian thinker of the past century. For those interested in the relationship of faith to thought and action, I am convinced that no spiritual writers have more to offer even today. Only time will assign Teilhard his proper place in the history of ideas. But those of us who believe that Christianity—for the sake of its credibility and even its survival—must eventually come to grips with science, and especially evolution, Teilhard continues to shine forth as a model of honesty, openness, and courage.

It is true that Teilhard draws less attention today than he did fifty or sixty years ago, but his thought is by no means obsolete. As theologian Jean Lacouture commented a half century ago, "The Catholic Church is in great need of the abrasive, energizing breath of a new Teilhard. Or in the interim (why not?) a return to Teilhard? Or, quite simply, a welcome for Teilhard?"[2]

During the Great War (World War I), having already studied geology as a seminarian and young priest, Teilhard became increasingly convinced that the evolutionary sciences require a new understanding of almost everything, starting with the universe itself. Each chapter of this book, therefore, brings out some of the changes in our understanding of God and the universe that Teilhard was beginning to consider essential in the light of evolutionary biology and cosmology.

These chapters are not intended to be an exposition or condensation of Teilhard's thought. Instead, they are an application of some of his main ideas about the cosmos to questions that still arise today when we reflect on the universe, life, thought, God, and other topics. Given the major shifts in cosmology that have occurred after Einstein, how is Christian theology going to approach the question of whether there are good reasons for our hope? What is the meaning of human existence? Will there be opportunities after Darwin and Einstein for the renewal of spiritual life? What shall we mean henceforth by the word *God,* if anything at all? What is the meaning of life, suffering, morality, religion, and the amazing phenomenon of thought?

Since Teilhard's death in 1955, new developments have taken place in biology, cosmology, and other scientific fields. So, one cannot expect that his books and essays will respond perfectly to all the questions we raise today about the religious and theological implications of science. Nevertheless, Teilhard left us with "lines of thought" whose general drift remains as exciting and liberating today as ever. The present book is not a scholastic reproduction of his ideas but a set of reflections on what his main ideas about the universe can mean for those who have felt the spirit of his powerful ideas. Let us begin by looking with Teilhard at how the cosmos has become the greatest story ever told.

1

COSMOS

When I was in graduate school in the late 1960s, I came across the following lines from Jürgen Moltmann's *A Theology of Hope*:

> From first to last, and not merely in the epilogue, Christianity is eschatology, is *hope*, forward looking and forward moving, and therefore also revolutionizing and transforming the present. The eschatological [hope] is not one element *of* Christianity, but it is the medium of Christian faith as such, the key in which everything in it is set, the glow that suffuses everything here in the dawn of an expected new day. . . . Hence eschatology [hope] cannot really be only a part of Christian doctrine. Rather, the eschatological outlook [hope] is characteristic of all Christian proclamation, of every Christian existence and of the whole church. There is therefore only one real problem in Christian theology . . . the problem of the future.[1]

To this day I believe that Moltmann, whose prolific writings continue to make him the greatest contemporary theologian of hope, is right on target in his understanding of what is most essential to Christian faith. His powerful writings still move me and many others. Yet, it was not through reading Moltmann that I first came to embrace hope and the coming of the future as the main theme of my subsequent theological efforts. It was through my studying the works of the Jesuit geologist and paleontologist Pierre Teilhard de Chardin.

A year or so before reading Moltmann, I had already begun wrestling critically with Teilhard's vision of the world, and it was his writings that first convinced me that the substance of Christian faith lies in its fundamental concern about the future. The future that Teilhard pointed to, however, is not just the final state of the individual soul or the goal of human history. More fundamentally, it is the future of the *cosmos*. Teilhard convinced me that the whole universe must now be set in "the glow that suffuses everything here in the dawn of an expected new day." Our personal hopes, he emphasized, find their true ambience and fullest satisfaction only in company with the fulfillment of *all things*, that is, in what the apostle Paul referred to as "the whole creation."

Teilhard situated his evolutionary worldview inside the ancient Pauline intuition that the entirety of creation finds its fulfillment in the universal Christ, "in whom all things consist" (Col 1:1). Teilhard's spiritual life was itself a search for what he called *consistence*, that is, something that holds all things together. Ultimately, "all things" are gathered up and held together by Jesus Christ, whose fullest being lies not in the past or present but in the future (Eph 1:15–22). For a time the scientist Teilhard wondered if the seeming solidity of elemental matter might not be the unifying principle that keeps the universe from falling apart, as materialists still claim. However, he soon came to realize that the more refined our analysis of matter becomes, and the farther back we look into the cosmic past with the tools of physical science, the more we discover that matter itself falls apart into subatomic bits, that is, into a state of incoherence.

As he grew in both scientific and theological understanding, Teilhard came to believe that the universe's true coherence belongs to the future, not the past or present. The Pauline Christ is for Teilhard the promise, center, and goal of cosmic process. Over the centuries, unfortunately, Christianity lost the sense that our own redemption is tied up with God's bringing the whole universe to a head, *anakephalaiosis* (cf. Eph 1:10 and, later, Irenaeus of Lyons), in Christ. Teilhard, more than any other recent Christian thinker, has brought back the ancient biblical and patristic sense that the whole universe is to be redeemed and renewed.

Moreover, what theology had formerly idealized as the primacy of spirit gradually became for Teilhard the primacy of the Future. A good name for this Future is "God." The idea that God *comes* from the future, of course, has long been associated with Abrahamic faith, but it took a Marxist philosopher (Ernst Bloch) and a creative young Christian theologian (Jürgen Moltmann) to remind us, in the twentieth century, that Futurity is God's *very essence*. So, we may now think of God, in the words of the Catholic theologian Karl Rahner, as the world's "Absolute Future."[2]

This does not mean that God is absent from the here and now. But God is present in the here and now as a gracious horizon of "futurity" that keeps inviting the universe, in ways that are always mysterious, to keep moving deeper into the territory of the "not-yet." God acts characteristically not by moving the world from out of the past or from above, but by opening up the past and present to new modes of being up ahead. God acts in the present not by overwhelming and dissolving the world, but by "going before" it as an endless source of opportunities for its becoming *more*.

God is the Future that empowers the world to exist as something distinct from God. But the "Power of the Future," as theologian Wolfhart Pannenberg refers to God, is also deeply incarnate in each present moment, generously opening it up to what is unprecedented and unpredictable.[3] Divine creativity provides an immensity of space and time in which the whole universe may constantly be made new. Although, in giving rise to human consciousness, the universe has already attained a most consequential outcome, the growth of the universe is not yet complete. Since the cosmos is always subject to drifting back toward the past state of physical dispersal, its emerging unity can be sustained only if it allows itself to be further created, that is, brought into deeper communion with God, the Center and goal of *all things*. Theologically, Infinite Love is the vital energy of this movement toward a new future for the universe. Love is the means by which the Power of the Future holds *all things* together even now, opening up for each person, for each living community, and for the whole cosmos, the prospect of deeper consistence and richer coherence up ahead.

The cosmos, Teilhard came to realize, gives rise to living and conscious syntheses only by being drawn toward the future amid "endless attempts and setbacks."[4] So, the universe becomes more alive and more conscious only by constantly resisting the drift backward toward the atomicity of its remote past. The attractive power that calls the universe into being and that sustains, unifies, and illuminates its passage in deep time is ultimately the divine Love incarnate in Christ. God's love works by opening creation to a new future, and so our human vocation is also that of opening up a new future for everything and everyone we profess to love.

Human love flourishes most fully and effectively where there is a sustained—indeed intergenerational—expectation that something really big is awaiting *all things* up ahead. In the contemporary intellectual world and its academic culture, however, it is hard to find such expectation. Even in Christian life and thought, cosmic hope seems weak. In the world of scientific thought we even find a general mood of despair about the cosmic future. This pessimism is unfortunate because wherever hope is absent, love scarcely has a chance to survive, let alone flourish. No doubt cosmic pessimists find some warmth in huddling together in the darkness of what they take to be a pointless universe. But can love find sufficient nourishment unless what we love has a future? And can we *fully* love the universe unless we place it in "the dawn of an expected new day"? Can we humans fully love one another unless, in some way, we are assured that *all things* have a future?

It is these questions that underlie Teilhard's novel thoughts about the cosmos and its growth. The universe, he points out, has not yet reached the goal of full consistence and coherence. It is still "on the way." The idea that nature can give birth to new kinds of being during the passage of time, however, should never have been disturbing to Christians. An impression that creation can change dramatically, and that life in some way "evolves," is an ancient one. Even St. Augustine (354–430) had proposed that new kinds of life come into being during the course of terrestrial time from "seed principles" sown by the Creator in the beginning. God is not only the one who initially creates and subsequently sustains the world's existence but also the one "who makes all things new" (Isa 42:9; Rev 21:5).

According to Teilhard, what evolution teaches us right away is that God makes things make themselves. Since creation is not yet finished, considerable doctrinal space remains in theological tradition to accommodate a Darwinian understanding of evolution. Consequently, scientifically enlightened Christians do not have to fear that there is any conflict whatsoever between the idea of evolutionary descent and the theological doctrine of continuous and new creation. Think of the Creator as bringing into being a world that can, in turn, give rise spontaneously to new life and lush diversity, and eventually to the human mind. The divine maker of such a self-creative world is arguably much more impressive—hence worthier of human reverence and gratitude—than is a "designer," who molds and micromanages everything directly.[5]

Theology long ago took it for granted that God keeps on creating in the mode of secondary causation, that is, through natural causes. Even in Genesis, God says, "'Let the *earth* bring forth living creatures of every kind: cattle and creeping things and wild animals of the earth of every kind.' And it was so" (Gen 1:24, emphasis added). God is the underlying creative principle, but creation comes about by relying on the lawfulness, consistence, and spontaneity of nature.

What evolutionary science implies, however, is that as the cosmos unfolds from one level of physical complexity to the next it passes through three distinct phases: divergence, convergence, and emergence. For example, as individual cells (single-celled forms of life) began to inhabit our planet, they spent a couple billion years simply spreading out over the face of the globe. This is the phase of *divergence*. But at a certain point a critical threshold is passed, and then the cells began to coagulate, first in loose associations, but later in tighter and more integrated forms of communion. This is the phase of *convergence*. Eventually, as the convergence of cells grows tighter, more complex organisms enter the cosmic scene. This is the stage of *emergence*.[6]

The same sequence—divergence, followed by convergence, followed by emergence—has repeated itself at every stage of cosmogenesis. So, let us move forward to the latest dominant development in life's evolution, the period during which humans began to take over the earth. Starting around 200,000 years ago, modern humans began spreading out, diverging into familial and tribal patterns of existence. Then, about five to eight thousand years ago, in places like the Nile River basin and Mesopotamia, the smaller individual tribes began to converge into tighter and increasingly complex social arrangements. The increasing compression of people led to the emergence of the ancient city-states and more recently nations. If we look at what has been happening historically, politically, economically, and technologically, the earth is now undergoing an increasingly rapid convergence. Human existence on our planet is now arriving at the threshold of a new phase of terrestrial and cosmic history. What, then, will the earth look like a million years from now, keeping in mind that a million years is not a very long timespan in evolution? Maybe a new and richer kind of emergence, now unpredictable, is eventually to take place on the horizon of the not-yet.

And what if intelligent life exists elsewhere in the universe? I think that if he were alive today, Teilhard would pay closer attention to this question than he did. His bold thoughts could be stretched in an age of SETI (the Search for Extraterrestrial Intelligence) to cover the whole cosmos. We know that, over the course of deep time, a gradual increase in organized physical complexity has been going on throughout the Big Bang universe starting with pre-atomic matter, followed by the birth of atoms, molecules, and then the carbon compounds that make up a good percentage of interstellar dust. We know without a doubt that the trend toward increasing physical complexity has advanced at least to the stage of distributing organic molecules throughout the vast cosmic expanses. We also know that, at least on earth, the process of complexifying matter has gone even further. Out of the organic molecules have emerged cells, organisms, vertebrates, and primates, including humans.

Presently, at least here on earth, a lively envelope of "thought" is beginning to take shape on a global scale. Who knows what else might emerge in the terrestrial and cosmic journey as it moves toward the not-yet? No doubt, engaging in such speculation seems premature for most people. Yet Teilhard provides an intelligible framework for those who dare to think large thoughts about our universe and its future possibilities. What remains undeniable, at least, is that the "human phenomenon" is now weaving itself collectively into a new "geological" stratum encircling our planet, taking advantage of the cultural complexity being spun by politics, economics, education, scientific developments, and especially communications technology. Teilhard, incidentally, is sometimes called the "prophet of the Internet" because he predicted that, through technological complexification, the earth would be increasingly encircled by "thought." He called this new planetary level of being the "noosphere" (from the Greek word *nous,* "mind").

Teilhard, as a devout Christian, had read the letters of the apostle Paul prayerfully. He took seriously Paul's sense that the whole universe is straining toward new creation. The Pauline cosmic vision is one that Teilhard developed using the evolutionary concepts of the twentieth century. What he saw happening on our planet reminded him of what had occurred a long time ago in evolution when the primate brain became sufficiently complicated to make the leap into "thought." Presently, we may notice that the social, political, informational, and technological complexification of our planet is analogous to the brain's evolution in complexity long ago. The earth is weaving around itself something akin to a brain. Is it also about to blossom into something new once again?

The formation of a noosphere is so recent that science does not yet know quite what to make of it. In evolution, after all, major innovations usually take millions of years, but the formation of the noosphere so far is a matter of only thousands. Perhaps in the long run it will turn out that the new sphere of "thought" is just barely dawning at present. The earth, having only recently given birth to the noosphere, could be moving in the direction of being unified and made new by the birth of a planetary consciousness. The sweeping movements of matter, life, and thought here on earth are also stages in an awakening universe. Teilhard interpreted this awakening, in his Christian cosmic vision, to mean that the whole of nature is the extended body of Christ, and that cosmogenesis is therefore Christogenesis. The universe's earliest coming into being is already oriented toward the birth of Christ. This is why, for Teilhard, evolution is holy.

But let us now add something more to this picture of an awakening universe. According to Teilhard, the growth of consciousness intensifies in direct proportion to the increase in organized physical complexity in the universe.[7] So, now that astronomers have good reason to suppose that many millions of earthlike planets exist in our Milky Way galaxy, and surely in others as well, the probability of extraterrestrial intelligent life increases far beyond what scientists could have surmised during Teilhard's lifetime. Teilhard only occasionally entertained such an idea, but now, on the basis of his general understanding of the correlation of growth in consciousness with a growth in physical complexity, we may reasonably speculate that extraterrestrial intelligence not only exists but also flourishes. If so, then something like extraterrestrial "noospheres" may also be in the process of formation. If the threefold sequence—divergence, convergence, and emergence—is operative on a cosmic scale, then the individual noospheres would be the fundamental units of a new stage in the recurrent three-stage pattern of cosmogenesis.

Are these thoughts too wild? Maybe so, but extrapolating from the development of terrestrial life and thought so far, the universe may still be moving toward something unimaginably momentous. We are each part of this universe, and especially in our religious aspirations, the whole universe may be awakening to something indestructible that is still dawning up ahead. In the arrival of the phenomenon of thought, we see that matter has already, at least locally, been transformed by natural processes into minds searching for timeless meaning, truth, goodness, and beauty. In our human drive to understand and, even more explicitly, in our desire for *right* understanding, 13.8 billion years of cosmic history are now reaching out for a meaning and truth for which we long but that is not yet in our possession.

So far, there is no evidence to confirm the speculation I have just indulged, but I believe Teilhard would rejoice that the search goes on. The cosmos elsewhere is unfolding in unknown ways, but at least here on earth it is awakening not only through scientific inquiry but also by way of religious faith. Faith *is* the universe in the process of awakening explicitly to the lure of an indestructible rightness, that is, to what Teilhard calls Omega. Consequently, we should now look at Christian faith and hope not only theologically, historically, psychologically, or sociologically, but also cosmologically. Faith and hope are ways in which the universe, now that it has reached the level of conscious self-awareness, continues its ageless search for an ultimate Center and Goal. Faith and hope are essential, therefore, to the cosmic drama of awakening to the future that is always coming but that is also "not-yet."

Thus, Teilhard brings a new breadth to the study of the cosmos. For him, the physical world, deep down, is nothing less than a grand awakening. In his cosmic vision the awakening by way of "thought" is essential to the universe and its future, whereas previously in both ancient and modern philosophies, mind, thought, and subjective experience have usually not been thought of as part of the cosmos. Teilhard emphasizes, however, that there is no basis for dualistically separating "mind" or "thought" from the cosmos. The cosmos is "mindful" from the start. Matter and spirit are terms that properly refer not to distinct substances, but to polar tendencies in cosmogenesis. "Matter" designates the inclination of nature to slide back toward the condition of dispersal that constituted the early subatomic stage of the universe's long journey. "Spirit," then, is the propensity of our awakening universe to converge toward unity in the form of future emergent complexity. Matter is spirit in the state of dispersal or decoherence. Spirit is matter in the state of emerging coherence. And "God" is the principle that creates the universe by bringing unity out of the state of multiplicity known as matter.

Cosmogenesis, to repeat, is Teilhard's name for the process by which the universe is still coming into being. So, if the cosmos, as science implies, is a work in progress, it still has a future. The cosmos is a promise that remains to be fulfilled. According to Teilhard, we cannot understand what the universe is unless we keep remembering that it has never been fixed or perfected in the past. We live in an always nascent, always ongoing process of cosmic movement. God is creating, therefore, not from "up above" but from "up ahead." By shifting to a futurist, hope-filled perspective, Christian thought connects cosmogenesis to the biblical promises of God.

The universe continues to be drawn toward the future by the attractive power of a God who creates the world by always offering it new possibilities for becoming *more*. The whole of creation is undergoing a transformation from simple to more complex modes of being. Perhaps, then, the universe carries a profound meaning that Christian faith can illuminate and that in turn can enliven Christian faith for our time. We shall see. The God of evolution continually creates the world anew not by pushing things from the past, but by drawing the world forward toward a new future from up ahead. The future is the primary dwelling place of God. Of course, God is present now and in the past, but God is intimately involved in each past and present moment precisely by opening it to a new future. The world leans on this future as its "sole support."[8]

GOD AND THE UNFINISHED UNIVERSE

As I see it, Teilhard's reflections run parallel to the biblical understanding of God as the one who makes and keeps promises. Teilhard adds, however, that in the age of science we may now realize that God's promises are not just for Israel, the church, and human history, but also for the entire universe. The church's mission now includes reminding people that the universe is "unfinished" and that its future is open. Only in the twentieth century did scientists find out that the whole universe is a story still going on. Teilhard, as it happens, was among the first of them. For the most part, however, even into the twenty-first century, Christian theology has failed to reflect deeply on what it means that we live in a still-becoming universe.[9] With rare

exceptions, Christian thought has not yet drawn out the implications of evolutionary biology, astrophysics, and cosmology for
our understanding of the world and God. Ecclesiastical officials
and religious educators still cling at least tacitly to ancient and
medieval images of a fixed universe, a primordial human innocence, a historical Fall, and a God who exists above or outside
of the natural world.

Most mainline Christian theologians, it is true, allow vaguely
for biological evolution and Big Bang cosmology, but religious
thought in general has scarcely begun to absorb the historical
understanding of the cosmos that has taken shape in scientific
thought after Einstein. For that matter, the wider intellectual
world, including the majority of scientists and philosophers, has
yet to realize that our minds are fully part of nature and that this
fact, as Teilhard emphasized, should make an enormous difference when it comes to our understanding the meaning of the
term *cosmos*. Stunted by a stale materialist understanding of life,
the reigning cult of scientific naturalism—the belief that the totality of being is reducible to what scientific method is capable of
finding out—has closed off contemporary intellectual life to the
most important implications of contemporary science, namely,
that the cosmos is new each day, that it may still be only at the
dawn of its creation, and that a vast and indeterminate future of
new creation lies open before it.

As far as Catholic theologians are concerned, our understanding of the meaning of God, human nature, Jesus, redemption,
and morality is still weighed down by an implicit preference
for prescientific cosmological assumptions. Most contemporary
Catholic thinkers, church leaders, and spiritual guides make little
use of new scientific discoveries in their thoughts about God
and the meaning of faith. The sense that we live in an unfinished
universe seems only incidental, even though, in fact, it is revolutionary, both scientifically and theologically. Scientific discovery
has demonstrated on multiple fronts that the cosmic process is far

from being over and done with, but most earthlings, including most theologians, have yet to explore carefully what an unfinished universe really implies for our spiritual and ethical lives.[10]

The universe, without doubt, is still coming into being. This, Teilhard insisted, "is the basic truth which must be grasped at the outset and assimilated so thoroughly that it becomes part of the very habit and nature of our thought."[11] Science's great new discovery of a still emerging universe, however, is far from having become habitual to most Christian thinkers. Teilhard often lamented the prevalent theological and ecclesiastical indifference to scientific discoveries. Were he with us today, he would be saddened by the ongoing unresponsiveness of most Catholic thinkers to science. Much to its detriment, Catholic thought still exhibits little appetite for real contact with the drastic transfiguration of cosmos and consciousness that science now reveals, and whose appropriation Teilhard rightly considered essential to the survival and vitality of Christian faith.

For some time now I have been arguing that Christian theology should be carrying forward Teilhard's pioneering work of revision. Given Christianity's increasing intellectual irrelevance to the aspirations of countless scientifically educated people, the task seems more urgent than ever. Science has given us a totally new picture of the universe, one that has vastly outgrown the images and concepts of God that most of us picked up in our youths. In view of recent cosmological discoveries, I believe, with Teilhard, that theology may now look for images and ideas of God more proportionate to our new sense of cosmogenesis.[12]

Something fresh and even startling is needed today to spark an intellectual revitalization of Christian faith and theology, beginning with a new sense of God. Catholicism, along with the rest of the Christian world, is now facing critical challenges: the spread of fundamentalism, the rising secularism in Western cultures, and the dominance of scientific naturalism in the intellectual world. Within Catholicism, powerful movements toward restoration—many of them officially endorsed by ecclesiastical leaders—seek to reestablish a spirituality that assumes prescientific—hence unnecessarily static and diminutive—representations of the cosmos. In the face of these and other trends, dramatic changes are needed for Catholic theology's intellectual acceptability in the age of science. What is needed now, especially in view of developments in science, is not "no God," as New Atheists and scientific naturalists propose, but a "new God," a revolution in our understanding of ultimate reality in the age of science.[13]

What, then, must our new thoughts about God be like in the context of an unfinished universe? The question needs to be asked not with the intention of moving outside of Christian tradition, but to facilitate its survival and thriving into the future. Unfortunately, the relatively few Christian thinkers who have been rethinking their faith in a way that takes advantage of science are seldom taken seriously by the faithful at large, or by seminary instructors, or by religious officials. The habitual neglect of science by most Christian theologians is not likely to cease soon, but I believe that the intellectual respectability of theology demands our bringing together in new ways current scientific understanding of the universe and the biblical hope for new creation.

Such a revision of Christian thought had a promising beginning with Teilhard, but he did not have the chance to develop his thoughts as fully as his faith and scientific understanding demanded. Even though his ideas were circulating at the Second Vatican Council, subsequently his synthetic efforts have had little influence on Catholic life and thought at large, not to mention on the intellectual world.[14] I hope in these pages to excavate, apply, and develop Teilhard's thought as it pertains not only to the cosmos, but also to other topics of concern to thoughtful people today. After Galileo, Darwin, Einstein, Hubble, and Hawking there can be no going back to a "fixist" cosmology with its assumption that "the heavens and the earth" came into being perfectly complete in an opening display of divine magic. Contemporary theology, as Teilhard would certainly agree, has scarcely begun to draw out the theological implications of science's relatively recent discovery of a universe still aborning.

2

FUTURE

In one of his loveliest poems Gerard Manley Hopkins (1844–89) exclaims: "Nothing is so beautiful as spring." The Jesuit poet is enraptured by "weeds in wheels," thrush's eggs like "little low heavens," birds' echoes that "rinse and ring the ears," and pear tree leaves and blooms that brush "the descending blue."

Hopkins asks: "What is all this juice and all this joy?" This seasonal excess, he answers, is "a strain of the earth's sweet being in the beginning; in Eden Garden." Sin has now corrupted the world's original innocence, but in the flush of springtime, sacramental reminders of a paradisal plenitude—of what Hopkins elsewhere calls the "dearest freshness deep down things"—break through the smudged surface of the earth. Springtime glory recaptures imperfectly and fleetingly the creation that had been made perfect by God in the beginning. We should hold fast, then, to these transient reminders of creation's primordial perfection: "Have, get, before it cloy . . . and sour with sinning."[1] Like generations of Christians before him, Hopkins displays, here, a spiritual orientation nourished more by sacramental reminders of an initially perfect creation than by a sense that nature is open to a new future. The universe is more epiphany than promise.

Teilhard de Chardin, Hopkins's fellow Jesuit, however, regards the passing glories of nature in a different light. The flowering of life need not turn us nostalgically back to "earth's sweet being

17

in the beginning." Evolution, after all, rules out the possibility that paradise ever actually existed in cosmic time or terrestrial history. Teilhard is more impressed by the new scientific evidence that the universe is still coming into bloom. Locally, this means that the earth has yet to become fully real. Nature's true being lies up ahead—in the future. Teilhard would agree with Hopkins that our world has been "bleared and smeared" and "bears man's smudge." The juice has indeed soured. To the Christian evolutionist, however, the vulnerability of our terrestrial home to sin's scourge is a signal that the creation still needs time to ripen. For Teilhard, autumn rather than spring was the happiest time of year. It is almost as though the shedding of leaves opened his soul to the limitless space of the up-ahead and the not-yet, liberating him from the siren charms of spring and summer.

The divergent spiritual sensitivities of Hopkins and Teilhard, both Jesuit priests, reflect a tension still alive in contemporary Christian spirituality. Both visionaries, melancholic by nature, felt the menace of despair, and they each scanned the natural world for hints of a perfection that would allow them to lift up their hearts. Both were intensely devout Catholics, but the solace and joy they each found in nature came to expression in different ways. Hopkins found spiritual comfort in seasonal reminders of a primordial innocence. He felt in the depths of nature an inexhaustible freshness now largely lost but still ready to break through unrestrainedly on occasion to remind us of the fullness of God's creation "in the beginning." Teilhard, more thoroughly schooled in the natural sciences as they had taken shape since Darwin, looked toward the future of a still unfinished universe for a reason to rejoice. He found an opening for hope in an awareness that "creation has never stopped," that it is "one huge continual gesture, drawn out over the totality of time." Creation, he believed, "is still going on; and incessantly even if imperceptibly, the world is constantly emerging a little farther above nothingness."[2]

It is toward the world's future, rather than toward a primordial past or an eternal present looming "up above," that the human soul may now strain to find that for which it truly longs. "The only thing that keeps me youthful and active," Teilhard wrote, "is the growing belief that there is something immense, something beautiful about to take place throughout the world, and that we must abandon ourselves to the mighty current of this development." This is because "our world contains within itself a mysterious promise of the future."[3]

Hopkins, though conversant with the science of his day, did not live long enough to ponder the religious meaning of the new story of nature that was emerging in the geology and biology of the nineteenth century. Teilhard's scientific training, however, implied that the natural world could never literally have played host to Eden. Unlike Hopkins, Teilhard had been exposed to the early twentieth-century arrival of Einstein's general theory of relativity (first published in 1916). He was aware, then, that Einstein's theory, as interpreted by Georges Lemaître and others, implied that the physical universe could not conceivably have come into full flowering in an opening instant of divine creativity that would later be soured by sin. Hopkins and Teilhard agreed that the universe—as it exists now—is not what it is intended to be, and that it is in need of redemption. The evolutionist shares the poet's sense of the brokenness of our world. If we follow Teilhard, however, it makes a considerable difference to Christian piety and theology, that creation was not completed "in the beginning" and that the world is still aborning. It means that there is a wide opening for unprecedented outcomes to take shape up ahead—in the cosmic future.[4]

AN UNFINISHED UNIVERSE

What does it really mean for Christian faith, then, that we live in an unfinished universe? At the very least, it means an end to the idea that God's creation has at any time in the past been perfect or paradisal. Once we have fully absorbed the scientifically incontestable fact that earth was not Eden in the beginning and that the cosmos did not first emerge in finished form, the future comes into view as never before.

How so? By making us realize that our lives here and now are tied into a *universe* that still has a future, the whole of creation appears to have room to become much *more* than it has been or is now. The cosmos as portrayed by contemporary science is a work in progress. This means that it may yet be subject to creative transformations that began around fourteen billion years ago and that are now winding their way toward who knows where. Each of us is part of an immense cosmic drama of *awakening*, a fact that may give new significance to our lives and efforts.[5]

Prescientific cosmology and metaphysics, as Teilhard understood them, cannot support the full liberation of human hope. Fullness of hope needs a horizon of expectation that links us physically to the universe's own future. Otherwise, we may easily underestimate the significance of our lives. A static cosmology orients our ethical and religious aspirations toward retirement in a timeless spiritual heaven above time and outside the physical universe. A universe that undergoes no significant transformation itself can only be "left behind" in the soul's search for final release from this "vale of tears." No doubt, an exclusively otherworldly expectation is understandable given the hopeless political and economic conditions in which so many human beings have found themselves. Nevertheless, an excessive preoccupation with the "next world," as the Second Vatican Council acknowledges, diminishes the ethical passion to build *this* world and hence to deal seriously with current political, social, economic, and environmental ills.[6]

A purely otherworldly optimism, moreover, provides no substantive resistance to contemporary scientific naturalism and its dogma that the universe is pointless. A pure supernaturalism is intellectually powerless to resist the current academically supported cult of cosmic pessimism. By cosmic pessimism I mean the belief that nature has no purpose and that whatever meaning exists in the world is our own perishable and illusory human creation. If the universe is still coming into being, however, none of us is in a secure position at present to declare, as the cosmic pessimists do, that the universe makes no sense whatsoever. We just have to wait and see.

Geology, evolutionary biology, and cosmology now situate the earth, life, and human existence within the flux of an immense cosmic *drama of awakening* that is still going on. Of course, in the history of life and the cosmos, there have been many instances of what may seem to be dead ends, where the universe seems to be destined for endless sleep. But these stages never last. There are temporary reversals, tensions, and conflicts, but these are completely consistent with a dramatic cosmos. The cosmic drama so far has been one in which at least a general drift from simplicity toward complexity has always been going on. Corresponding to this loose directionality, the cosmos has trended from less consciousness to more consciousness, from less being to fuller being.[7]

Once we realize clearly that the drama of creation is still going on, therefore, it is not inevitable that we take the route of despair. Nor is it required that Christians today have exactly the same thoughts about the Creator, sin, virtue, and the meaning of life and human destiny as did our religious ancestors. If the cosmos is still emerging, we need no longer think of Christ and his mission in exactly the same way as previous ages did. The church's formerly static sense of the cosmos and its analogical sense of God may now be transfigured by an anticipatory awareness that the universe is still coming into being. The church's worship, sacraments, and spirituality may now take on meanings that our religious ancestors could never have envisaged on the basis of what Teilhard calls their "fixist" understanding of the natural world.

Fidelity to traditional theology and spirituality will, of course, be essential to the reshaping of Christian religious identity in an unfinished universe, but we shall not feel obliged to imprison our souls and aspirations in depictions of the cosmos that are simply too small for scientifically educated persons. With Teilhard, we need to examine more carefully than ever before the metaphysical and cosmological assumptions at the root of the church's persistently pre-evolutionary understanding of nature and God. Certainly, Hopkins's lamenting of the souring of innocence by sin, and of our need for redemption, will still be relevant. In the context of an unfinished universe, however, our awareness that "things are not what they should be" may arouse a new kind of hope and spiritual adventure.

Christian faith and theology will seem increasingly uninteresting to thoughtful people unless we reflect more deliberately on the vast and still aborning universe exposed by contemporary science. Christians who profess to love God and to have been saved by Christ will lose nothing and gain everything by transplanting their sacramental spirituality to an incalculably larger cosmic setting made available by science. Our sense of the Creator, the work of the Holy Spirit, and the redemptive significance of Christ can now grow wider and deeper by immense orders of magnitude. The Love that rules the stars will now have to be seen as embracing over two hundred billion galaxies, a cosmic epic of fourteen billion years duration—and perhaps even a multiverse.

A METAPHYSICS OF THE FUTURE

Thinking about human life, ethics, and worship without also taking into account science's picture of an unfinished universe has two negative consequences. First, it perpetuates the unfortunate impression that Christian faith is intellectually implausible. Second, it "clips the wings of hope"[8] and saps the "zest for living" that any theological vision must sponsor if it is to prove challenging enough to make a difference in the world.[9]

If hope is to have wings and life to have zest, nothing less is needed than a theological vision that opens up a new future, not just for Christianity or the church, but for the whole universe. In this book, I am calling such a vision a *metaphysics of the future*[10]—in other words, a way of understanding that gives primacy to what is yet to come, to what corresponds to hope rather than to pessimistic "realism." No doubt philosophers and theologians conditioned to thinking of the world and God in the context of ancient and medieval notions of "being" will raise conceptual objections to the notion of a metaphysics of the future. They will assume that, since the future does not yet "exist," it cannot be foundational to our understanding of God and the world. However, those who take seriously both the fact of an unfinished universe and a biblical understanding of time based on the ancient Hebrew discovery of the future can hardly object. Those who dwell within a worldview rooted in the Abrahamic motifs of promise and hope will rightly suspect that Platonic, Aristotelian, Thomistic, and most other ancient, medieval, and modern philosophies have blunted the futuristic edge of Israel's prophetic faith and the earliest stage of Christian thought.[11] The God we are looking for is one who, in some sense, is *not-yet*. As long as we think about the universe only in prescientific static and purely spatial terms, divine transcendence means *not-here*. But since the universe after Darwin and Einstein is temporal through and through, divine transcendence may in some sense mean yet-to-come.[12]

No matter how brilliant or conceptually attractive the traditional systems of thought may have been, most of the philosophical systems that theologians have tried out for more than two thousand years are not readymade to frame adequately either the universe of contemporary science or, for that matter, the kind of expectation that animated the lives of our biblical ancestors. Consequently, I freely employ the intellectually un-settling expression *metaphysics of the future* to designate Teilhard's worldview and to highlight theology's need for a cosmic vision that can accommodate synthetically both biblical hope and contemporary science.

The idea of a metaphysics of the future may be conceptually unclear, but there is a reason for its opacity, a reason rooted in the nature of reality itself. A sense of darkness, a realization that the intelligibility we seek is always partly obscured by shadows, is inevitable in any universe that is still *in via*. As long as the cosmic journey is not yet over, as Teilhard points out, it cannot possibly be fully intelligible to those traveling along with it.[13] Full intel-ligibility is something human minds can anticipate, not possess. Meaning is something for which we must—in some way—al-ways wait. If it is to be a constant source of nourishment, we can only draw upon it, never master or control it. Accordingly, I believe a metaphysics of the future is an appropriate philosophi-cal setting for contemporary theology as it reflects with Teilhard on human existence in an unfinished universe.

In any case, a new worldview is needed to counter two domi-nant metaphysical alternatives that have persistently "clipped the wings" of hope. I call these rivals respectively the *metaphysics of the past* and the *metaphysics of the eternal present*. The first and most deadening of these prevalent alternatives is the *metaphysics of the past*. This is the physicalist worldview that now dominates scientific thinking and much intellectual life all over the planet. It is the largely unquestioned sense of reality ensconced in most of the world's universities and research centers.[14] It is the main intellectual roadblock, however, to a truly hopeful vision of reality. I am referring to it as a metaphysics of the *past* because it assumes that the foundation of all being—and the ultimate explanation of all present actualities—can be found only by digging back into the cosmic past, all the way back to the mindless physical plasma that reigned for a long period of time during the earliest stages of the cosmic process. According to the modern materialist and atomist worldview, the only reliable way to understand the natural world here and now is to retrieve the earliest episodes of cosmic history—to recover and retrace the stages that have led gradually, blindly, and deterministically from the past to the present.

It was not in science, then, but in a doctrinaire metaphysics of the past that Teilhard encountered secular thought's hostility to his vision of the universe. The modern materialist worldview professes to explain all present realities completely by going far back temporally, and deep down analytically, to gather up the subatomic units that over the course of cosmic history have led to atoms, then molecules, cells, organisms, and eventually human brains and their cultural products. Materialism takes for granted that we can arrive at the goal of complete understanding of nature by viewing present reality—including life and mind—as nothing more than past elemental simplicity now "masquerading" as present complexity.[15]

According to this starkly reductionistic worldview, human inquiry can find an adequate explanation of present evolutionary outcomes *only* by using the analytical tools of contemporary science to uncover the "really real" province of lifeless and mindless elements that made up the earliest chapters of the cosmic story. Contemporary adherents to a metaphysics of the past profess to have planted human thought on the firmest ground excavated so far in the history of human inquiry: pure matter. Scientific thinkers now take for granted that nonlife rather than life is the ground state of being. Scientific materialists and atomists now assure us that, ever since cosmic beginnings and for all subsequent ages, there can be no real novelty in the universe but only a reshuffling of the original elemental bits. Nature's outcomes were already set in stone from the start.

This inherently pessimistic view of the universe is still the most imposing intellectual challenge to Christian hope, although even developments in physics and cosmology have for some time been raising questions about it. Nevertheless, as Teilhard rightly points out, the materialist enshrinement of an inanimate and mindless physical past as the goal of our long human search for complete intelligibility is the result of an "analytical illusion."[16] That is, contemporary physicalism and cosmic pessimism are based on the uncritical belief that only by breaking things down into their subordinate parts can we finally satisfy the human craving to understand them.

Scientific method, of course, does require the use of analysis.[17] Analysis by itself, however, fails to provide an ultimate explanation of anything. Analysis can help provide a scientifically essential map of the universe's particulars and constituents, and it can help us temporally piece together, chapter by chapter, the long cosmic story of the universe. But ever since antiquity the analytical method has led human minds downward and backward into an atomic dispersal that becomes increasingly diffuse and incoherent the farther back or the farther down we look.

The second unsatisfactory alternative to a metaphysics of the future is a *metaphysics of the eternal present.* This vision of reality is rooted in Platonic, Aristotelian, and Neoplatonic philosophies that, to one degree or another, have provided the intellectual setting of most traditional Catholic thought. For centuries this system of thought has located the fullness of being in a domain of timelessness immune to all becoming. It has given metaphysical primacy to an immaterial world lurking everlastingly within, above, beyond, or behind the transient sphere of terrestrial and cosmic becoming. No doubt this second metaphysical alternative has given solace to individual souls, but it holds out no hope for rescuing the physical universe from the threat of nonbeing.[18]

If a metaphysics of the past forbids in principle anything truly new from ever happening in the universe, so also does a metaphysics of the eternal present.[19] The latter allows little room for our world's becoming *more*—since creation is said to be fully complete from the outset. The idea that ultimate reality is an "eternal now" is hard to reconcile with a robust hope for a future in which creation can become *truly* new. Indeed, a metaphysics of the eternal present is content to let the universe eventually undergo complete annihilation as long as immortal souls can escape from its embers.

This classical, prescientific worldview seems plausible whenever we take literally the biblical narrative about a primordial befouling of "earth's sweet being in the beginning." The idea of a "Fall" from primordial innocence can have the effect of turning human action into a project of *restoration* rather than renewal. In doing so, the myth of the world's initial perfection risks divorcing our moral lives from the joy of cooperating with divine creativity in bringing about what is unprecedented.

A metaphysics of the eternal present traditionally conceived of nature as a static hierarchy of levels of being, each graded ontologically according to the degree of its sacramental participation in the eternal perfection of God. At the lowest level of the sacred hierarchy lies the obtuse realm of matter. Then in ascending order come the higher levels of plants, animals, human beings, angels, and finally God. This Great Chain of Being has been the latticework around which the vine of Catholic spirituality has wound itself for centuries.

Despite Vatican II's acknowledgment that our understanding of the world has now moved from a static to an evolutionary understanding, a metaphysics of the eternal present still underlies most contemporary Catholic theology, ethics, and spirituality. Whole universities, institutes, and television networks are devoted to keeping it foundational to Catholic faith and theology. Consequently, contemporary Catholic thought and culture remain generally indifferent to the scientifically demonstrable notion of a universe still coming into being. In company with

Teilhard and Vatican II, however, I am suggesting that medieval metaphysics, though not without important insights, is conceptually inadequate to hosting a theology that professes awareness of our unfinished universe and the promissory core of biblical faith.

IMPLICATIONS FOR HOPE AND LOVE

In contrast to both the metaphysics of the past and of the eternal present I am proposing that Christian theology now requires the renewal implied in a biblically based *metaphysics of the future.* Teilhard himself professed to be weary of metaphysics, but he turned out to be thoroughly metaphysical in the sense that, like other profound thinkers, he was looking for a bedrock solidity and unassailable "consistence" upon which to rest his vision of reality. He found it eventually only by turning toward the future. At one time Teilhard had looked for a spiritual foundation in the apparent durability of "matter," but he soon realized that matter granulates into atomic and subatomic bits, and then disintegrates completely, when subjected to ever more refined scientific analysis. In other words, the farther analytical science digs into the world's physical past, the more the world falls to pieces before our eyes. By dissolving reality into scattered individual units, a purely atomistic philosophy of nature leads our minds downward in space and backward in time toward final unintelligibility.[20]

It is only by arriving at a sense of their coherence that things become intelligible to us. So, because the components of our universe are still coming together, our sense of its intelligibility belongs to the future. Contemporary scientific atomism, however, builds its sense of "reality" on the cosmic stage of physical de-coherence. This "analytical illusion," as Teilhard calls it, has seduced countless educated people into embracing the fantastic belief that breaking material complexity down into its most indivisible subatomic components or—what amounts to the same thing—by traveling back to the remotest cosmic past, we shall finally be able to make complete sense of the universe.[21] Instead of leading our minds toward what is truly intelligible, however, pure analysis only makes the world ever more unintelligible.

Teilhard, moreover, challenges not only the metaphysics of the past implied in contemporary scientific atomism but also classical theology's assumption of a perfectly completed initial creation. We encounter true "consistence" not by escaping intellectually into a world of Platonic perfection, but by waiting and actively working toward a fullness that is not-yet. If the cosmos is still unfinished and hence still being drawn toward deeper and richer syntheses up ahead, then its intelligibility is something we cannot possess but only *anticipate*. The world's coherence lies in the future rather than in the past or in an eternal present.

In his dissatisfaction with the fixist or "immobilist" theology of the Scholastics, and his frustration at the failure of scientific naturalism to account for evolution's becoming *more*, Teilhard calls for a "new God." God, he proposes, may now be thought of as the ultimate center of convergence for an unfinished universe rather than as an overseer of a creation that had once been perfect but is now spoiled by sin and ravaged by time. As the ultimate center and goal of cosmic convergence, God creates the world by drawing it forward from up-ahead (*ab ante*) rather than "pushing" it into existence from out of the remote past (*a tergo*). God is both Alpha and Omega, of course, but God is more Omega than Alpha.[22] Consequently, in our unfinished universe the metaphysical search for what is "really real" leads in the direction of the "not-yet" rather than backward toward "the already" or upward toward the *nunc stans,* the "standing now." Remarkably, the scientifically established fact that our universe is still in process invites Christian theology to think in new ways about God, creation, suffering, death, incarnation, sin, evil and redemption, grace and freedom, eschatology, and the virtues of faith, hope, and love.[23]

A necessary condition for the *full* exercise of our capacity to love, for example, is that we must first put on the virtue of hope.[24] Hope, however, as the Protestant theologian Jürgen Moltmann puts it, "has the chance of a meaningful existence only when reality itself is in a state of historic flux and when historic reality has room for open possibilities ahead."[25] It is a great gift to Christian faith, therefore, that science has now provided irrefutable evidence that our universe is historical, that it is still becoming, and that it is open to realizing new kinds and degrees of coherence in the future. The assumption of an essentially finished and perfected universe, on the contrary, would not allow for such openness, no matter how one looks at it. As long as Christians are given the impression that everything important had already been accomplished in an initial creative instant, can anything really worthwhile still remain for us to do—as more than one modern philosopher has asked? Might not the assumption of an initially completed universe unconsciously suppress the creative vitality needed to sustain both hope and vigorous moral effort?

For now, I leave this as a question for each reader. I only wish to suggest, with Teilhard, that the traditional theological idea of an initially completed creation based on a literal interpretation of Genesis—and fortified by ancient and medieval metaphysics—not only diminishes the space for hope but in doing so circumscribes arbitrarily the field of love's effectiveness. The assumption of an initially completed creation also limits the impact of ethical life by sometimes diverting it into practicing virtuous habits that have no other goal in mind than that of meriting eternal life after death.

The moral life after Darwin and Einstein, Teilhard tells us, must amount to much more than this. As long as the universe is reduced to timeless primordial subatomic particles, or as long as the universe is embalmed in an eternal now, the possibility of real love is diminished—because such a world exists without new possibilities that can arrive only from out of the future. A purely prescientific theological understanding of virtue has had little to do with "building the world," a motivation that Vatican II made essential to Christian ethical life.

If the creation "in the beginning" had ever actually been in a state of "sweet being," what would be the point of moral imperatives here and now? If we assumed, along with most classical Christian theology, an initial "Fall" from a primordial integrity, then pursuit of the ethical life would perhaps be motivated by a sense of shame at our rebellion against God or by the need to restore by expiation the perfection that had been defiled. Our practice of virtue, however, would have little to do with the great work of contributing to the ongoing awakening of the universe or to the creation of something truly new.

The myth of an initially finished creation and primordial innocence followed by narratives of sin, expiation, conversion, practice of virtue, and the restoration of innocence still defines the spiritual and ethical itinerary of countless Christians. Admittedly, this narrative allows for exemplary lives and a kind of spiritual adventure fraught with perils and garnished with momentary triumphs. It can give a sense of worthwhileness to individuals as they struggle from exile toward paradise. Nevertheless, since the traditional Christian understanding of innocence, sin, and redemption is tied so tightly to the prescientific assumption of an initially complete creation, it seems right to ask now what Christian spiritual and moral life would be like if we accepted the fact of an unfinished universe?[26]

The sense of creation's "sweet being in the beginning" underlying Hopkins's spiritual aspirations still has great appeal. But it can no longer be taken literally and with full intellectual sincerity by scientifically informed believers. The idea of an initially fixed and finished universe, one that fits a metaphysics of the eternal present, seems more appropriate to the nurturing of nostalgia than to the full liberation of our native need for reasons to hope. Certainly Hopkins's "Spring" is a moving expression of the universal religious sense that the world at present is not what it is intended to be, and this is why we may still profit spiritually from meditating on religious classics built on a metaphysics of the eternal present. But evolutionary biology teaches us that a strain of souring was present in the universe long before the sinning. Consequently, we need to ask whether classical Christian theology can rightly account for this Fault before the Fall. Furthermore, if the universe had been essentially complete in the beginning, wouldn't our lives in time consist at best of participating in a labor of recovery or restoration? Our longing for fuller being, or for the infinite, might then too easily express itself in premature mystical flights *from* the universe rather than in longsuffering hope *for* a cosmic fulfillment still far off.

The science-based idea that the universe is still coming into being offers a promising—and I believe realistic—framework for understanding biblical hope and for a correspondingly fresh understanding of the practice of love. Teilhard's embrace of an unfinished and still-awakening universe is one of the main reasons why his writings mysteriously lift the hearts of his readers and make room for a new thrill of hope—an *extensio animi ad magna*—that they had never experienced so palpably when reading and meditating on prescientific theological and spiritual works. The ancient and medieval habit of thinking about God only as an eternal now is spiritually restrictive because it ignores or suppresses the primary matrix of Christian faith, namely, the ancient Abrahamic religion of expectation and the prophetic trust in God's promises of a new future.

Classical Christian spirituality, moreover, has assumed a static, hierarchical picture of the universe, one in which nothing much, other than decay, is going on across the reaches of time. The classical metaphysics of the eternal present, which Hopkins takes for granted, interprets the beauties of nature as reminders of a lost innocence rather than as anticipatory signs of a cosmos still coming to birth. Scientific naturalism's metaphysics of the past, meanwhile, assumes that anything that seems new is really no more than a different state of the inanimate dust into which analytical scientific research typically resolves the universe.

A still-emerging universe, furthermore, is more congenial to meaningful hope and effective love than are its two main metaphysical rivals. Both science and biblical faith open up our understanding of the universe to new possibilities and hence to a worldview in which love, by virtue of the opportunities revealed by hope, has a chance to make the world new. From a Christian perspective, if determinism reigned and the cosmic future were already closed, or if the fullness of being were already actualized in an eternal now, would this not blunt the good news that something radically new is still coming? Let us keep this question in mind as we move forward.

3

HOPE

The grandeur of the river is revealed not at its source but at its estuary.
—Teilhard de Chardin, *Hymn of the Universe*

So far, we have seen how science has given us the portrait of a universe that is still open to realizing new possibilities in the future. An essentially finished and perfected universe would not allow such openness. Not only would it clip the wings of hope, but it would also stunt the expression of love. Human effort and the aspiration for more-being would be channeled into flight from the universe rather than journeying along with it. If the universe itself had no truly new future up ahead, the hope that springs eternal would look for ways to escape from it—perhaps by premature mystical excursions into the beyond.

Viewed from a biblical perspective, Christian theology should have been prepared to embrace the recent scientific discovery that the cosmos is thoroughly historical and open to a new future. Instead, as Teilhard has observed, Christian faith's native Abrahamic openness to the future is forced to compete nowadays not only with an academically sponsored cosmic pessimism but also with a theological tradition's long marriage to Neoplatonic otherworldly optimism.

It may be helpful, then, to consider how Teilhard's own life makes the transition from a traditional Catholic piety to a spirituality of cosmic hope. From his earliest days Teilhard had a deep affection for the natural world, and his wide-eyed perceptivity carried over later to a career in the natural sciences, especially geology and paleontology. He was fascinated by rocks because these symbolized the permanence he sought in the midst of perishing. His entire life thereafter became a constant search for something incontestably solid to which he might fix his natively anxious sensibilities. Although he confessed to being temperamentally inclined to tie his life to the fixity of the past, he eventually realized that the remote cosmic past dissolves into the sandy flats of scattered elemental bits the farther we journey back in time. Increasingly, as his life went on, Teilhard became convinced that whatever "consistence" the universe has—whatever it is that holds everything together—lies in the future, not the past. The solidity he sought throughout his life gradually shifted from the false fixity of the cosmic past to the unifying power of the cosmic future. The real coherence he was looking for lies not in the past or in an eternal present but on the horizon of what lies "up-ahead." It is in the direction of what is not-yet that Teilhard eventually looked for the world's meaning and its metaphysical foundation.[1] Increasingly, his religious feelings merged more cohesively with the biblical sense of hope and promise than with the materialist's obsession with physical simplicity or traditional theology's all-too-Platonic love of timelessness.

While his valor as a stretcher-bearer in World War I was earning him entry into the Legion of Honour, Teilhard was becoming increasingly disillusioned inwardly with the conventional naturalistic belief that the cosmos can best be understood by tracing its physical makeup back to the elemental simplicity of its atomic past. Taking such an analytical line of inquiry, he warned, ends up leaving our minds stranded in an original state of cosmic incoherence. Instead, the universe's real intelligibility, he claimed, emerges only as it is being borne along by a breeze that blows toward the future. Hence, the intelligibility we seek in the cosmos, both scientifically and spiritually, resides in the irreversible flow of time toward the future, not in the past or present:

> Like a river which, as you trace it back to its source, gradually diminishes till in the end it is lost altogether in the mud from which it springs, so existence becomes attenuated and finally vanishes away when we try to divide it up more and more minutely in space or—what comes to the same—to drive it further and further back in time. The grandeur of the river is revealed not at its source but at its estuary.[2]

Emboldened by hope in the cosmic future, Teilhard sought to share with his fellow humans what he thought he could see happening up ahead. He wrote prolifically, but his religious superiors did not permit him to let most other scientific and theological experts see what he saw. His most widely known book, *The Human Phenomenon*, appeared in print only after his death.[3] While no great writings can escape the historical limitations of their original formulations, there are exceptional works that attain the status of classics to which subsequent ages recurrently turn for nourishment. I believe, along with many others, that Teilhard's *Phenomenon* merits such acclaim. Like any other great thinker Teilhard was fallible, and so neither scientists nor theologians can accept every aspect of his work. Nevertheless, any serious Christian discussion of faith and science today can hardly afford to overlook his contributions.

During his scientific career Teilhard worked for a quarter century as a geologist in China—from the 1920s until after World War II. It was during his China sojourn that he wrote not only the *Phenomenon* but also smaller pieces on evolution and faith. Until after his death, however, his writings remained largely unknown to all but a few friends and acquaintances. Returning to France in 1946, he was offered a prestigious academic position at the Collège de France, and—not for the first time—his superiors refused permission. Following this disappointment he traveled to the United States, where he found employment at the Wenner Gren Foundation of Anthropological Research. He participated in two more paleontological expeditions and died virtually alone and unknown in New York City on Easter Sunday, 1955.[4]

Why were his writings suppressed? Apparently, at least in the eyes of his ecclesiastical censors, it was because Teilhard's ideas on evolution and Christianity required too radical a reinterpretation of doctrine. In the aftermath of Vatican I's declaration of papal infallibility and the later official condemnations of Modernism, a defensive atmosphere had settled into the official church at the very time during which Teilhard was developing his breathtaking new vision of Christianity and the cosmos. Church officials feared that the idea of evolution, along with many other innovations in the world of thought, could end up destabilizing Christian doctrine and confusing the faithful.

Anxiety about evolution not only in the Vatican but also among theologians in general was especially pronounced in Teilhard's day. Consequently, his enthusiastic embrace of geology, biology, paleoanthropology, and new developments in astronomy and cosmology seemed dangerous, not least because these sciences required a new theological understanding of the whole universe as an unfinished story of creation. Even today, despite Pope John Paul II's positive embrace of evolution in 1996,[5] many if not most Christians, including theologians, are still reluctant to look closely and consistently at the possible implications of evolution for Christian faith. It is still difficult to find Christian theologies of nature that are as comfortable with the Darwinian revolution as Teilhard was.[6]

EVOLUTION AND HOPE

In his religious interpretation of life Teilhard's starting point was a deeply orthodox trust in the Christian doctrines of creation, incarnation, and redemption. But the theoretical context of his reflections was a scientifically informed understanding of nature quite different from that of early and traditional Christianity. Not unlike many other great Christian thinkers and writers, Teilhard wanted to make sense of Christian teaching in terms of the intellectual currency of his own historical period, even if it proved difficult. At the very least, he thought, understanding Christian faith in our own time requires facing up to the discoveries of evolutionary biology and scientific cosmology. A full and frank encounter with the new scientific cosmic story would be a shock to the religious sensibilities of many people, Teilhard realized, but it is an encounter that honest people must be prepared to undergo nonetheless.

In my opinion there is no better place for Christians to undertake theology after Darwin and Einstein than by entering through the portals of Teilhard's way of *seeing* life and the universe. At first, one may find certain aspects of his vision curious, or at least in need of clarification, whether scientifically or theologically. But a Christian theology of nature can learn not only necessary truths but also gain courage and honesty from Teilhard's refusal to fortify faith against science. It is worth noting that Teilhard's reflections on the meaning of Christian faith are probably no bolder or more innovative in his own time than those of Justin, Irenaeus of Lyons, Gregory of Nyssa, and Thomas Aquinas were in theirs.[7] If daringness of vision were an impediment to good theology, this would have disqualified many thinkers whose perceived excesses have served to shape Christian tradition.

In any case, Teilhard's expert grasp of natural history convinced him of the need for a radical reinterpretation of Christian teachings about God, Christ, creation, incarnation, redemption, and eschatology in the light of evolution.[8] He became convinced that evolution is not a stumbling block to Christian faith, but the most appropriate framework available for understanding its meaning in depth. As he saw it, the new scientific understanding of nature does not contradict Christian tradition, as many fear. Instead, evolution brings into the open—with more depth and breadth than ever before—the linkage of Christian *hope* to the new scientific understanding of the universe.

Whatever one's criticisms of Teilhard's thought may be, there is no question that his writings have made it possible for many scientifically educated people to remain Christian. This is partly because his ideas arouse hope for the universe and the future of life, thus differing substantially from the acosmic and stylishly pessimistic literature of his own day as well as ours. More than fifty years ago theologian Ernst Benz expressed what many other readers of Teilhard have felt:

> [Teilhard's] main importance lies in the fact that he opened again the dimension of hope for our time. The opening of the theological aspect of the theory of evolution occurred at a time when the world, or at least the European and American world, got tired of existentialism and theological dialectics. This turning back to an analysis of one's exis-tence, this scorpion-like contortion of the poisonous sting against oneself, this flirting with evil, this digging in the unfathomable depths of one's being, has led to a petrifac-tion of thinking.[9]

Teilhard provides an alternative to this world-weariness. Benz re-minded his readers that a whole generation of intellectuals who became famous right after World War II were similar to Lot's wife. Like her, they "could not look away from the picture of decline and destruction." They "became mesmerized by the abyss of human aberrations" and "got lost in the constricting numbness of fear and defeat." Thought during the postwar period had "turned to stone."[10] Writing in the mid-1960s, however, Benz remarked that his contemporaries were growing tired of cosmic pessimism and were now paying attention to "thinkers who open their hearts for the beauty of the world and humanity."[11] In 1962, theologian Jean Danielou had also expressed this resurgent mood of hope: "One of the great diseases of the modern mind," he wrote, "is the 'enjoyment' of misfortune, the '*goût du malheur.*' Teilhard detests this with all his heart. And he is right. I wish it were possible to eliminate forever these poisonous miasmas of a decadent Western intelligentsia!"[12]

As most theologians now realize, Christian thought, especially in the West, had over the course of centuries lost touch with the biblical theme of hope. The passionate eschatological expectation that shaped Jesus's religious vision and the spiritual life of the earliest Christian communities had become clouded, prior to the Second Vatican Council, by centuries of otherworldly spirituality and the corresponding assumption that nothing of lasting significance could possibly be happening in the physical world itself. The eyes of the faithful had been looking upward toward the "next world," while "this world" was mostly thought of as a place to prepare for the soul's journey to paradise. What happens in natural history, therefore, had no permanent importance other than providing a "waiting room" in which souls might get ready for heaven. Even today, countless Christians assume that the future of the universe matters little, if at all, as far as the meaning of hope is concerned. Many still doubt that human persons are fully part of the natural world or that their own destiny is inseparable from that of the whole universe.

Modern biblical studies have demonstrated, however, that the prophets, Jesus, St. Paul, and other New Testament writers did not think of human destiny as a radical break with the physical universe. Generally speaking, early Christian expectation was focused on the coming of a new age that would transform or recreate our world, not provide an avenue of escape from it. Accordingly, it was the advent of God from out of the future that the early Christian communities awaited, in an intensified version of the anticipatory spirit of Abraham, Moses, and the prophets.[13]

Mostly as a consequence of the Platonizing of Christianity, however, Abrahamic hope gave way to an increasingly dualistic and acosmic brand of expectation. In Teilhard's lifetime biblical scholars and theologians were still embarrassed by the eschatological enthusiasm of Jesus and the early Christians. They had rediscovered the passionate hope of Jesus, the Synoptic Gospels and Paul, but they did not know quite what to make of it. Prominent Christian thinkers even proposed that eschatology be thoroughly demythologized so that God would be thought of more as an eternal present than a destabilizing future.[14] Teilhard, however, can be credited with a vision that tries to keep hope alive for the whole universe. He saw in evolution and post-Einsteinian cosmology a fresh opportunity to link the entire story of life, as well as the history and destiny of the whole universe, to the biblical anticipation of new creation.

Evolutionary science makes good sense, Teilhard thought, if we locate it in a metaphysical setting that gives priority to the future rather than the past. The experimental data underlying evolutionary science become less, not more, intelligible when interpreted mechanistically or materialistically, that is, by explaining the life story exclusively in terms of the earlier and simpler physical causes lying in the dead past. Only by looking toward the estuary, not the source, of the evolutionary river will life and the universe begin to disclose their true meaning. As I noted in the preceding chapter, Teilhard was seeking to replace the materialist metaphysics of the past with a metaphysics of the future, a worldview more in keeping with the Abrahamic and early Christian intuition that ultimate reality comes into the present from out of an ever-replenishing future. Teilhard thought that such a view of reality is needed now in order to highlight the fact that evolution is bringing new being, or "more-being," into the cosmos.[15]

Much of the negative press Teilhard has received from scientific critics, therefore, has less to do with disagreement about his scientific qualifications than with his deliberate espousal of a worldview opposed to modern scientific materialism. Teilhard knew the difference between science and scientific materialism, but most of his scientific critics have failed to see the distinction. This is probably why, for example, the biochemist and Nobel laureate Jacques Monod, an avowed mechanist, cast scorn on Teilhard for refusing to go along with materialism's decisive expulsion of subjectivity and purpose from nature.[16] Similarly, the late Harvard paleontologist Stephen Jay Gould, annoyed by Teilhard's conviction that there is an overarching directionality to evolution, gratuitously linked him to a notorious scientific hoax.[17] More recently the highly respected American philosopher Daniel Dennett has labeled Teilhard a "loser" simply because he does not go along with Dennett's overt materialism and his claim that evolution entails atheism.[18] The biologist Julian Huxley and the renowned geneticist Theodosius Dobzhansky were enthusiastic supporters of Teilhard both as a scientist and visionary, but the American evolutionist G. G. Simpson, despite his enjoyment of Teilhard's friendship, would certainly have considered the Jesuit scientist to be deluded in attributing theological meaning to a universe that evolutionary science, at least to the hardcore materialist, had exposed as manifestly pointless.[19]

Teilhard's professional scientific papers have never been controversial, and most scientists today would still find them impressive.[20] It is Teilhard's philosophical and religious reflections on evolution, such as those in the *Phenomenon,* that have raised objections from some scientists. Nevertheless, the late Harold Morowitz, a Nobel Prize–winning biochemist, gave a very positive scientific assessment of the *Phenomenon*,[21] even though he did not subscribe to Teilhard's religious vision. Unlike Monod, Dennett, and Gould, Morowitz was fair in distinguishing clearly between Teilhard as a scientist and Teilhard as a religious thinker. In fact, Morowitz thought the *Phenomenon* contributed substantially to the scientific understanding of evolution. He correctly observed, for example, that many years prior to the theory of "punctuated equilibrium" formulated by Stephen Jay Gould and Niles Eldredge, Teilhard had already devised an insightful way to account for the paucity of transitional forms in the fossil record.[22] Morowitz also wondered why Gould, a reputable Harvard paleontologist, had savagely attacked Teilhard by tying him without any evidence to the notorious Piltdown hoax.[23] We should also credit Teilhard for having debunked long ago the crude anti-Darwinism so visible today among creationists and "intelligent design" proponents. For Teilhard, the reversion by some Christians, including religiously devout scientists, to a pre-Darwinian idea of a divine magician performing acts of special creation diminished rather than exalted the creative power of God. Teilhard, on the contrary, saw a tight alliance between life's evolution and the biblical theme of hope.

TEILHARD'S UNIVERSE: WHAT DID HE "SEE"?

Teilhard was one of the first scientists in the twentieth century to realize that the entire universe, and not just the life-story, has a historical character. He took for granted that, on our planet at least, natural processes have successively brought about the realm of matter (the *geosphere*), then life (the *biosphere*), and most recently the *noosphere*, the "thinking layer" of earth history, a network made up of human persons, societies, religions, and other cultural, intellectual, artistic, and technological developments. Teilhard complained that scientists, in studying the universe, have failed to *see* that the noosphere is one of the most interesting developments in the history of the universe. Even though the recent emergence of the noosphere is clearly a part of *cosmic* history, ironically it has not yet become a focal topic for cosmology or even earth history. This is puzzling because a geologist is conditioned to look for emerging levels or layers in planetary evolution, and surely the noosphere is one of these. Yet most geologists, along with cosmologists, have failed to view the noosphere as a new layer or a new chapter in natural history continuous with the entire becoming of the universe. Behind this caution lies a scarcely suppressed (dualistic) suspicion that the world of thought, the world of human subjectivity, is not really part of the universe after all.

The phenomenon of thought, more often than not, remains off the maps of nature drawn up by scientists and philosophers of science.[24] But for Teilhard, the phenomenon of thought is fully part of nature rather than an alien intruder. The domain of thought is no less a flowering of nature than are rivers and trees. It is not science but the materialist metaphysics of the past that promotes the modern assumption that the universe is essentially mindless and hence that our own minds do not belong to the physical universe. Teilhard, however, considers it irrational to separate subjectivity or thought from nature. After all, the recent emergence of thought in evolution is tied seamlessly into the entire cosmic history, so Teilhard rules out any dualistic severance of mind or spirit from the physical universe. An essentially mindless realm of matter has never actually existed since, from the point of view of the new cosmic *story*, matter was already pregnant with mind (and spirit) from the very beginning of the universe. The universe is not just a place but a promise of more-being, and it has always been so.

As noted earlier, matter and spirit, in Teilhard's cosmology, are labels for two polar *tendencies* in nature's evolution, not two separate types of substance: *matter* is the tendency of nature to fall back toward a state of sheer multiplicity and incoherence;

spirit is the tendency of nature to move toward unity up ahead. For Teilhard, it is spirit, not matter, that gives consistence to the cosmos. Ultimately it is God the Creator who is the Center that initiates and grounds the world's inclination toward future coherence. It is by unifying things *ab ante*, from up-ahead, that God creates the universe. Since science has informed us that the universe is a still-unfolding process, we may think of nature as suspended between two poles, one toward fragmentation (the past), the other toward communion (the future). So, theology should no longer think of the world as divided into separate domains, matter and spirit. Before science had discovered that the universe is still coming into being, it was easier to indulge in such partitioning, but we now realize that the cosmos has always been in the process of awakening. From its beginning the cosmos has been gradually giving birth to thought.[25] How can this cosmic awakening fail to give us good reasons for hope here and now?

Thus, Teilhard writes, "The cosmos could not possibly be explained as a dust of unconscious elements, on which life, for some incomprehensible reason, burst into flower—as an accident or as a mould."[26] Since there has always been a cosmic tendency toward the emergence of mind and spirit, the universe has never been essentially mindless, or spiritless, or devoid of promise.

Teilhard continues:

[The universe] is *fundamentally and primarily* living, and in its complete history is ultimately nothing but an immense psychic exercise. From this point of view man is nothing but the point of emergence in nature, at which this deep cosmic evolution culminates and declares itself. From this point onwards man ceases to be a spark fallen by chance on earth and coming from another place. He is the flame of a general fermentation of the universe which breaks out suddenly on earth.[27]

Scientific materialism, by contrast, claims that the universe is essentially mindless and spiritless. It is especially a materialist view of reality that so many modern thinkers have made the foundation of their repudiation of Christian faith and hope, but Teilhard is intent on exposing the shallowness of the materialist creed. He attributes it to a tendency to view nature "under too great a magnification." The "analytical illusion" of materialists supposes that we can get to the bottom of the phenomena of life and mind by mentally decomposing them into lifeless droplets of "matter."[28] However, concretely, there is no such *thing* as matter; when materialists think they are giving a fundamental explanation for life and mind by pointing to their molecular and atomic makeup, they are fallaciously mistaking abstractions for concrete reality. Scientific materialism, with its message of cosmic pessimism, is the consequence of a failure not only of vision and hope but also of logic.

A NEW SPIRITUALITY OF HOPE

Everything that we can make out in the cosmic past with the help of science suggests that the universe has always been open to further increase in being and value. And there is no reason to think that this openness to *becoming more* has now been spent. Theologically, the universe is still being created, and the body of Christ is still in the process of formation. Every eucharistic celebration is a declaration that "what is really going on" in the universe is that Christ continues to gather everything, including our labors, joys, and diminishments, along with the entire cosmos into his own body.[29]

The intensifying of consciousness, unity, diversity, beauty, freedom, and love—all of which Teilhard refers to as the birth of "spirit"—is the supremely important set of events going on in the universe, all of it still open to redemption, transformation, and fulfillment in Christ. And so, it would be a pity for

Christians to go through life without an awareness that we are all being invited at each present moment to involve ourselves in the great work of increasing the universe's own being, that is, of making the cosmos, as the extended body of Christ, *more* than it has been before. This Christian vision of nature and its destiny gives a value to our secular pursuits that previous theology has seldom acknowledged, but which not too long ago was brought to our attention by the Second Vatican Council.

Without our *seeing* that something momentous is already going on in the universe, our hopes and moral aspiration will lack power, drama, zest, and the spirit of adventure. Like Teilhard, therefore, I believe that the greatest shortcoming of contemporary spirituality—religious or secular—is our failure to connect our need for hope to the story of the universe that science has set before us. Failing to see that our own lives are part of a cosmic stream that is flowing toward the estuary of more-being, our moral efforts and capacity for love lack an adequately energizing incentive. Consequently, we begin to drift aimlessly on a silent sea. In "Mass on the World," Teilhard prays: "Shatter, my God, through the daring of your revelation the childishly timid outlook that can conceive of nothing greater or more vital in the world than the pitiable perfection of our human organism."[30] The meaning of our lives amounts to much more than proving ourselves virtuous. Teilhard wants us to feel deeply the sense of purpose and responsibility that comes from our being part of the grand drama of cosmic awakening about which our religious ancestors knew nothing.

Perhaps these days we may understand the importance of cosmic hope as we look for a unifying basis for a global and ecologically responsible ethic. Until not long ago, a serious concern about cosmic destiny has been virtually absent in otherwise noble attempts to arrive at a planetary moral ecological consensus. It still seems that many ethicists overlook the fact that the earth is part of a much larger universe in which something unimaginably immense, beautiful, mysterious, and momentous may be working itself out. Spiritual directors likewise have failed to emphasize that our worship, prayer, and action may be redirected and invigorated by an awareness that our planet has an important part to play in a much larger, indeed cosmic and Christic, drama of creation.

The general assumption in most modern and contemporary spirituality has been that what is going on in the universe has little to do with what is going on terrestrially, ecologically, nationally, and religiously, as well as in our personal and family lives. However, the human phenomenon, as Teilhard emphasizes, is a "function of sidereal evolution of the globe, which is itself a function of total cosmic evolution."[31] To overlook the cosmic roots of life, thought and moral existence, he thinks, is to leave ourselves intellectually, ethically, and spiritually stranded.

How many of us consistently take into account in our thoughts about God and Christ the cosmic context of our hope? Feeling deeply connected to the cosmic story of creation would in no way entail the forsaking of time-tested religious doctrines or virtues such as humility, gratitude, moderation, justice, and love. Rather, in a dynamic cosmic setting, these would now have fresh meaning, transfigured by cosmic hope. In a cosmic setting, ethical activity and worship would mean that our faith, hope, and love are participating in the ongoing creation of a *universe*. For Christian spirituality and ethics it would mean connecting our search for the kingdom of God or our building the body of Christ to the ongoing creation of the heavens and the earth. A cosmically reformed hope does not mean that we would stop doing the small and often monotonous things we have always had to do. But at least we may now connect even the most mundane duties and obligations to our hope for the fulfillment of the entire universe.

Teilhard was deeply troubled by the persistent religious dualism that separates the moral responsiveness of religious people from the universe itself. This severance only "sickens" Christianity, preventing it from feeling the enlivening sap that rises up from cosmic roots. A "zest for living" must be the underpinning of all serious ethical endeavor, but such vitality requires the conviction that our efforts have the backing of the universe.[32] For healthy and robust hope to exist, there must always be room for something *more* to happen, since nothing "clips the wings of hope" or subverts the incentive to enthusiastic moral action more severely than the assumption that everything important has already occurred in some splendid mythic or cosmic past, and that the most human effort can accomplish is the restoration of what once was.[33] In fact, only a "passion *for being finally and permanently more*," says Teilhard, can sustain our hopes and actions.[34]

It is into a still awakening universe, not into a large lump of inert matter, that the incarnate God has descended. The God incarnate in Christ is the longed-for consistence, the Future on which the universe has always leaned "as its sole support." Theologically, what is *really* going on in evolution is that God is becoming increasingly incarnate in the world and the world is exploding "upward into God."[35] Beneath the surface of what science has discovered in nature there is the eternal drama of God's creativity, incarnation, and saving promise.

DOES ANYTHING LAST FOREVER?

For Teilhard, the incentive to do good becomes most invigorated when it is motivated by trust that our efforts can have a *lasting* impact on the whole of things—that is, on the continuing story of the universe. But since the universe itself will eventually perish, there must be a permanent guarantee that the *whole* of things is not sentenced to an "absolute death." If we thought that our spiritual aspirations and moral efforts were ultimately futile, we would lose heart. This is why Teilhard places the virtue of hope at the very foundation of his cosmic vision. He takes for granted the Christian belief in a God who saves everything from absolute perishing. Otherwise it would be unreasonable to trust that the long cosmic story of creation would add up to anything significant in the end.

As an informed scientist, Teilhard does not deny that the laws of thermodynamics predict an eventual termination of the physical universe. But the prospect of a "total death" of the universe, he adds, would "immediately dry up in us the springs from which our efforts are drawn."[36] By this he means that, corresponding to the outside scientific story of the universe, there is an "inside story" that weaves itself *permanently* into the resurrected body of Christ and hence into the everlasting life of God. Each of us is explicitly aware of only a small slice of the inside story. But our own inquiring minds, along with our moral and spiritual aspirations, as argued later, are intertwined with the inside story of the whole universe. And this inside story, Christians hope, will be gathered up, transformed, and made new by the everlasting love of God.

Because it has taken 13.8 billion years of physical and bio-logical ferment to generate the cerebral complexity that allows humans now to ask questions about meaning and truth, no sharp line of demarcation separates the story of the universe from our interior lives. Likewise, our capacity to hope is not, as skeptics insist, an escape from reality. Rather, human hope is a special way in which the whole universe keeps reaching toward what is truly real.

Let us continue these reflections immediately in the following chapter by reflection on the meaning of human action and moral aspiration.

4

ACTION

Shatter, my God, through the daring of your revelation the childishly timid outlook that can conceive of nothing greater or more vital in the world than the pitiable perfection of our human organism.

—Pierre Teilhard de Chardin,
"The Mass on the World"

The philosopher Immanuel Kant thought that each of us needs to keep asking three big questions: What can I know? What must I do? What may I hope for? Today, though, we may add another: What's going on? What's going on in the universe?[1] In order to act responsibly, Teilhard instructs us, it is not enough to know only what's going on in one's life and the human community but also what's going on in the universe at large. Teilhard's contemporary importance, I believe, consists in great measure of his almost unique realization last century that understanding the universe is not irrelevant to right action. Having a sense of the drama of awakening already going on in the universe can give us a new "zest for living," a sense of being part of a great cosmic adventure, and this awareness can refocus our moral lives. We may experience a new jolt of moral aspiration especially once we realize that we are part of a great cosmic project of bringing about "more-being."[2] Looking carefully at what has already been transpiring in the wider universe, starting long before we arrived in earth history, we may discover general guidelines and new incentives for what we should be doing with our lives here and now.

Secular ethicists, for the most part, have been trying to decide what to do with their lives without looking any deeper for guidance than what goes on in the biological, social, political, and economic spheres. Likewise, religious ethicists have also weighed the question of what to do without paying much attention to the cosmic context of their lives. In Christian thought today the cosmos still functions predominantly as a neutral background for human action rather than as a drama of continuing creation where giving birth to more life and more thought transforms the whole meaning of responsible human action.

Until recently, post-Enlightenment thought had shown little interest in actually *seeing* the universe to find out what is going on. The natural world may have been of theoretical interest to physicists and cosmologists, but for most people it remained a relatively featureless backdrop in their struggle to find meaning in their lives and actions. After Darwin, principled thinkers even turned their eyes deliberately away from the cosmos because of what they took to be the immoral and uncaring workings of natural selection.

Traditionally, of course, the Abrahamic faiths assumed that the universe is inherently meaningful. They took it to be the expression of divine power and creativity, and this belief gave human lives at least a vague sense of belonging to something of great importance. Modern thought, however, has taken for granted that the universe is essentially mindless and pointless, and as such it cannot be a source of moral guidance. Most of our religious ancestors had considered the universe and our lives to be timelessly grounded in a transcendent principle of meaning and goodness—*Dharma*, *Rta*, *Tao*, *Logos*, *Brahman*, *Yahweh*, *Allah*, *Wakan Tanka*, and so on. Religious lives were shaped by an assurance that the cosmos was at heart governed by a principle of "rightness," and a religious sense of belonging to this indestructible sphere of being was essential to ethical aspiration. Modern science, however, seems to have divested the universe of inherent meaning altogether.

Ideals that shape the ethical sensitivity of most humans today, including religious skeptics, still draw weakly and unknowingly from the moral heroism of ancient predecessors whose lives were shaped by religious trust in a meaningful cosmos. The obedience by most nonreligious people to the demands of justice and compassion is tacitly tied to cultures of the past that were themselves shaped by a religious sense of indestructible rightness. Today, however, powerful intellectual forces maintain that science has rendered obsolete the ancient religious convictions that we inhabit an ultimately meaningful cosmos. The natural sciences, especially Darwinian and neo-Darwinian biology, have made it hard for scientifically educated people to feel the deep connection our ancestors experienced between moral life and the universe. Some of them insist that any universe that allows for the ragged evolutionary story of life must be indifferent to values that shape our moral lives. Since evolution occurs by way of countless accidents, aimless struggle, abundant suffering, and the elimination of the weak by impersonal natural selection, nature now seems more indifferent to our own moral ideals than ever before. The physical universe, as it is understood especially by contemporary biologists, is blind, non-directional, and hence utterly devoid of moral significance.

WHY AND HOW TO ACT

With his eyes fixed on the achievements of science, however, Teilhard developed a vision of reality in which *seeing* what's going on in the universe (and not just in the life-story) is essential for understanding what we must be *doing* with our lives, ethically speaking. He spied something momentous coming to birth in the cosmos, and this great drama—if we only had eyes to *see* it—includes at least general instructions for shaping—or reshaping—human action. A scientifically informed awareness that our own lives and labors are woven into an awakening universe can give new zest to life and hence to moral aspiration.

With Kant, Teilhard asks: "Why act—and how to act?" He admits:

> So long as our conceptions of the universe remained static, the basis of duty remained extremely obscure. To account for this mysterious [moral] law which weighs fundamentally on our liberty, men had recourse to all sorts of explanations, from that of an explicit command issued from outside to that of an irrational but categorical instinct. In [an] evolutionary scheme of the universe, such as we have here accepted, the answer is quite simple. For the human unit the *initial* basis of obligation is the fact of being born and developing *as a function of a cosmic stream*. We must act, and in a certain way, because our individual destinies are dependent on a universal destiny. Duty, in its origins, is nothing but the reflection of the universe in the atom.[3]

For Teilhard, the universe, as given to us after Einstein, has had an overall tendency to become *more* throughout its long history. In Teilhard's futurist cosmology "becoming more" means becoming more alive, more conscious, and more liberated from blind determinism. Teilhard calls this process of liberation from the fixed past the emergence of *spirit*. Here, *spirit* does not mean something "immaterial." It is not a supernatural layer added to the physical. Rather, spirit is a name for the awakening now going on in the very same cosmos that earlier gave rise to molecules and living cells. It includes the new terrestrial dimension of thought, the intensifying of our sense of beauty, our religious longing for meaning, and our natural creativity including our technological inventiveness—anything that elevates the cosmos beyond the state of slavery to what has been.

The need to act arises in our hearts, then, when we experience how our own lives are webbed into the great cosmic work of intensifying life, consciousness, and spirit that is already under way. The universe is giving birth even now to more-being, and so, morally, our human vocations, whatever they may be specifically, must universally be that of contributing to the arrival of fuller being in the grand drama of a cosmic awakening.

Underlying Teilhard's bold sense of an awakening cosmos, of course, is a profoundly religious vision. Unlike contemporary evolutionary naturalists, Teilhard would never have contemplated separating the cosmos from a transcendent principle of creativity and care that allows for emergent novelty and guarantees the worthwhileness of the world's becoming. In the final analysis, life, human effort, and the cosmic process would be vacuous apart from a principle of care that saves the world from absolute perishing. Something great is afoot in the cosmos ultimately because it has always been intimately related to the life of God. For Teilhard, the cosmos is the matrix of emergent complexity, life, consciousness, personality, and spirit. Such outcomes are possible, however, only because of a favoring divine influence operative at a level of reality too deep for ordinary science to grasp. It is this dimension of divine creativity that awakens the universe and justifies human action.

Why, the naturalist will ask, need one invoke the idea of God at all? In the first place, at least for Teilhard, there has to be an eternal ground of all the possibilities that become actualized in the course of the unfolding of the world, whether as life, consciousness, or spirit. The ultimate source of these possibilities can be nothing less than what Christians refer to as God. Second, cosmic process and human action can have deep significance only if there exists a transcendent principle that is *preservative* of all the events that make up cosmic process. Christian hope for redemption, Teilhard proposes, must cover the whole universe and not just the individual soul's destiny. Along with the life of Jesus, divine compassion assimilates everything that transpires in the story of the universe, not just in human history. God is the savior of the *entire* universe, and God is the constant stimulus to the universe's becoming more. Teilhard even allows that God, without in any way undergoing diminishment, is in some sense *changed* by what happens in the world. If so, this is a deeply significant reason for right human action. Teilhard agrees with traditional Christian teaching that there is a sense in which God is self-sufficient, but in reality "the universe contributes something that is vitally necessary to [God]."[4] What happens in the world truly matters to God, and our own actions, no matter how small they may seem to us, are taken into God's life—everlastingly.

Were it not for a religious intuition that the universe, despite its transience, is intertwined with something everlasting, we could never attain a profound sense of the importance of our moral lives and human action. A zest for living is essential to serious moral existence, but there can be no such zest without a conviction, first, that something of utmost importance is already occurring in the universe and, second, that our lives and struggles are so enmeshed with the universe that they make a *permanent* difference to the encompassing cosmic drama of awakening and hence to the life of God. A purely stoical heroism, appealing though it may be to our sense of nobility, is not enough to undergird a lasting sense of obligation. Only a "passion *for being finally and permanently more*" can lead to a consistently enthusiastic participation in right action.[5]

Such aspiration, however, will eventually go limp apart from a belief that the universe has a meaning that is sealed into it everlastingly. The materialist assumption that the universe, and we along with it, are destined for absolute oblivion would eventually quench the fire that enkindles moral action. To all cosmic pessimists, therefore, Teilhard writes:

> Promise the earth a hundred million more years of contin-
> ued growth. If, at the end of that period, it is evident that
> the whole of consciousness must revert to zero, *without its
> secret essence being garnered anywhere at all,* then, I insist, we
> shall lay down our arms—and mankind will be on strike.
> The prospect of a *total death* (and that is a word to which
> we should devote much thought if we are to gauge its de-
> structive effect on our souls) will, I warn you, when it has
> become part of our consciousness, immediately dry up in
> us the springs from which our efforts are drawn.[6]

A persistent challenge to Teilhard's religious and ethical enthusiasm is the unthinkable prospect of an eventual total death
of the cosmos as predicted by contemporary astrophysics. If
we really believed that the universe, including the totality of
our labors, will eventually be reduced to nothingness, then
moral incentive will eventually vanish. Fortunately, the minds
and hearts even of the most extreme cosmic pessimists do not
embrace, deep down, the belief that human action is ultimately
futile. Teilhard believes, however, that to invigorate human action
robustly, we need to believe formally that the "secret essence"
of the universe is being "garnered" somewhere. Everything that
exists in time eventually perishes, including the universe itself.
But everything that takes place in time, including our own lives
and actions, is imprinted in God's compassionate "memory" and
transformed by divine creativity into a beauty to be enjoyed
both by God and ourselves everlastingly. If so, there is no reason
to suppose that what occurs in the cosmos and human history
is ultimately "pointless" and that our own efforts are ultimately
empty.

Attuning our minds and hearts in acts of faith and hope to the promises of God comports fully with our new awareness of a universe that is still coming into being. Awareness of a still-awakening universe can have a bearing not only on the meaning of moral life but also on our acts of worship:

> To worship was formerly to prefer God to things, relating them to him and sacrificing them for him. To worship is now becoming to devote oneself body and soul to the creative act, associating oneself with that act in order to fulfill the world by hard work and intellectual exploration.
>
> To love one's neighbor was formerly to do him no injury and to bind up his wounds. Henceforth charity, without losing any of its compassion, will attain its full meaning in life given for common progress [where "progress" means the emergence of more-being in the arrival of life, consciousness, and spirit].
>
> It used to appear that there were only two attitudes mathematically possible for man: to love heaven or to love earth. With a new view of space [and time], a third road is opening up: to make our way to heaven *through* earth. There is a communion (the true communion) with God through the world; and to surrender oneself to it is not to take the impossible step of trying to serve two masters.[7]

Such an understanding of worship, Teilhard goes on to say, "has no taint of the opium which we [Christians] are accused with such bitterness (and not without justification) of dispensing to the masses."[8] His reinterpretation of moral action and worship in the light of evolution and cosmology may seem too radical and too "secular" for many Christians, but Teilhard was convinced that a serious commitment to Christian life requires henceforth a cosmically transformed sense of both worship and moral obligation.

SCIENCE, FAITH, AND MORALITY

Again, "Why act? And how to act?" Teilhard was convinced that good answers to these questions require a new synthesis of science, cosmology, and faith. It is doubtful, after all, that moral aspiration can be kept alive intergenerationally apart from a vision of the universe that makes human action permanently, and not just temporarily, worthwhile.[9] We first have to be reassured, however, that life is worth living, and worth living well, if our ethical lives are to have a solid foundation. To live life zestfully, we must first have a conviction that our efforts and struggles can have lasting repercussions in bringing about something "more" and in giving new shape to the whole of things. Our moral energy drains away whenever we suspect that our efforts have no permanent significance. Sustained moral commitment can exist only in the expectation that by acting we are contributing something of lasting value to whatever it is that is coming to birth in the cosmos itself.

Teilhard thought that if we look at the universe with the eyes of both faith *and* science, we may find that the cosmos can teach us something about how to act. By observing carefully what has already been going on in the universe, namely, the gradual emergence of consciousness and spirit, we can gain a sense of direction as to what we must do. He insists that to get through life courageously, we need "an absolutely certain biological and moral rule." The universe provides that rule by directing our actions and lives to the goal of bringing about greater degrees of being and consciousness.[10] That is, our moral lives can be animated by a sense that our actions can contribute to the ongoing awakening of the universe.

The intensifying of consciousness, spirit, and hence the bringing about of more-being is the supremely important set of events going on in the universe. Consequently, "we should use the following as an absolute principle of appraisal in our moral judgments: 'It is better, no matter what the cost, to be more conscious than less conscious.'" "This principle," Teilhard assumes, "is the absolute condition of the world's existence." It is also the foundation of a moral vision for the age of science after Darwin and Einstein. Nevertheless, Teilhard complains, "many contest [this principle], implicitly or explicitly, without any idea of the enormity of their denial."[11] This blindness stems from the questionable modern belief that our moral instincts have nothing whatsoever to do with the universe as revealed by science.

Today, as well as in Teilhard's lifetime, prominent scientific skeptics continue to deny that humans can learn anything at all about what we must do by looking at what's going on in the universe. Starting with Darwin and T. H. Huxley, evolutionists, for example, have asserted that nature has nothing to teach us about how to conduct our lives. Modeling behavior on the story of life's evolution, we are instructed, would lead only to social Darwinism and other evils. George Williams, a renowned contemporary biologist, even refers to nature as a "wicked old witch" because of the heartless and wasteful way in which it lets blind natural selection do the job of creating diversity. Contemporary biological understanding of the role of genes in the life process seems to support Huxley's intuition that we must not look to the natural world to find out how to act or what to do. As Williams puts it:

With what other than condemnation is a person with any moral sense supposed to respond to a system in which the ultimate purpose in life is to be better than your neighbor at getting genes into future generations, in which those successful genes provide the message that instructs the development of the next generation, in which that message is always "exploit your environment, including your friends and relatives, so as to maximize our genes' success," in which the closest thing to a golden rule is don't cheat, unless it is likely to provide a net benefit?[12]

The late Harvard paleontologist Stephen Jay Gould, one of Teilhard's most hostile critics, has also insisted that the "cold bath" of Darwinism should have convinced us once and for all that nature can teach us nothing about what we must do or how we should act. "The factual state of the universe, whatever it may be," he writes, "cannot teach us *how we should live* or *what our lives should mean*." Gould then goes on to say that "Darwin . . . liberated us from asking too much of nature, thus leaving us free to comprehend whatever fearful fascination may reside 'out there,' in full confidence that our quest for decency and meaning cannot be threatened thereby, and can emerge only from our own moral consciousness."[13]

Teilhard, however, would reject the claims by Huxley, Williams, and Gould that the natural world has nothing to teach us as far as duty is concerned. Such a prejudice is the product of an inability or refusal to gain a wide enough vision of the cosmos. No doubt, when we study life's evolution narrowly—in isolation from the rest of the cosmic story—Darwin's science can hardly set an adequate standard for human action, as Teilhard would surely agree. But the story of life's evolution must now be set within the larger context of a cosmic drama of awakening. And, if one has the breadth of vision to take in the larger story, the Darwinian episodes may not be as ethically disturbing as evolutionary materialists have often made them.

In laying out the cosmic context for Christian ethics, Teilhard soundly rejects his critics' separation of the story of life and mind from the larger cosmic narrative. The narrow perspective on the universe typical of evolutionary materialists, he observes, is a product of the modern *analytical illusion*,[14] a way of looking at nature that puts it "under too great a magnification."[15] Scientific observers tend typically to view the universe atomistically, that is, by imaginatively breaking everything down into elementary units that evolution then blindly gathers into the shapes of living organisms. Then, when these aggregates eventually fall to pieces, as inevitably they do, it seems to materialists that nothing remains of what had been achieved in the earlier syntheses. For the scientific atomist or "pluralist," death by dissolution is the final destiny of all organic assemblies, not to mention the universe itself.

However, Teilhard responds:

> Seen under too great a magnification, the finest of paintings is reduced to shapeless blotches, the purest curve to divergent strokes, the most regular of phenomena to disordered turbulence, the most continuous movement to jerks. Bearing that in mind we can hardly wonder that under the solvent . . . of analysis the living being, in turn, is reabsorbed into unconsciousness, chance and determinisms, while all the rest—all, I mean, that is specifically living—slips through the mesh of the filter.[16]

By being so narrowly and analytically fixated, most scientific thinkers fail to see the larger drama going on in the universe. It is hardly to be wondered at, therefore, that specialists cannot see or reflect deeply on the vast cosmic drama in which the universe has always been struggling to become more. The eyes of the geologist or paleontologist are conditioned to look for distinct *levels* in the record of earth's evolution, but they have unfortunately overlooked the relatively recent cosmic eruption of conscious thought, the new *geological* level that is now enveloping our planet. They cannot see the forest of cosmic awakening going on in the background because they are too tied up with the troubled trees in the foreground.

The cosmic process has passed through pre-atomic, atomic, molecular, unicellular, multicellular, vertebrate, primate, and human stages of awakening. In the course of this passage, it has produced a measurable increase in the terrestrial store of consciousness. It has brought about more-being. The human brain and its capacity for thought, for example, are outcomes of a *cosmic* trend toward increasing complexity and consciousness. A general directionality in cosmic becoming is there to be seen, as is the universe's tendency to sponsor an increase in organic complexity and the intensity of subjectivity. The cosmic trend toward deeper subjectivity and consciousness instructs us that our own moral lives also should be committed to the cause of enhancing life and intensifying the cosmic awakening.

When we are deciding why and how to act, we do not have to be blind to what is going on in the universe. A hidden but powerful moral imperative already resides inside the universe: it is always good to increase the world's awakening. Of course, *at their own levels of explanation*, the laws of natural selection, physics, and chemistry can account for the emergence of complexity without any mention of the deeper drama of an awakening universe. So, to become aware that the universe is a drama of awakening, Teilhard was convinced, we need a wider empiricism and a deeper understanding than science conventionally utilizes. Biology and other sciences can arrive at a more or less accurate account of the outward complexification of life. But what needs our attention also is the fact that this outward complexity is accompanied by the emergence of interior awareness, including eventually human thought. The arrival of thought in the cosmic drama brings with it the obligation for us to contribute to its growth in whatever way we can.

For several centuries science has been pretending, in effect, that consciousness is not part of the *real* world.[17] In modern times a number of scientists and philosophers, in a desperate attempt to make the cosmos appear completely mindless, have even denied that subjectivity or consciousness has any real existence at all. While this pretense may be methodologically advantageous in some phases of scientific research, a complete concealment of the dimension of subjectivity prohibits a full and *objective* understanding of the universe that is now waking up. Unfortunately, the picture of the natural world devised by modern materialist thought is typically one in which no room exists for subjects of any kind. Consequently, when evolutionary biology locates the roots of our own existence in what it takes to be a mindless universe, the only way to fit humans seamlessly into the rest of nature is to deny in effect that subjectivity is part of nature.

To return subjectivity to its rightful place in the natural world, therefore, Teilhard calls for a "hyperphysics," a wide way of looking at the universe in which subjectivity is understood to be inseparable from matter. By ignoring subjectivity, modern thought has passed over the larger story of awakening that is the most important thing going on in the universe. Even worse, it has reduced the cosmic story to a mere reshuffling of atoms. By focusing only on elemental physical units, analytical materialists have failed to see anything significant working itself out in the universe. They have encouraged "enlightened" people to assume that the universe is essentially mindless and that an absolute death awaits everything in the end.

If this outlook were accurate, no good reasons could be given as to why we should attribute lasting importance to our own actions and moral efforts. Today, unfortunately, it is mostly from within a cosmically pessimistic intellectual atmosphere that ethicists, ecologists, economists, politicians, and social scientists are trying to decide "what we must do." The persistent separation of mind (or soul) from physical reality runs contrary to Teilhard's cosmic vision, according to which our intellectual, moral, and religious lives are fully part of a still emerging and unfinished universe. By failing to see the universe as a story of becoming *more*, and therefore as having dramatic importance, modern thought has ignored the connection between the cosmos and human moral obligation.

Any attempt to decide what we must do without looking simultaneously at the drama of awakening that gave rise to our capacity for moral aspiration in the first place is ethically shortsighted. By acknowledging that human subjectivity is an outcome of a dramatically awakening universe, however, Teilhard realizes that what goes on in the cosmos cannot be insignificant ethically or spiritually. Once the sharp line between the history of matter and the emergence of subjects including the human "soul" dissolves, the modern materialist belief that the universe is an essentially mindless realm of matter is seen to be pure fiction. There is no real separation between the morally sensitive human "soul" and the physical universe. "If God . . . is to *make a soul*, there is only one way open to his power: to create a world."[18] And if that soul awakens to moral values, it is not by being liberated *from* nature, as Gould and other evolutionists claim, but by being an indispensable instrument in the dramatic cosmic awakening to indestructible rightness.

5

SPIRITUALITY

In 1612, John Donne wrote the sonnet "Anatomie of the World," in which these famous but anxious lines appear:

> And new Philosophy calls all in doubt,
> The Element of fire is quite put out;
> The Sun is lost, and th'earth, and no man's wit
> Can well direct him where to looke for it.
> 'Tis all in peeces, all coherence gone.

Just two years earlier, Galileo Galilei, whom the poet may have met in Padua, had published the first scientific bestseller, *The Starry Messenger*. This was Galileo's initial public announcement that the heavens are not organized the way almost everybody had previously thought. A half century earlier, in 1543, Nicolaus Copernicus had already made the sun change places with "th'earth," but not too many people had taken him seriously. Those who paid any attention at all typically interpreted Copernicus's new model as a hypothesis, useful for making astronomical measurements and predictions but not representative of the real world. Galileo, however, did not hold back. For him, the Copernican system was not just a geometric experiment but an accurate portrayal of the way things are.

Donne's lyrics are of interest to students of Teilhard because they express the anxiety that ensues when the picture of nature presupposed by a religious tradition is turned topsy-turvy. Today, for example, in the Christian (and Muslim) experience nothing has twisted the serene face of nature more grotesquely than developments in biology over the last century and a half. Charles Darwin's science, as we have already seen, rattles the faith of many devout believers. Evolutionary biology's portrayal of life is not what the faithful had come to expect from their Creator. The high degree of accidents, the impersonality of natural selection, and the wasteful immensity of time essential for the gradual emergence of living diversity—these three ingredients of evolutionary thought have rendered traditional providential pictures of life suspect. Just as John Donne felt spiritually disoriented at losing his spatial grounding, so people today worry about whether and how a spiritual life can find a proper place in an unfinished and unpredictable universe.

Spirituality can have many meanings, but at the very least, it is a quest for something to which we can lift up our hearts, something that can give us what Teilhard calls "the zest for living." For centuries the geocentric model of the universe had functioned as the framework for the spiritual journey, while ancient Greek philosophy provided a powerful theoretical setting for the lifting up of hearts. The circular movement of the heavens and the faultless spherical shape of the sun and moon offered at least an inkling of the timeless perfection that dwells beyond the imperfections of our shadowy world. So central was the ideal of perfect circularity in the heavenly spheres that even Galileo hesitated to abandon this ancient aesthetic prejudice.

The "new philosophy"—by which Donne means what we now refer to as the Copernican revolution—called "all in doubt." With the newer measurements of celestial motion by early modern astronomers, the heavens underwent a series of demotions that eventually blunted their capacity to symbolize the perfection people need to anchor their spiritual lives. The birth of modern science initiated a seismic upheaval in the topography previously underlying spiritual life, and we are still feeling the aftershocks.

In the ancient world Aristotle had portrayed the heavens as a quintessential (fifth) kind of reality far surpassing in value the four mundane elements—earth, air, fire, and water. But the early modern astronomer Tycho Brahe (1546–1601) demonstrated to his disappointed contemporaries that comets and supernovas—both implying change and novelty—existed beyond the moon, in the domain of allegedly unchanging perfection. Johannes Kepler (1571–1630) calculated that superlunary planets move in "ugly" ellipses rather than perfectly circular orbits. And Galileo (1564–1642), peering at the skies through his newly upgraded telescope, delivered a final blow to the assumption of astronomical perfection. Venus, he discovered, goes through phases and changes dramatically over time. Jupiter turned out to have satellites that circle not around the earth but around an extraterrestrial heavenly body. And even more disturbing, Galileo discovered that the most excellent heavenly body of all, the sun, is blemished by sunspots. The heavens are mediocre, not "quintessential." "The Element of fire is quite put out," writes Donne, and all visible things both beyond and beneath the moon's orbit are just average.

Now that the heavenly canopy turns out to be subject to the corrosiveness of time, it is no more to be privileged than is our terrestrial place of pilgrimage. Apart from perishable seasonal flowerings that let in the light of divine love for sensitive souls like those of Hopkins and Donne, is there any steady, enduring emblem of perfection in the natural world to which our spiritual longings might now cling? If everything else in nature, including celestial bodies, is bedeviled with impermanence, to what may we now lift up our hearts?

Our prescientific ancestors could sample eternity simply by turning their eyes to the changeless heavens. After Copernicus,

Darwin, and Einstein, however, the whole cosmos seems tied to irreversible time. The whole of nature, as Einstein aided by other cosmologists has demonstrated, is inseparable from time and perishing. Are there any sacraments of perfection in the natural world today, then, that are as spiritually elevating as the changeless heavens had been since antiquity? In the age of science, amid all the transient seductions and bitter sorrows of our own temporal lives, can we find any quality in the natural world that may lead us to lift up our own hearts and link us hopefully and joyfully to the permanent beauty for which we long?

And can science help us in this search? One might not think so immediately. Scientific method, after all, thrives on making what seems remarkable at first seem unremarkable after subjecting it to analysis. To the scientific naturalist, everything in nature turns out to be explainable in terms of tiny atomic bits and invariant physical principles. Analysis makes nature seem utterly mundane. So, is there anything about our new scientific understanding of the universe that can arouse throbs of joy in our hearts and charge us with a new zest for living?

Yes. The universe, as Teilhard never tired of saying, is still coming into being, and our own existence is part of an enormous and still unfinished epic of creation. The new scientific picture of an unfinished universe can make a difference in our spiritual lives. Science has opened up before our eyes a 13.8-billion-year-old cosmic story of creation about which the ancient and medieval spiritual guides knew nothing. The dramatic new story of the universe, because it is not yet over, may now provide a brand-new horizon for religious aspiration.

How so? Scientific discoveries, as we have learned over the last two centuries, clearly imply that nature is narrative to the core and that the story of cosmic creation is far from over. The universe may still hold the promise of eons of new creation up ahead. I agree with Teilhard that this promise should be a source of spiritual joy. By unveiling a four-billion-year-old journey of life in a fourteen-billion-year-old cosmic drama, science now makes it possible for us realistically to lift up our hearts, not just to the heavens above but, even more, to the open and mysterious *future* dawning from the up-ahead. The cosmos is a transformative story of gradual awakening into which we may now weave our own lives, moral aspirations, and spiritual longings as never before.

The whole universe, as it turns out, is being called into a new future, and we along with it. Together with Abraham, the prophets, and Jesus, we can taste the kingdom of God today not so much through contemplation of an eternal present, or by nostalgia for an imagined past state of primordial cosmic perfection, but by *anticipation* of a new future for the entire cosmos. We look forward not to "another world" but to the transformation and new creation of this one.

GAUDIUM ET SPES

As we shall come to appreciate throughout this book, our own personal destinies may now merge self-consciously with what is going on in the whole physical universe. Christian faith is inseparable from hope for new creation, and one of the great recent instances of such hope, I believe, was the stirring in Pope John XXIII's heart and mind as he sought, in a phrase often attributed to him, "to open the windows of the church to let in some fresh air." A new sense of the future was arriving during Vatican II and, before that, in biblical and theological studies that influenced the council's invitation to renew our faith in light of Christianity's foundational documents. Many of us who were around when the council took place cannot forget the sense that something never seen before was breaking into our world during that period. Over a half-century later we may still draw strength from the council's mood of expectation, one that revived the wave of hope that swept over the ancient world with the early arrival of Christianity's resurrection faith. The council left us with a deeper conviction than ever that Christianity is essentially forward looking and that God, in the words of theologian Karl Rahner, is the Absolute Future.

I believe with Teilhard that scientific discoveries during the last two centuries invite us to expand and intensify our personal hope for the coming of this Future. The startling picture of an expanding, still-unfinished universe can provide a new anticipatory setting for the lifting up of hearts. In his hope-filled "Closing Message of the Council" (December 8, 1965), Pope Paul VI addressed, among other audiences, those whose lives are devoted to science: "Continue your search without tiring and without ever despairing of the truth," he said. "Happy are those who, while possessing the truth, search more earnestly for it in order to renew it, deepen it and transmit it to others. Happy also are those who, not having found it, are working toward it with a sincere heart. May they seek the light of tomorrow with the light of today until they reach the fullness of light."[1]

The council's closing words are encouraging: "Never perhaps, thank God, has there been so clear a possibility as today of a deep understanding between real science and real faith, mutual servants of one another in the one truth. Do not stand in the way of this important meeting. Have confidence in faith, this great friend of intelligence. Enlighten yourselves with its light in order to take hold of truth, the whole truth."[2]

The council's 1965 document *Gaudium et Spes* (*Pastoral Constitution on the Church in the Modern World*) had already expressed both the fruit and the promise of a new encounter of Christian faith and hope with the sciences. After noting that the "scientific spirit exerts a new kind of impact" on culture and thought, the document makes two provocative claims that express the importance of recent scientific discoveries for spiritual life. The first is that "the human race has passed from a rather static concept of reality to a more dynamic, evolutionary one. In consequence there has arisen a new series of problems . . . calling for efforts of analysis and synthesis" (no. 5). The second proposition, relying implicitly on the first, is that "a hope related to the end of time does not diminish the importance of intervening duties but rather undergirds the acquittal of them with fresh incentives" (no. 21).

The council goes on to emphasize, in the spirit of Pope John XXIII's encyclical *Mater et Magistra*, that Christian hope does not lead to withdrawal from the world but instead to "bettering" (no. 21) and "building" it (no. 34). These two statements provide a promising theological departure for implementing the pope's and the council's expectation of a rich future convergence of the seemingly separate worlds of science and Christian hope. For some of us the words of the council seem so familiar now that we may fail to reflect deeply enough on their revolutionary spiritual implications.

No doubt those present-day Christians for whom modernity seems essentially evil and spiritually regressive will ignore the two claims just cited. The statements seem to be a path toward the dead end of secularism. Why, some Christians are still asking, should we want to reconcile faith and theology with an evolutionary worldview? Evolution, after all, is an idea that strikes many as equivalent to materialism and atheism. It is an idea that appears dangerous theologically because it has been alloyed so often with shallow and even murderous "visions" of progress and social engineering. Did not Hitler and Nazi eugenics, for example, appeal to Darwinian ideas? And what exactly are the "fresh incentives" that Christian hope for final redemption gives to our "intervening duties" of "building the world"? What does our hope for final redemption imply for our moral decisions and duties here and now?

It is impossible for me to ponder the council's words about evolution and building the world without thinking of Teilhard. In a variety of posthumously published writings, Teilhard had

anticipated the spirit of the council and outlined ways to renew Christian thought and spirituality in the age of science.[3]
Consequently, a close look at Teilhard's many writings, although
they were composed long before the Second Vatican Council,
can still guide us as we reflect today on the council's overtures
to women and men of science.

There can be no doubt that Teilhard's ideas on faith and science are transparent in *Gaudium et Spes*. The document clearly
endorses, at least in principle, Teilhard's call for transplanting
Christian thought from its former cosmological setting—a static,
pre-Copernican and pre-Darwinian understanding of nature—to
a dynamic, evolutionary one. The renowned theologian Henri
de Lubac, SJ, confirms this impression in his postconciliar remark
that *Gaudium et Spes* expressed "precisely what Pére Teilhard
sought to do."[4] The Teilhard scholar Robert Faricy, SJ, rightly
refers to Teilhard's influence on the document as "a dominating
one."[5] And it seems that a Teilhardian spirit of hope and a new
"zest for living" informed the council in other ways as well. So,
more than half a century later, as I am arguing throughout this
book, we may fruitfully examine anew Teilhard's efforts to frame
a spirituality for the age of science.

During Teilhard's own lifetime, we may recall, church censorship had prevented the publication of his innovative reflections
on science and Christian faith. Ostensibly, it was Teilhard's early
and undeveloped attempts to reconcile original sin with evolution that had first alarmed his superiors. It seemed convenient
to the latter, therefore, to let the brilliant young Jesuit scientist
spend a quarter of a century virtually exiled in China, far from
his beloved Paris, where he was already becoming controversial.
The long period in China, however, only served to nurture Teilhard's sense of the need to render Christianity relevant in terms
of geology, evolutionary biology, and cosmology, sciences that are
giving us an entirely new awareness of an awakening universe.

The Vatican's banning the distribution of Teilhard's writings during his lifetime is consistent with the fact that church officials and even many Catholic theologians were then highly skeptical of evolutionary science in general. They were equally alarmed at Teilhard's world-affirming spiritual vision, sometimes suspecting (wrongly) that it was more communist than Christian. Remarkably, however, by the end of the council, a mere decade after Teilhard's death, his church had acknowledged the need to take the new evolutionary view of the world seriously and to redefine our Christian vocation accordingly. By the end of the council, Pope Paul VI is reported to have said: "Fr. Teilhard is an indispensable man for our times; his expression of faith is necessary for us!"[6]

Yet how many Catholics and how many theologians, seminarians, catechists, and spiritual advisers have looked deeply enough into *Gaudium et Spes* to taste the Teilhardian "zest for living" that animates it? Teilhard would certainly have applauded the council's closing message that we are on the verge of "a deep understanding between real science and real faith, mutual servants of one another in the one truth." But just how enthusiastic today are most Catholics and other Christians about the council's call for a fruitful, in-depth conversation between science and faith?

If Christian faith is to survive intellectual scrutiny in the age of science, as Teilhard had rightly come to see, it simply must come to grips with science, in general, and evolution, in particular. In our own day, perhaps even more than in that of John Donne, an honest embrace of scientific discoveries requires a spiritual adjustment that seems too dramatic for many religious believers. In many ways Christians the world over are still pre-Copernican or "fixist" in their religious and theological sensibilities. At times they tolerate evolution, but how often do they truly celebrate it as the intellectual backbone of a new spiritual vision? Darwinian biology and Big Bang physics seem to have called all in doubt when in fact they may lift up our hearts in a new epoch of discovery—both scientific and religious. The fear remains strong among many Christian thinkers that evolution is the slippery slope to philosophical materialism, cosmic pessimism, and outright atheism. This fear, however, is not a reasonable alibi for avoiding the task of "analysis and synthesis" for which the council calls.

Teilhard died in 1955, but by the time of the council his ideas on science and Christian faith had become familiar, either directly or indirectly, to at least some of the theologians and bishops at the council. The *Phenomenon* was becoming a bestseller in the area of religious thought for Harper & Row, so it was hard to ignore. *The Divine Milieu* appeared in French in 1957 and in English translation in 1960. Its spirituality of "divinizing" human action in the world is reflected in the council's exhortation not to let our hopes for final redemption diminish the importance of "intervening duties" in our present existence.

Teilhard, of course, was not the only Catholic thinker to have made action and "building the world" essential components of Christian spirituality and ethics, but the force of his integration of Christian faith with human effort and hope for the world's future is unsurpassed in its combination of spiritual depth and intellectual power. It was Teilhard more than any other religious thinker of his time who brought the discoveries of the natural sciences to bear on the quest for a wholesome spirituality. Most remarkably, he made cosmogenesis the loom on which to weave any future Christian vision of hope. It was Teilhard who, even while digging ever deeper into the remote geological past, could announce that the world "rests on the future as its sole support."[7]

Only a cosmic sense that something really big is taking shape up ahead, Teilhard thought, can let us lift up our hearts in such a way that it may add incentive to our "intervening duties." By harnessing nature's own leaning toward the future Christian spirituality after Galileo, Darwin, and Big Bang cosmology can motivate our actions in a way that is fully consistent with the

Christian doctrines of incarnation and redemption.[8] Understanding St. Paul's cosmic Christ as the goal of the world's natural evolution, and locating his "new God" as the "Omega" of cosmogenesis, Teilhard and his followers can remain completely tied to the natural world without suspecting that they are thereby turning their backs on their creator.

The council, moreover, affirmed the Teilhardian view that what Christians may hope for is no longer reducible to having their souls transported from earth to heaven. And furthermore, after Darwin and Einstein, we may look for the glory of God not only in the design of living cells and organisms, but even more in the drama of a whole universe still coming into being in surprising but hidden ways. Science now allows Christians to respond to the threat of spiritual suffocation not only by lifting their eyes to the spatial immensity of the heavens but also, and even more, in the spirit of the apostle Paul, by hoping for the redemption, liberation, and full awakening of a not-yet-perfected universe.

In my opinion Catholic Christianity has largely failed to take spiritual advantage of Teilhard's synthesis of science, on the one hand, and faith in the future, on the other. Interest in Teilhard's cosmic vision, for no justifiable reason, has waned since the time of the council. In 1967, Archbishop Fulton J. Sheen wrote: "It is very likely that within fifty years when all the trivial, verbal disputes about the meaning of Teilhard's 'unfortunate' vocabulary will have died away or have taken a secondary place, Teilhard will appear like John of the Cross and St. Teresa of Avila, as the spiritual genius of the twentieth century."[9] Regrettably, this prophecy has yet to be fulfilled. More than half a century has elapsed since Archbishop Sheen ventured his bold prediction, but Teilhard's synthesis of Christianity and evolution remains largely unknown and undigested by most Catholics, including the majority of theologians. Even those who have given notional assent to evolutionary science have been reluctant to think out carefully, as both Teilhard and the council encouraged, what it really means that we have "passed from a rather static concept of reality to a more dynamic, evolutionary one." And Catholic thought has yet to undertake on a large scale what the council called new efforts of "analysis and synthesis."

ANALYSIS AND SYNTHESIS

To appreciate the constructive advice of *Gaudium et Spes,* it may be helpful to recall here several of Teilhard's pioneering ideas, some of which I touched on earlier. First, Teilhard claimed that it is theologically, spiritually, and ethically important to seal into our hearts and minds the fact that in each moment of each day the world is "raised a little further above nothingness."[10] In keeping with the ideas of Darwin and Einstein, the cosmos shows itself to be more open than ever to a future of ongoing creation. In the cosmic journey something new and significant is always taking shape up ahead.[11] Evolution, viewed theologically, implies that the universe is always capable of *more-being*. So our intervening duties may have new meaning to the extent that they are contributing to the awakening of a universe that is always being called by God toward *fuller being*.

If we had been present in the early universe and been able to survey it when it was still only an undifferentiated sea of radiation, how many of us would have predicted that the primordial plasma held the promise of eventually becoming stars, supernovae, carbon, life, thought, art, morality, and the capacity to make and keep promises? Yet, even in its remotest origins, all of these outcomes were already beginning to stir undetectably. Four billion years ago, when microorganisms first quietly emerged on earth, the web of life was already beginning to weave itself into a *biosphere*. And after the biosphere appeared, an even newer sphere of mind and thought, of culture, morality, freedom, literacy, science, and technology was already waiting on the horizon of the future. The *noosphere*, our planet's new envelope of *thought*, was beginning to take form. What, then, awaits our universe right now?

It is by way of building communities, both nonhuman and human, that the universe advances. Through the increasingly intense connections and interrelationships of atoms, molecules, cells, and organisms, the universe has become *more* during all of its major transitional stages to the present. So now that conscious persons have recently emerged in evolution, it is only by way of interpersonal communion among these unique centers of thought and action that we may expect more-being to be actualized. Only mutual love, along with "a great hope held in common," can bring these distinct personal centers together into a rich and differentiated communion. The cosmic function of Christian faith, hope, and charity is to foster the building of community and in this way contribute to the ongoing growth of the universe.[12]

Our new scientific awareness that the world is still coming into being can serve, then, to lift up our hearts and give new incentive to our spiritual lives in the age of evolution. In giving reasons for our hope, Teilhard pointed to what he saw as a discernible direction in evolution and a general drift in cosmic process toward increasing complexity-consciousness. Evolution in the eyes of biologists may seem to resemble a drunken stagger, but the overall movement of the *universe* has been in the direction of increasing physical complexity, a point that even atheistic evolutionists now accept. The long cosmic journey gives evidence of a measurable intensification of organized complexity accompanied by a corresponding degree of awakening. One can only wonder what this mysterious tendency toward complexity and consciousness may lead to in the future.

In any case, as visible matter has become more complex outwardly, an invisible subjectivity, interiority, centricity, or "insideness" has also become gradually more intense, leading the universe toward increasing sentience and consciousness.[13] Having arrived recently at the level of human consciousness, there is no reason to assume, therefore, that the universe's hunger for more-being and fuller awakening is now fully satisfied. The universe still has the opportunity to become more, especially by reaching toward a transcendent Center of attraction.

For Teilhard, the incarnation of God in Christ continues to stir up the world. The entire cosmic process of creativity is always being called irreversibly and everlastingly into the life and redemptive compassion of God. Nothing in the story is ever lost or forgotten. Evolution means that creation is still happening, and that God is creating the world not *a retro*, that is, from out of the past, but *ab ante*, from the up-ahead.[14] All things are still being brought together in the Christ who is coming. As a devotee of the apostle Paul, Teilhard was convinced that what is *really* going on is that the "whole creation" is groaning for the renewal wrought by God in Christ through the power of the Holy Spirit (Col 1:15–20).

It is in the cosmic Christ that all things "hold together." Our spiritual hope, our "resting on the future," therefore, is simply the flowering of what has always been an anticipatory universe. Now, through the spiritual longings of each human heart, the universe shows that it is still restless for further creation. Is it not possible that something really big is still taking shape up ahead? And are not our visions of the coming kingdom of God and the building up of the body of Christ expressing through us the universe's own ages-old anticipation of more-being? Can anything lift up our hearts more forcefully than a sense that our "intervening duties" are contributing, no matter how insignificant our individual offerings may be, to the emergence of more-being on the horizon of the cosmic future? The universe, as science has taught us, has always been ripening toward a new future, long before human beings arrived on the terrestrial scene. Today, the church of Jesus should be the first to applaud science's great discovery that the universe is still pregnant with promise.

Teilhard was one of the first scientists to have noticed that the cosmos is a still-unfolding drama. He was among the first Christian thinkers to realize that the universe is not just a stage for the human drama, but that the stage is *part* of the drama. Our spiritual life appears now in an entirely new light and our own lives are part of a larger creative cosmic process. Theologically, this means that what we do with our lives is of consequence for the larger narrative of creation, as St. Paul seems to have implied when he understood our own redemption by Christ as something for which the whole of creation has been waiting (see Rom 8:18–21).

So, the Second Vatican Council was justified on both scientific and biblical grounds in connecting our "intervening duties" to the final destiny of the universe in God. After Darwin and Einstein, our action in the world matters because it contributes both to the deeper incarnation of God and to the redemptive gathering of the whole world—and not just human souls—into the body of Christ. Reflecting on both the new scientific story of the universe and St. Paul's cosmic Christology, Teilhard notes how wondrously the doctrine of God's incarnation converges with the new scientific sense of a still emerging universe.[15]

Finally, as Teilhard was aware, for many sincere scientifically educated people, the universe has apparently outgrown their sense of God. It is encouraging, therefore, that even in the early twentieth century, Teilhard was emphasizing that evolution and scientific cosmology provide new resources for Christian spirituality. In this and many other ways Teilhard's thought still has an important role to play in the implementation of the council's encouragement of a spirituality proportionate to our age of remarkable new scientific discoveries.

The world's religions, at least during the period of their emergence, knew nothing about Big Bang cosmology, deep time, or biological evolution. Generally, they have yet to catch up with these realities. Even in the scientific West, the findings of evolutionary biology and cosmology continue to lurk only at the fringes of contemporary theological awareness. The sensibilities of most believers in God, including theologians, have been fashioned in an imaginative context defined either by ancient cosmologies or, if philosophically tutored, by equally timeworn metaphysical systems that are static and hierarchical. Our religious sense of ultimate reality, our thoughts about the meaning of human existence and destiny, our intuitions about what is ultimately good and what the good life is, and our ideas of what is evil or unethical—all of these at least originally took up residence in a human awareness that was still innocent of the implications of deep cosmic time and largely unaware of the possibility that the universe is presently only at the dawn of its eventual journey through time.

How, then, are we to think about God, if at all, in terms of the new scientific understanding of biological evolution and cosmic process? Probably the majority of scientifically educated people have given up on such a project, settling into their impressions that the immense universe of contemporary natural science has outgrown for good what astronomer Harlow Shapely once referred to as the anthropomorphic, one-planet deity of our terrestrial religions. Theology, meanwhile, has only barely begun to reconsider the idea of God in a way that would render it consonant with up-to-date evolutionary science and cosmology.[16]

The making of conscious subjectivity has been going on, with no sharp breaks anywhere along the way, ever since the earliest cosmic moments. Subjectivity—essential to an awakening universe—was already being stitched into the universe by virtue of the physical conditions and fundamental constants that came onto the cosmic scene in its opening moments. A universe that has for so long been awakening still has plenty of room for our own patient and longsuffering cosmic hope. Awareness that the universe has a long future ahead of it and that its "secret essence" is being "garnered" in God may let us lift up our hearts in a new way.

If determinism reigned and the cosmic future were closed, Jesus's proclamation of the good news and his constant encouragement to trust would seem irrelevant to our understanding of creation and of what is going on in the universe. Christianity might then be reduced to a world-escaping fairytale and, at best, heartwarming fiction. Teilhard's cosmic vision, however, allows that people of faith need no longer compromise with cosmic pessimism as they have often done in the past. We are born into, and borne along by, a general drift of the entire cosmos in the direction of a full awakening to God in Christ. Our new awareness of nature's immensities—in the domains of space, time, and organized physical complexity—provides us with the opportunity to enlarge our sense of God far beyond that of any previous age.

6

GOD

As his thought matured, Teilhard increasingly complained that traditional theology's understanding of God as *being* (*esse*) does not connect comfortably with the dramatic new scientific sense of a world still in the process of *becoming*. Christian theology has previously conceived of God too much in terms of Aristotle's notion of a Prime Mover pushing the cosmos into being from the past (*a retro*). Evolution, however, demands that we think of God as attracting the world into being from out of the future (*ab ante*), drawing the whole cosmos forward into the realm of the not-yet. Creation is a process of gathering the thin strands of cosmic beginnings into increasing complexity located not so much up-above as up-ahead. To create, therefore, is to unite. Creation is a process in which past multiplicity is being drawn toward future, increasingly richer, forms of coherence. For Teilhard, as for the author of Revelation, God is both Alpha and Omega. But after Darwin and the new cosmology, God is less Alpha than Omega: "Only a God who is functionally and totally 'Omega' can satisfy us," Teilhard exclaims. But then he asks: "Where shall we find such a God?"[1]

Over six decades after Teilhard's death we are still looking for an answer to this question. For the most part theologians still think and write as though Darwin, Einstein, Lemaître, and Hubble never existed. Theological attention is fixed almost exclusively on questions about the meaning of human existence, human history, social justice, hermeneutics, gender issues, or the individual's spiritual journey—with little attention to the universe and its future. The traditional topics are all worthy of attention, of course, but except for a smattering of ecologically interested theologies, the meaning of natural history still fails to command much religious or theological interest. In the Christian churches, redemption and eschatology are still typically thought of in anthropocentric terms, as a saving of human souls *from* the universe, rather than as the coming to fulfillment of an entire cosmic story.

GOD, EVIL, SIN, AND REDEMPTION

Paul Tillich (1886–1965), one of the most influential Christian theologians of the twentieth century, was aware of modern theology's failure to take the natural world into account, and he sought to address this failure, especially in the third volume of his *Systematic Theology*. He even felt the need for a theology of the inorganic world, and I have often wondered what such a theology would look like had Tillich become more familiar with the writings of Teilhard. Toward the end of his life Tillich indicated that he had become acquainted with some of Teilhard's ideas, and although he considered Teilhard's vision of the universe too "progressivistic" for his own tastes, he nevertheless felt "near" to the modest Jesuit in "so many respects."[2]

Tillich did not say exactly what attracted him to Teilhard, but I suspect that he found in Teilhard a forward-looking Christian thinker who mirrored many of his own theological interests. For example, Tillich and Teilhard both sought a Christian spirituality in which we do not have to turn our backs on the natural world in order to enter the kingdom of God. Additionally, they agreed that life in a finite universe is inevitably, and not just accidentally, riddled with ambiguity, and that the estrangement of the universe from its essential state of being somehow coincides with the very fact of its existence. They both wrestled in creative ways with how to balance the vertical (transcendent) and horizontal (this-worldly) dimensions of human aspiration. They both looked for ways in which the human person could experience religious meaning without "heteronomy" (Tillich's term for our being subjected to a law alien to our authentic being and freedom). That is, they longed for a kind of communion with God that allows human selfhood to flourish and freedom to thrive. They held in common the intuition that love is the key to healing an estranged universe, but that *agape* should never be separated from *eros*. Similarly, they both recognized that scientific materialism is, in Tillich's words, nothing less than an "ontology of death."[3] And they both sought to counter materialism without reverting to a vitalistic separation of life from matter. Above all, they wanted religious thought to open itself to the category of the New.

Both Tillich and Teilhard were also extremely sensitive to the ways in which dualism and "supra-naturalism" had weakened Christianity. Although Teilhard was not directly influenced as much by Friedrich Nietzsche as was Tillich, he was sensitive to the Nietzschean accusation that Christian piety has too often fostered a hatred of the earth that saps human existence of the "zest for living."[4] Tillich and Teilhard also agreed that Platonic influences in Christian thought had robbed the world's "becoming" of any real significance.

In the end, however, Teilhard no less than Tillich found the Nietzschean atheistic outlook suffocating. Nietzsche understandably longed for a fresh beginning to human history, but his cosmological claim that everything that happens is part of an "eternal return" leaves no room for what is truly new. Any vision of things that ultimately closes off the world to *new being* is ill-adapted to the human soul and religious adventure. Neither the classical metaphysics of the eternal present nor the modern materialist metaphysics of the past provides breathing room for freedom, creativity, and the zest for life. Classical theism assumes that everything important has already happened in eternity, and materialism explains everything "new" on earth as nothing more than a reshuffling of the atoms of old. Both systems of thought have the effect of stifling hope and deadening human effort.

Another point of comparison is on the meaning of original sin. Aware that the traditional explanation of a historical "Fall" of humans from an original paradise could no longer be taken literally as the explanation of our estrangement from true being, both Tillich and Teilhard tried out new ways of accounting theologically for the ambiguities of life and the oppressiveness of evil. They wrote their main works at a time when biblical scholarship and a growing awareness of evolution had already debunked literalist readings of Genesis, and they received harsh criticism from conservative Christians as they sought deeper meanings in the biblical myths of origins.

On the question of "original sin," what still requires theological discussion is the role of human freedom and responsibility in accounting for evil. Both Tillich and Teilhard moved decisively in the direction of interpreting sin, evil, suffering, and death as tragic, or as "somehow" inevitable. Their intention in each case was to widen the scope of the redemption of the world in Christ. A one-sided anthropocentric interpretation of evil diminishes the breadth of divine love, but thinking of evil as somehow a cosmic phenomenon raises troubling questions about how much responsibility human persons have in contributing to the existence of suffering and evil.

More than most other Christian thinkers, Teilhard resisted the idea that evil is due only to human sin. In one of several early notes not intended for publication (writings that may have led at least indirectly to his being virtually exiled to China by his religious superiors) Teilhard wrote:

Original sin, taken in its widest sense, is not a malady specific to the earth, nor is it bound up with human generation. It simply symbolizes the inevitable chance of evil (*Necesse est ut eveniant scandala*) which accompanies the existence of all participated being. Wherever being *in fieri* [in the process of becoming] is produced, suffering and wrong immediately appear as its shadow: not only as a result of the tendency towards inaction and selfishness found in creatures, but also (which is more disturbing) as an inevitable consequence of their effort to progress. Original sin is the essential reaction of the finite to the creative act. Inevitably it insinuates itself into existence through the medium of all creation. It is the *reverse side* of all creation.[5]

For Teilhard, the most noteworthy theological consequence of this universalizing of evil is that it considerably enlarges the scope and import of the redemption in Christ:

If we are to retain the Christian view of Christ-the-Redeemer it is evident that we must also retain an original sin as vast as the world: otherwise Christ would have saved only a part of the world and would not truly be the center of all. Further, scientific research has shown that, in space and duration, the world is vast beyond anything conceived by the apostles and the first generations of Christianity.[6]

It follows that by failing to expand our minds in a way that represents the temporal and spatial immensities revealed to us by the new scientific cosmic story, we will also inevitably fail to do justice to the significance of Christ and the scope of divine redemption: "How, then, can we contrive still to make first original sin, and then the figure of Christ, cover the enormous and daily expanding panorama of the universe? How are we to maintain the possibility of *a fault as cosmic* as the Redemption?"[7] Teilhard's answer: "The only way in which we can do so is by spreading the Fall throughout the whole of universal history."[8] And he adds: "The spirit of the Bible and the Church is perfectly clear: the *whole* world has been corrupted by the Fall and the *whole* of everything has been redeemed. Christ's glory, beauty, and irresistible attraction radiate, in short, from his *universal* kingship. If his dominance is restricted to the sublunary regions, then he is eclipsed, he is abjectly extinguished by the universe."[9]

As a still-classical theologian, Tillich would surely sympathize with Teilhard's attempt to widen the scope of redemption. In fact, for Tillich, redemption extends not only over the whole of the physical universe and its history, but also into the very heart of *being* as such.[10] However, for Tillich no less than for Teilhard, the question remains as to whether, by universalizing the primordial fault and correspondingly the compass of redemption, he has unduly lessened the role of human responsibility in accounting for evil. Many theologians have resisted a broad extension of the scheme of redemption to the nonhuman world precisely because such expansionism seems to dilute and even nullify the role of human freedom in accounting for the most horrendous evils in our world.[11]

Although Teilhard does not pretend to have responded adequately to the mystery of evil, he rightly claims that the reality of evil has a cosmic dimension; and evil appears to be not quite the same thing when viewed in the context of evolution and contemporary scientific cosmology as it is when interpreted in terms of a static universe. We may ask, then, whether even as significant a theologian as Paul Tillich has taken evolution and the idea of an unfinished universe sufficiently into account in his own understanding of God and redemption.

Cosmic and biological evolution, as Teilhard instructs us, mean that we live in a universe that is not yet fully created. The incompleteness of cosmic becoming—that is, of cosmogenesis— implies logically that the universe and human existence have never, under any circumstances, been perfected. In an evolving cosmos *created* being, as such, has *not yet* achieved the status of full integrity. Moreover, this is nobody's fault, including the Creator's (as we shall see again in Chapter 9), because the only kind of universe a loving and providential God could conceivably create in the first place is an unfinished one. For God's love of creation to be actualized, after all, the beloved world must be truly *other* than God, and an initially perfected universe would have been only an emanation or appendage of deity. A perfectly designed universe would not be sufficiently independent of God to have its own existence and distinct identity. It could never have established sufficient autonomy or dialogical distance from the Creator to be lovingly espoused by God or to love God. The idea of a world perfectly constituted *ab initio* (from the beginning) would, in other words, be logically incompatible with the belief that the universe is the free gift of God.

Unfortunately, the prescientific idea of an initially perfected, non-evolving universe has tended to generate scapegoating quests for the "culprit" or "culprits" who ruined the initial harmony. If creation had been originally a fully accomplished affair, after all, we would understandably want to expose whoever or whatever it was that messed things up so badly for us. The assumption of an originally perfected creation has, in fact, led Christians to blame and demonize communities, nations, political parties, persons, genders, and other seemingly alien entities for allegedly defiling the primordially perfect creation. We cannot help wondering, then, what would happen to religious thought and Christian spirituality were they to take evolution and cosmogenesis seriously.

In 1933, Teilhard observed, in words that apply to Christian thought even today:

In spite of the subtle distinctions of the theologians, it is a matter *of fact* that Christianity has developed under the over-riding impression that all the evil round us was born from an initial transgression. So far as dogma is concerned we are still living in the atmosphere of a universe in which what matters most is reparation and expiation. The vital problem, both for Christ and ourselves, is to get rid of a stain.[12]

As long as we had assumed that creation was fully formed instantaneously in an initial creative divine act, the only way we could make sense of present evil and suffering was to posit a secondary distortion. But this assumption interprets suffering essentially as punishment, fostering an ethic of retribution and scapegoating. Such a twist can only render expiation an interminable affair, thereby robbing suffering of the possibility of being interpreted as part of the process of ongoing creation itself. "A primary disorder," Teilhard says, "cannot be justified in a world which is created fully formed: a culprit has to be found. But in a world which emerges gradually from matter there is no longer any need to assume a primordial mishap in order to explain the appearance of . . . evil."[13]

Evolution and cosmogenesis, to come back to our starting point, imply that the world is unfinished. But, if it is unfinished, we cannot justifiably expect it ever previously to have been perfect. It *inevitably* has a dark side as long as it is still coming into being. Redemption, therefore, if it means anything at all, must include the healing of the *tragic* evil that accompanies the existence of any universe whose journey is not yet over. What would it mean, then, if the creator had fashioned a universe whose *original status* was one of full paradisal perfection? Then the evil that we experience here and now would have to be attributed to a contingent occurrence or perhaps a "culprit" that somehow spoiled the primordial cosmic splendor, causing it to lose its original integrity. This, of course, is how evil and suffering have often been accounted for by Christian theology in the prescientific past. Accordingly, "salvation" could easily be thought of as a repairing and "restoring" of the original cosmic state of completeness. And although the *re*-storation may be garnished at its margins with epicycles of novelty, it will be thought of essentially as a *re*-establishment of the assumed fullness that once was and is now no more.

Paying close attention to evolution, however, no longer allows us to imagine that the universe was at one time—in a remote historical or mythic past—a fully perfected state of being. Instead, as we look with Teilhard back into the universe's most distant past, we see nothing paradisal, but only multiplicity fading into nothingness. But with the help of contemporary astrophysics, we may now at least notice that, even in the very earliest phase of its history, the cosmos is accompanied by an almost imperceptible straining toward the future. The mathematical values, physical constants, and initial conditions are precisely those that will allow for the eventual arrival of life. From the beginning the universe is a promise, one that remains to be fully actualized.

In that case, then, a scientifically informed Christian theology of redemption (soteriology, as it is called) may no longer plausibly make the themes of restoration or recovery dominant. The remote cosmic past, after all, consists of what Teilhard calls "the multiple," that is, fragmentary monads not yet brought into relationship or unity with others. The notion of an unfinished universe still coming into being opens up the horizon to a new, unprecedented future for the natural world. In doing so, it does away in principle with the religious obsession with expiation as a reasonable response to the fact of evil. This is partly why evolution is potentially such good news for theology.

IS TILLICH'S THEOLOGY ADEQUATE TO EVOLUTION?

How well, then, does Tillich's theology function as a context for understanding and appreciating the reality of evolution?

Unfortunately, even Tillich, despite his awareness of the biblical theme of new creation, embeds his cosmic soteriology and eschatology in the atmosphere of "*re*-storation." Tillich, no doubt, goes beyond most previous versions of classical theology and leads us at least in the general direction of a metaphysics of the future that the logic of evolutionary understanding now requires. His expectation of New Being points us toward an understanding of God that can at last take evolution seriously.

But does it take us far enough? While Tillich's system of theology is open to New Being, we may still wonder whether it has fully absorbed the impact of Darwin, Einstein, and others who have introduced us to evolution and an unfinished universe.[14] Can Tillich's classical theology of "being" move us fully beyond a restorative and expiatory understanding of redemption? Tillich distinguishes the actual state of our world from what he refers to as its "essential" being. Both he and Teilhard think of finite existence as a state of separation from what is essential, but they differ on the meaning of *essential*. For Tillich, the existing universe is estranged from what he calls the "ground of being," a very earthy metaphor for God.[15] For Teilhard, however, the universe is estranged from its future, from what is not-yet.

For Tillich, creation can be healed, and evil overcome, only by the creature's *re*-union with essential being or with the ground of being. This reconciliation is brought about by the coming of "the New Being" symbolized in the birth, life, death, and resurrection of Jesus the Christ. In Christ, the New Being overcomes the estrangement of the world from its essential being. Tillich's theological language, centered on the idea of being (*esse*), still allows, like most pre-evolutionary classical theology, the subordination of the theme of redemption to the motif of *restoration*. Even though Tillich's thought tries to introduce us to New Being, it is still in terms of a rather futureless notion of "being" that he articulates the newness.

In Tillich's theology the New Being is defined as "essential being under the conditions of existence."[16] Teilhard would comment that Tillich's preference for a theology of "being" cannot stop us from thinking of God in pre-evolutionary terms. The notion of being suppresses the dimension of the future, of the not-yet, toward which biblical expectation turns us. In Tillich's thought, as in the classical metaphysics of pre-evolutionary theology, the futurity of being is subordinated to the idea of God as an eternal *present*.

From a Teilhardian perspective, in other words, Tillich's theology still lends support to the prescientific assumption that nothing truly new can ever get accomplished in the world's historical unfolding, since the fullness of being is portrayed as already realized in an eternal present. Such a concept, as Teilhard explains, will only "clip the wings of hope." This is why, for Teilhard, the essential fullness of being always lies in the future. The "essential" is not a state of being that lurks either in an eternal present or in some misty, mythical past (*Urzeit*)—that is, in an unimaginable state of being before time or outside of time. For Teilhard, that which is essential is always in some sense not-yet. The world's true being awaits it up-ahead. The foundation of all things is not primarily a "ground" of being sustaining the creation from beneath, but a power of attraction drawing the multiple toward unity up ahead.

"The universe," as Teilhard proposes, "is organically resting on . . . the future as its sole support."[17] This suggestive way of locating ultimate reality arouses a religious imagery and affectivity quite different from Tillich's notion of God as *ground* of being or as the *eternal now*. The gravitational undertow of Tillich's powerful metaphor of "ground"—together with his other earthy images of God as "depth" and "abyss"—tends to pull his theological reflection toward the expectation of a *return* to what already *is*. Tillich's metaphors for God as ground, depth, and abyss do respond to Teilhard's concern that theology need no longer stake out the dwelling place of God in an arena "up above" or completely outside of time. Instead, the Jesuit evolutionist looks for God preeminently on the horizon of a future that has never been before.

In a world not yet fully completed, it is important for theology still to acknowledge with Tillich that the actual condition of finite existence is indeed one of estrangement from its essential being. But the being from which the finite world and finite human persons are "estranged" must be, at least in the light of evolution, in some sense not-yet-being. God arrives faithfully from the region of the not-yet—*ab ante*. There remains in Tillich's theology a spirit of tragic resignation that is hard to reconcile with Teilhardian hope. The New Being central to Tillich's theology enters *vertically* into the context of our estrangement and reconciles us to itself. Consoling as such an idea may be to a certain kind of Christian piety, however, it still bears the weight of metaphysical traditions innocent of evolution and at least to some extent resistant to the biblical motif of promise.

CONCLUSIONS

Tillich's presentation of Christ as the New Being does indeed give breadth to the theology of redemption, and in this respect his theology goes a long way toward meeting the requirements of a theology of evolution. However, although Teilhard would be appreciative of Tillich's broadening of the scheme of redemption, he would still wonder whether the philosophical notion of "being," even when qualified by the adjective "new," is adequate to the reality of evolution. For Teilhard, it is less the concept of *esse* (being) than that of *fieri* (becoming) or *uniri* (being brought into unity) that a theology of creation attuned to a post-Darwinian world requires.[18]

Even in his earliest reflections on God and evolution, Teilhard expressed disillusionment with the Thomistic metaphysics of being, and he did so at a time when it was unusual for a Catholic thinker to express such disenchantment. But the young Teilhard realized even then that evolution requires nothing less than a revolution in our sense of what is truly real. As I have repeatedly suggested, Teilhard's thought calls for a full-blown metaphysics of the future. Here, I am arguing that Tillich's metaphysics of being, even his notion of new being, does not fully satisfy this requirement.

For Teilhard, the "essential" from which the universe, including humans, is now separated, is the Future, the Up-Ahead, the Omega who creates the world *ab ante* rather than *a retro*—the God, who saves the world not so much by rooting it more fully in an eternal now, but by being the world's unceasingly faithful and always surprising Future. The *essential*, therefore, is not for Teilhard an original fullness of being from which the universe has become estranged, but instead a yet-unrealized ideal toward which "the multiple" is being summoned into deeper unity. In this dynamic futurist setting—one that renders Teilhard's thought more biblical than Tillich's—the universe can be thought of as a promise, not just a sacrament. Correspondingly, nature may be seen as anticipative of the ultimate Future on which creation leans, rather than analogically revelatory of an eternal present. If we still wish to view the cosmos as participative being, then what it participates in is not a fixed past or present plenitude, but a pleroma (fullness) yet to come. And its present ambiguity is of the sort that we might associate with a promise still unfulfilled rather than with the traces of a primordial wholeness that has now vanished into eternity or into a forgotten past.

Instead of nostalgia for a lost innocence, evolution demands a posture of genuine hope that ennobles creative human action in the world. Our existence as finite beings involves more than just waiting for an alleged reunion with Being-Itself. The true "courage to be" is not simply that of conquering the threat of nonbeing, but of orienting our lives toward the insecurity of the not-yet. Concretely, this includes "building the earth" in a responsible manner as our small contribution to the ongoing creation of the cosmos. After Darwin, the power of being is the power of the future, and we affirm our human existence coura- geously by allowing ourselves to be grasped by this future rather than by returning to the static fixity of the past.

According to Teilhard's metaphysics of the future, sin is the consequence of our free submission to the deadening pull of the multiple, to the fragmented past states of a universe whose ultimate communion with God-Omega has yet to be realized and for which we shall have to wait and work with patient expectation. In an unfinished universe humans remain accom- plices of evil, of course, even of horrendous forms of evil. But our complicity in evil may now be interpreted less in terms of a hypothesized break from primordial innocence than as our deliberate refusal to participate in the ongoing creation of the world.

The creative process is one in which the originally dispersed elements of a nascent cosmos are now being drawn toward ulti- mate unity. Our own sin, then, is that of spurning the invitation to participate in the adventure of a whole universe being drawn toward its future—the God-Omega, the New God—upon whom the universe leans as its foundation.

Here, sin means our resistance to the call toward "being- more." Sin is our deliberate turning away from participation in what is still coming into being. Thus, there is ample room in a metaphysics of the future to affirm the traditional emphasis on personal sin and the need for redemption. But we can acknowl- edge our sinfulness without expecting retribution in the form of endless expiatory suffering and self-hatred. We can address our sinfulness not by paying for our misdeeds in a proportionate measure of pain, but by seeking reasons for hope in a cosmic future that can give new zest to our ethical aspirations. Here, we may define original sin as our shared human tendency to place ourselves outside of the cosmic awakening to which we already belong. Original sin, from this point of view, is the accumulation in human history and culture of our habitual refusal to assume responsibility for contributing to the ongoing creation of a universe.

Original sin is not the defilement of a primordial cosmic perfection but the residue of a habitual human history of turning away from the world's essential being. Original sin is the cumulative history of "falling" backward into the decay of disunity and of being content with monotony as the status quo. The stain of cosmic pessimism touches all souls and threatens to erode the faith and hope of all human beings. Nevertheless, past emergent achievements—such as the arrival of life, sentience, and thought in the universe—provide reasons for hope that the forces of unity can emerge victorious in the future. Even if the physical universe eventually succumbs to entropy, as Teilhard predicts it will, something of great significance—he called it "spirit"—is "garnered" and transformed everlastingly in the heart of a divine compassion. And the coming of more-being in cosmic history is rescued from nonbeing and absolute loss by being taken permanently into the Absolute Future we may call God.

7

DESCENT

The innumerable species, genera and families, with which this world is peopled, are all descended, each within its own class or group, from common parents, and have all been modified in the course of descent.

—Charles Darwin,
On the Origin of Species

The topic of human evolution and what it means in the context of Christian faith requires consideration of how to understand the venerable teaching that human beings are created in the "image and likeness of God." If our species has descended in a continuous way from a nonhuman animal ancestry, can Christians now justify their traditional claim that human beings have a special standing among created beings? Of course, other theological questions also arise in connection with the theme of human evolution—and the present chapter makes brief allusions to some of them—but the main focus here is on the question of whether and how to measure human worth after Darwin. As we pursue this question, we shall find that Teilhard's cosmic vision allows us to understand the value of human life and human dignity in a way that was not yet available to our religious ancestors.

EVOLUTION AND THE IMAGE OF GOD

By the time Charles Darwin had published *On the Origin of Species* in 1859, many naturalists in Europe and America had already concluded that all extant living beings have a common ancestry. Even Charles's own grandfather Erasmus Darwin had expressed the opinion that life has unfolded and diversified gradually from a single common source over a long span of time. Furthermore, according to traditional theology, God's creativity is not limited to the beginning of time. There is *original* creation, of course, but there are also *continuous* and *new* creation. The Creator works not only at the time of origins but also over the course of time, allowing for new beings to come into existence spontaneously during the course of natural history. This creativity can take place, moreover, without disturbing the regularity of natural laws.

St. Augustine of Hippo (354–430) proposed long ago that new kinds of beings, including unprecedented forms of life, can come into existence quite naturally after the initial creation of the world (*De Genesi ad Litteram*). According to Augustine, the Creator planted "seed principles" (*semines rationales*) in nature in the beginning, and these potentialities blossomed into actualities only later on. Nowadays, it is standard Christian theology to acknowledge that the world is still being created with the complicity, rather than the evasion or violation, of natural causes. To maintain that natural laws can proximately explain the existence of various phenomena is not to deny that God is the ultimate explanation of the existence of the heavens and the earth. In the biblical understanding of creation, God continues to create by making all things *new* (Isa 42:9; Rev 21:5). Such a religious understanding of nature is, in principle, completely consistent with an evolutionary account of human emergence.

Consequently, Christians are not contradicting their fundamental beliefs or theological traditions when they embrace the scientific idea of life's common descent. According to most

Christian evolutionists, especially Teilhard, Darwin's new science now makes it possible to think of God's power to create as more impressive than ever. A creator who brings into being a world that in turn gives rise to new kinds of being from out of its own resourcefulness is certainly more impressive than a hypothesized "designer" who molds and micromanages everything in the world directly. As Charles Kingsley (1819–75), Frederick Temple (1821–1902), and Teilhard have all expressed, the wonder of creation consists not only of the fact that God makes things but, even more, that God makes things that make themselves.

Long before Darwin, Christian theology had already proposed that God, the primary cause of the world, characteristically creates by way of secondary or instrumental natural causes. Even in Genesis, God is portrayed as creating through natural causes. Darwin, who was in no way the atheist some contemporary evolutionists have made him out to be, also occasionally employed the classic theological distinction between a primary creative cause (God) and secondary, or instrumental, natural causes. The latter include the causal agency that Darwin and neo-Darwinians have referred to as natural selection. The creation of human beings by natural causes, therefore, does not diminish the creative role of God in bringing about a world inventive enough to produce, by evolutionary processes, not only living beings but conscious, moral, and religious beings as well.

However, what can it mean, after Darwin, that human beings are created in the image and likeness of God? This is a question we must also pose to Teilhard. According to the Bible, we are special in the context of creation (see Gen 1:26), but evolutionary theory seems to challenge this status by washing out what were earlier thought of as clearly defined lines of discontinuity between ourselves and other living beings. Evolution situates humans in an unbroken line of descent involving millions of other kinds of living beings that share our metabolic, genetic, and chemical constitution. Even though traditional Christian theologies of creation possess a doctrinal latitude sufficient to accommodate Darwin's theory of life's gradual descent, many believers remain troubled that human life has emerged only recently, and apparently without any sharp breaks, from a non-human line of descent going back millions of years. The evolutionary proximity of human life to that of primates and other mammals has been especially hard for countless Christians to embrace enthusiastically.

According to virtually all paleontologists, human beings did not appear on earth abruptly, but only stepwise, from a long lineage of hominids going back to a latest common ancestor with primates six to eight million years ago. Teilhard embraced this scientific perspective without hesitation. He was even an important participant in the discovery of Peking Man.[1] Most scientists agree that contemporary human beings have descended most recently from anatomically modern forebears who migrated out of Africa as recently as 200,000 years ago.

So, because of our own evolutionary proximity to nonhumans, the question arises as to whether we can legitimately claim to be special in any significant sense. How are we to understand such declarations as those of Jesus that we are of "more value than many sparrows" (Matt 10:31), or of the psalmist that we were created only slightly lower than the angels (see Ps 8:5)?

There should be no theological difficulty accepting common descent, but I recognize that for countless believers, such as Darwin's nemesis, the highly respected Anglican bishop Samuel Wilberforce (1805–73), the idea of human evolution provokes a palpable sense of disgust. A good many Christians still agree with Wilberforce's sermon on the implications of Darwinian science: "man's derived supremacy over the earth; man's power of articulate speech; man's gift of reason; man's free will and responsibility; man's fall and man's redemption; the incarnation of the Eternal Son; the indwelling of the Eternal Spirit—all are equally and utterly irreconcilable with the degrading notion of the brute origin of him who was created in the image of God."[2]

Darwin did not dwell on the idea of human descent in his *On the Origin of Species* (1859), even though the notion is clearly implicit there, as Wilberforce rightly grasped. However, Darwin's later book, *The Descent of Man* (1871), made human evolution its main theme. Many, if not most, of Darwin's contemporaries interpreted *The Descent of Man* as a subversion of the ageless Christian teaching on the exceptional dignity of human beings. By the beginning of the early twenty-first century, as a result of impressive post-Darwinian developments in biology and other sciences such as geology, paleontology, ecology, archaeology, and especially genetics, evolutionary science appears to have erased any decisive historical line of demarcation between the human species and its animal past.

Consequently, if Darwin and contemporary evolutionary biologists are right, religious and theological inquiry cannot help asking such questions as whether human moral activity, even in its most noble expressions, is fully distinguishable from the instinctive and adaptive behavior of nonhuman animals. The human commitment to living a serious moral life would seem to require that people think of themselves as endowed in an exceptional way with freedom and responsibility, but doesn't evolution undermine this belief? The conviction most people have of an interior freedom suggests that human persons are qualitatively distinct from nonhuman forms of life, but evolutionary science challenges any such assumption. Isn't freedom an illusion, and haven't our own moral tendencies been inherited by way of a gradual modification of the adaptive behavioral repertoire of animals that in previous ages seemed to be stuck morally far beneath us in nature's hierarchy of beings?

The human treasuring of personal freedom and the sense of moral responsibility have traditionally reinforced the assumption of human dignity. Yet, if one assumes that human beings are linked in a continuous biological chain of inheritance to the simplest forms of life, can human beings still claim to be qualitatively different from their evolutionary progenitors? According to Darwin, all the various orders, families, genera, and species of life, including *Homo sapiens,* have descended slowly and gradually from a single common ancestor over an immensely long span of time. The mechanism for change is said to be a combination of accidental organic variations (now traceable especially to genetic mutations) and natural selection. At what point in evolution's long unbroken descent does freedom or responsibility enter? Or, as traditional religious believers would ask, at what point in the process do immortal souls take up their dwelling within the newly evolved bodies of human beings? Moreover, how can the combination of accidents and impersonal selection give rise to beings endowed with freedom, self-awareness, moral seriousness, and religious longing—qualities that at least appear to make us quite special in a world otherwise ruled by fate, as the ancients named it, or by inviolable natural laws, as contemporary scientists suppose?

Not only are persons tied tightly to the evolutionary continuum, but their existence seems to have required no special divine creation or intervention in the evolutionary process. Long before Darwin, Carolus Linnaeus (1707–78) classified living beings in the static categories of distinct genera and species. In his binomial system all species are qualitatively distinct from one another due to their separate creation by God. Linnaeus's crisp distinctions, however, have now given way to the idea of life as a continuously rolling stream of genetic experiments and recombinations subject to impersonal natural selection. Contemporary gene-centered biology pictures life as a simple matter of genes flowing aimlessly—that is, without any intelligent direction— from one generation to the next.

This "gene's eye" perspective is the result of combining Darwin's notion of natural selection with the Mendelian discovery of discrete units of inheritance now known as genes. According to this modern biological synthesis, sometimes labeled *neo-Darwinism*, genetic mutations provide the raw material for most evolutionary change. The genetic changes, moreover, are said to be accidental, in the sense of not being directed by any intelligent agency toward any specific result. It is the function of combinations of genes (segments of DNA) to instruct proteins how to take specific organic forms. A relatively small number of these organic experiments prove to be adaptively fit, in that they give form to living beings that can survive long enough to reproduce.

Moreover, as evolutionary materialists like to point out, both genes and proteins are composed of complex molecules that, in turn, are resolvable into arrays of lifeless atomic units. Consequently, another disturbing question arises for theological reflection on human specificity: Is there really any clear distinction between life and lifeless matter? Each of the following two sections, one on "information" and the other on Teilhard's cosmic vision, proposes a way for theology after Darwin to respond to what might seem at first to be a decisively materialist victory over religious or ethical attempts to justify the theologically indispensable Christian belief in special human dignity.

THE SIGNIFICANCE OF "INFORMATION"

The science of genetics allows theology to consider the question of human dignity and the meaning of being created "in the image and likeness of God" in a new way. Information science, especially as applied to genetics, can neutralize the claims of those evolutionists who take the historical arrival of Darwinian biology of descent to be the final defeat of all religious claims to human specificity. With the arrival of life, there quietly emerged in natural history an "information explosion," as Holmes Rolston III has put it.[3] When applied to living beings, "information" means the encoding and transmission of messages in the letters of the genetic code. The DNA molecule in the nucleus of each cell, for example, comprises a patterned series of the "letters" A, T, C, G, and sometimes R, embodying various informational sequences. Chemical and biological processes translate the "messages" embedded in these sequences into corresponding arrangements of amino acids. The latter are the constituents of the proteins whose three-dimensional patterns make up the diverse bodily types in the realm of life.

Were it not for the informationally distinct sequences in the nucleus of living cells, there would be no evolution by natural selection, and hence, no speciation in the story of life on earth. By recognizing the role of information in the life process, modern science has finally bumped into a dimension of nature radically different from the purely physical causes that, according to scientific materialists, provide the ultimate explanation of literally everything going on in the natural world. Materialists, those who believe that matter is ultimately "all there is," take the DNA molecule to be "just chemistry." However, at another level of understanding, it is something nonmaterial—namely, the informational *sequence* of letters (A, T, C, and G)—that we may now take to be the most remarkable aspect of the living cell. The *specific sequence* of nucleotides determines whether the coded organism will turn out to be a vegetable, monkey, or human being. The specific arrangement of letters (nucleotides) in the DNA molecule does not violate the laws of chemistry, and the informational content goes unnoticed by the physical sciences. From an informational perspective, however, the specific sequence of letters in DNA is all-important.[4]

Why so? The arranging of letters in DNA creates sharp distinctions in the specific sequence of nucleotides of different species, say, radishes, alligators, chimpanzees, and human beings, even though physically, chemically, biologically, and historically they are all made of the same stuff. Human beings, for example, share with other species a common evolutionary history, as well as similar molecular and metabolic characteristics. However, even a quantitatively small difference in the specific sequence of letters in the human genome, or that of any other species, makes it qualitatively distinct from other kinds of life. Even if human beings and chimpanzees have descended only gradually from a common living ancestor, and although their respective genomes differ only fractionally from each other, even a small informational divergence is enough to make each species and each individual within a species ontologically unique. We need not deny the atomic, physical, and chemical continuity, or the biological kinship humans have with all other forms of life, in order to claim with logical consistency that even minuscule informational differences can render each species and each member of a species qualitatively distinct from all the others.[5]

The relatively new appreciation of information by life-scientists is significant for our question of human dignity. By itself the fact of informational differences cannot provide the foundation of human dignity, but it is a necessary condition for doing so. The informational component implies that no living organism is simply reducible to mindless matter. Logically, biologists can no longer claim to have gotten to the very essence of life simply by resolving living cells into lifeless chains of atoms and molecules. The irreducible informational dimension in the cell implies that life is not "just chemistry." After all, nothing in the science of chemistry or physics is able to specify or explain precisely the *particular* patterns of letters in the DNA of a particular species.[6] Another "reading level," one capable of detecting informational differences, is required.

Materialist biologists, including Francis Crick and James Watson, the co-discoverers of the double helix formation of DNA, assumed that their discoveries meant that all life is now reducible to physics and chemistry.[7] Further reflection, however, demonstrates that this assumption is logically mistaken. It is not the chemistry at work in the cell but instead the specific sequence of letters in DNA that determines why an organism is a carrot, amoeba, monkey, or human being. DNA, as we now realize, carries a considerable amount of "junk" segments, but this in no way rules out the specificity resident in the sequence of letters in a DNA molecule. Even though there is atomic and molecular continuity, the element of information crisply differentiates one species from another.

Scientists must not attribute this sequence to supernatural intervention or to anything miraculous. However, the fact of information does require a richer understanding of the resourcefulness of nature than has been customary in mechanistic and atomistic philosophies of life. An informational perspective shows, at the very least, that modern humans can be qualitatively differentiated from all other species, including other primates, despite the fact that they share physical, chemical, and biological factors. The genome of one species has the same alphabet and the same lexicon but not the same "message" as others. Seen in terms of coded information, even a slight modification of the sequence of letters and "words" carried by the DNA of a chimp is enough to differentiate it sharply from anatomically modern humans.

We may clarify this with a simple analogy. In writing an essay, any author employs the same alphabet, lexicon, and grammatical rules as others. As far as relying on these ingredients is concerned, there will be no important differences among writers. But at a higher reading level, that of the specific sequence of letters and words, their essays differ considerably from one another. Likewise, in the domain of life, even a quantitatively slight difference in the sequence of letters and words, say, in the respective genomes of chimps and humans, can generate a disproportionately large difference when this information is expressed at the level of the whole organism in a specific environment. Figuratively, the genetic alphabet, lexicon, and syntax can be shared across species. Yet, at a different level of understanding from that of chemistry and physics, information's openness to an endless variety of arrangements allows for sharp discontinuity among species. This is why the natural sciences, including biochemistry and evolutionary biology, cannot by themselves settle the question of whether humans are created in the image and likeness of God. Even after Darwin the informational dimension in life and its descent leave ample logical space for a theological interpretation of what it means to be specifically human.

TEILHARD: THE PERSPECTIVE OF COSMOLOGY

As we have just noted, an informational perspective provides one framework within which human dignity can, at least in principle, be affirmed without conflicting with scientific accounts of evolutionary descent. In doing so, it offers an alternative to the narrowly materialist perspective on life that has dominated biology since the time of Darwin.

In a radically different way recent discoveries in the fields of astronomy and cosmology also open a new window onto the specificity of human life and evolution within the larger history of nature. Big Bang cosmology now implies that the emergence of life and the ongoing story of biological evolution are part of a much larger cosmic drama than our species had ever known about prior to the twentieth century. In this recent and more sweeping cosmological setting evolution may be understood to carry a meaning that accentuates our human difference and dignity in a surprising new way. In a word, a contemporary cosmological perspective allows us to realize that, at least on our planet, it is through human beings that "critical consciousness," along with freedom, moral aspiration, and religious longing, has broken into the sphere of finite being and into the story of the universe. The perspective of biology, as I have pointed out in previous chapters, is now complemented by that of cosmology.

By placing biology in the context of cosmology, science has now shown that human beings have recently sprung into existence out of a physical universe that is estimated to be 13.8 billion years old. Moreover, judging from all that the physical sciences have discovered recently, this universe is still coming to birth, as Teilhard appreciated. In theological terms the cosmos is still being created. It may be instructive, therefore, to locate the question of human significance, as Teilhard suggests, within the framework of the newly revealed cosmic drama. Christian theology may now ask what human evolution means in terms of an awakening universe.

It is only recently that scientists and theologians alike have been able even to raise the question of human specificity in this cosmological way. Thanks to developments in recent astrophysics, however—as Teilhard had earlier emphasized—the existence of human consciousness in nature entails a very different kind of *universe* from that of modern materialism. Astrophysics now confirms that our universe possesses just the right physical features for the eventual emergence of "thought." Thus the question of human specificity now merges with the much larger question of cosmic specificity: Why *this* particular universe?

Many scientists have now conceded that the Big Bang universe has been pregnant with life and mind from its very inception. Contrary to what materialist philosophies of nature have traditionally held, our universe has never been essentially mindless or soulless. The emergence of beings endowed with the capacity for thought—for understanding, reflection, and decision—begins during the first microseconds of the universe's existence. We humans have appeared, scientists now agree, from out of a cosmos whose primordial physical makeup was such as to render the eventual appearance of life and thought highly probable. Even though human minds have arrived relatively late in the cosmic story, the physical prelude to this emergent wonder was already quietly in play from the very start of the symphony. During the earliest moments of cosmic existence, mind was already beginning to stir, as it were, in the very heart of matter.[8]

The relatively recent debut of life 3.8 billion years ago, and of conscious self-awareness only a few million years ago, points to a drama of cosmic awakening—still in progress—in which the universe is now becoming conscious of itself through the complex brains of members of our own species. In our specifically human mode of existence the universe is finally bringing one of its deepest potentialities into the open, at least here on earth. Perhaps our place in the universe is to be unique agents and instruments of a cosmic awakening.

As Teilhard's numerous writings demonstrate, the phenomenon of *thought*, of reflective self-consciousness—in the medium of self-aware human persons—gives the universe a definition it would not otherwise possess. The appearance of thought on the cosmic stage may seem unimpressive from the perspectives of physics, chemistry, and even biology, since no laws of nature are bent or broken in the process. Cosmologically, however, the recent emergence of conscious self-awareness, accompanied by moral, aesthetic, and religious sensitivity, is the most dramatic development ever to have occurred in the long journey of our universe, at least up until now. Looking with Teilhard at human evolution panoramically, as part of the impressive drama of cosmic awakening, the arrival of our species is hardly the trivial occurrence that entrenched scientific materialists take it to be.

CRITICAL CONSCIOUSNESS
AND HUMAN DIGNITY

Along with the emergence of consciousness, of course, other human propensities associated with the *imago Dei,* such as freedom, creativity, the ability to form deep relationships, and the capacity to love and keep promises, have also made their way into the universe. Despite the claim by Darwinian materialists that the high degree of accident and blind necessity in biological evolution renders humanity nothing more than a fluke of nature, the cosmological perspective proposed here provides a wider perspective and a necessary corrective. Indeed, after Einstein, an exclusively Darwinian understanding of human existence turns out to be unnecessarily cramped. A cosmological perspective like Teilhard's, of course, does not render Darwinian biology irrelevant to our understanding of human specificity. It does, however, challenge the common assumption that biology is the most comprehensive intellectual setting within which to discern the meaning of human existence in the age of science.

Biology's inability to take into account the much broader cosmological context of human emergence has often led contemporary scientific thought and philosophy to the dubious conclusion that the human phenomenon is nothing more than an absurd and unintended product of an essentially pointless universe. Cosmologically understood, however, the arrival in natural history of consciousness, freedom, and moral sensitivity is how the universe dramatically reveals its true being and potential.

Of course, the universe expresses its inner depths uniquely in the emergence of every form of life, and not just in the arrival of modern humans. Nevertheless, in the recent emergence of human beings—and any other instances of thought or consciousness that may exist in extraterrestrial zones—the universe has made a momentous narrative leap. And now, through the medium of human thought, it is beginning to reflect on itself and on the many possible ways it may continue to unfold in the future. In producing beings that have the capacity for thought, reflection, and moral sensitivity, the universe demonstrates that it still has the reserve to become even *more* than it has thus far.

The fact that we humans can contribute in countless diverse ways to the universe's becoming more implies that we have a special standing within the whole of creation.[9]

In our creativity, our openness to new relationships, and our capacity to act responsibly, we mirror the image of God in an exceptional way among other creatures. In view of astronomy and astrophysics, members of our species may now realize that the cosmos is a still unfolding, unfinished drama, and that the very meaning of our lives consists, at least in part, of our awareness that we may now take a deliberate role in the continuation of this drama. It is mostly to Teilhard's cosmic perspective that contemporary Christian thought owes this fresh perspective on the nature and dignity of human beings.

Like freedom, creativity is one of the traits that grounds our sense of self-worth. While other species may, to some degree, be sentient and even conscious, there is no evidence that they perceive themselves as having a special cosmic vocation and responsibility. They do not appear to possess a self-conscious concern about who they are, about what they should be doing with their lives, or about what their destiny is. Nor is their specific mode of awareness developed to the point where they can ask what is *really* going on in the universe and whether the universe has a purpose or meaning.

For this reason it seems silly to maintain that there is nothing special about human existence. A cosmological window onto human evolution challenges the nearsighted claim that Darwinian biology has now deposed humans from some illusory perch that they may formerly have occupied, reducing them to mere accidents of nature in an ultimately absurd universe. The dangers of anthropocentrism are, of course, always present and subject to criticism, but instead of depleting our self-confidence, the new cosmological perspective has the potential to revive and reinforce it.[10]

CONCLUSION

Situating biology and anthropology within the context of a universe that is still awakening renders dubious all the shortsighted assertions by contemporary evolutionary materialists that biology alone can make adequate and ultimate sense of human nature. Unfortunately, the separating of scientific disciplines from one another in an age of over-specialization has led many scientists and philosophers to exaggerate the explanatory power of their own particular areas of expertise. This narrowing of perspective has been especially the case with scientists and philosophers who maintain that Darwinian biology is the ultimate and adequate framework for making (adaptive) sense of human existence, thought, morality, and the human capacity to worship.

The absence of a cosmological perspective on humanity has led to a biological obscuring of human specificity. The arbitrary decree that biological evolution is now the ultimate explanatory context for all living beings, including humans, inevitably makes human existence seem profoundly superfluous and vocationally futile. The ultra-Darwinian debunkers have assumed—on the basis of the impersonal way in which natural selection seems to work—that any universe that sponsors a Darwinian mode of creating diversity is an indifferent and even hostile setting for the story of life and humanity.[11] Nevertheless, as suggested earlier, natural selection may also be interpreted cosmologically. A cosmological perspective situates life and evolution within the context of a universe that is held together by a whole suite of reliable and predictable habits known as natural laws. In such a context, natural selection should be no more theologically troubling than are the physical and chemical laws functioning impersonally in the emergence of life and mind. The evolutionary materialists have failed to notice that the universe itself is the fundamental drama and that events of dramatic significance are happening on a much larger scale than physics, chemistry, and evolutionary biology can capture.

Consequently, by moving our main point of view from biology to that of cosmology—following Teilhard's sense of an unfinished universe—the birth of life, thought, moral aspiration, and religious faith are the most dramatic episodes ever to have occurred in the unfolding of the cosmic story (or in the multiverse, if it turns out that there exists a plurality of worlds empirically cut off from our own Big Bang cosmos). Unfortunately, however, apart from Teilhard and his followers, most Christian thinkers, rather than widening their scientific vision of nature, have been content to ignore cosmology as irrelevant to their understanding of human specificity. Christian thought traditionally affirmed human dignity by appealing to classical dualistic schemes in which the human "soul" is said to be separable from the body, just as matter seems separate from spirit. This dualistic understanding has provided an excuse to avoid any deep reflection on human specificity within the framework of a still unfolding universe. The typical approach of Christian education has been to salvage human dignity after Darwin by first allowing that our bodies may be the products of evolution but that an immortal soul has been infused in each person directly by God. Accordingly, even if humans and chimps have emerged from a shared ancestry, and even if our existence is part of a larger cosmic adventure, it is the divinely created human soul that assures us of our special value.

To those content with this interpretation, there is little or no interest in theologically connecting human identity tightly to the story of the universe. As far as traditionalist theological anthropology and eschatology are concerned, the only important future that awaits human souls lies in an extraterrestrial heaven with no lasting connection to the history of matter. Accordingly, there is no need to worry too much about our relationship to the natural world during the period of our terrestrial exile. To those whose spiritual aspirations are limited to the "next world," both evolution and cosmology seem religiously inconsequential. So, to countless Christian believers, Teilhard's cosmological interpretation of human existence will likewise seem religiously irrelevant.

Nevertheless, as Teilhard suggests, the idea of a directly infused human soul can scarcely be theology's last word on the relationship of humans to nature and God. Is there not some way in the age of evolution and Big Bang physics that Christianity may affirm human dignity without trying to outflank biology and cosmology altogether? The longing for an eventual divorce of humanity from the cosmos, after all, is quite unbiblical. The apostle Paul rejected such dualism when he declared that the *whole* of creation longs for the redemption proclaimed by Christian faith (Rom 8:21–23). In Christianity's foundational phase, devotees of Christ did not separate the Redeemer's destiny or their own from that of the universe.

Contemporary cosmology, as Teilhard's many writings witness, provides the opportunity for a fresh theological valuation—in terms of cosmology and not just biology—of who we are and what our lives are all about. Cosmic reflection on human dignity by theology has barely begun, but even now, at the very least, it seems reasonable to acknowledge that the natural sciences provide no justifiable reasons for Christians to abandon hope for the liberation of the entire creation to which they belong. On the contrary, biology and cosmology together can help reenergize the belief that the grand story of life and the universe is being called to participate in the drama of fulfillment proposed by the Christian gospel. The following chapters consider in more detail what it means that we humans belong to an unfinished universe.

8

LIFE

Scientists and philosophers today often claim that evolutionary biology provides so complete an understanding of life that it renders all religious and theological explanations superfluous. This assumption is especially interesting to those of us who are impressed by the work of Teilhard, who could not make complete sense of life apart from the idea of God.

Before Darwin, it was easy to understand life theologically. The Platonically influenced Western mind had situated life and its various manifestations within a vertical, hierarchical picture of the cosmos. Before modern times, theology and philosophy located matter at the bottom of the cosmic hierarchy. Then, above matter—in increasing degrees of value—came the higher levels of plants, animals, humans, angels, and God. This scheme made the natural world seem highly intelligible while providing a framework for spiritual adventure as well. The meaning of authentic human life consisted of struggling virtuously against the lure of materiality, making one's way up the ladder of being to final union with God after death.

Christian spirituality had for centuries tied itself tightly to some version or other of this cosmic hierarchy. Human beings occupied a relatively high level in the "Great Chain of Being," and our elevated status confirmed the sense of our exceptional value. Evolutionary biology, however, in company with other natural sciences such as geology, paleontology, and cosmology, now seems to have washed out the ancient lines of hierarchical discontinuity among the grades of being, destroying any timeless foundation for affirming the value of life and the special dignity of human persons.

Scientists now assume that after life came about—by pure chance—it handed itself over to the well-known Darwinian recipe for evolution. Evolution's three main ingredients are unplanned accidents, impersonal natural selection, and an enormous amount of time. For evolutionary naturalists these three components are enough to explain *ultimately* what is going on in life, including human life. Accordingly, it would appear that no room remains for a theological understanding of life such as Teilhard's.

Evolutionary naturalists today believe that Darwin's three-part recipe, updated by genetics, can account fully for *every* aspect of life. Descent, diversity, design, death, suffering, sex, intelligence, morality, and religion—these aspects of life all lend themselves now to an exhaustively evolutionary understanding.[1] The exquisite "design" of organisms, for example, seems completely intelligible in evolutionary terms, thus rendering unnecessary any attempts to explain the organized complexity of cells and organisms by reference to God, creation, divine wisdom, or providence. If organisms had been designed by "a beneficent Creator," they should have no design flaws. Yet evolutionists observe that most organisms are not perfectly designed. Design flaws are abundant, and that means an intelligent divine Designer cannot possibly exist.[2]

David Barash, an evolutionist at the University of Washington, for example, writes that religious believers are required to attribute the intricate design in living organisms to an intelligent designer since "only a designer could generate such complex, perfect wonders." However, Barash continues, "the living world is shot through with imperfection." All adaptations, in other words, have design flaws. Consequently, "unless one wants to attribute either incompetence or sheer malevolence to . . . a designer, this imperfection—the manifold design flaws of life—points incontrovertibly to a natural, rather than a divine process, one in which living things were not created *de novo*, but evolved." After Darwin, Barash contends, organisms and species require no explanation other than biological evolution. Darwinian science is sufficient.[3]

Evolutionary naturalists often point out that the "design" of living organisms is frustratingly awkward and inefficient. Any human engineer could do a better job in the fashioning of life, they observe. The human digestive tract, for example, is so convoluted that one can only be amazed that food makes its way from one end to the other. An engineer, according to science writer Chet Raymo, would at least streamline the design of digestive mechanisms: "Roll that small intestine up into a nice neat coil. Straighten out those kinks in the large intestine. Can you imagine the exhaust system of your car in such a tangle?"[4] Judging by an engineer's standards, the digestive system is a failure. How could it be attributed to an intelligent designer?

Consider also the twisted "design" of the human ear. From an engineering perspective, it too seems needlessly complicated. "Hammer, anvil and stirrup: Where did those crazy little mechanisms come from? Five separate membranes. And three fleshy loops that seem, on the face of it, superfluous." Indeed, Raymo continues:

Much of the human body is an engineer's nightmare, showing little in the way of intelligent design: which is just what you'd expect if our bodies evolved by a process of incremental changes acted upon by natural selection. The thing about evolution is this: Inevitably it moves toward ever more finely adapted organisms, but the end is not foreordained and the journey is something of a drunken stagger.[5]

As Raymo goes on to say, however, the waywardness of evolution harbors a deeper wisdom than first meets the eye. Although he is agnostic on theological matters, Raymo does not jump immediately to the conclusion that the absence of perfect design entails a godless universe, as other evolutionary naturalists, such as Barash, almost always claim. Raymo is more skittish:

> Before you accuse me of tossing an Intelligent Designer out of the picture, consider this: For all of the improvements an engineer might suggest for the human body, the body is still a thing that no engineer could hope to equal. Fabulously resilient. Capable of stunning feats of endurance. Exquisitely attuned to the environment. Agile, disease-repelling, self-repairing, purposeful, cunning. Evolution by natural selection, for all of its jerry-rigged solutions, for all its failed experiments and blind alleys, is a wonderfully efficient way to populate a universe with diverse and interesting creatures. If I were an Intelligent Designer, and I had a hundred billion galaxies (at least) to fill with wonders, I can think of no way more efficient to do it than by genetic variations and natural selection of self-reproducing organisms. You want intelligent design? Try evolution.[6]

Raymo, nonetheless, remains a skeptic theologically, even though he is more religiously inquisitive than most other scientific materialists. A graduate of the University of Notre Dame and a longtime professor of physics at Stonehill College, Raymo now questions the existence of a personal God. Even though he still cultivates a nostalgia for the sacramental Catholicism of his youth, when he speaks of "intelligent design" (ID), he is far from accepting the anti-Darwinian views of Michael Behe, William Dembski, and Philip Johnson, three famous champions of ID. Nevertheless, he is drawing our attention to something much deeper and more theologically interesting than ID, namely, what I am calling the *drama* of life and the universe.

A drama, unlike architecturally interesting instances of design, is, at least in principle, able to carry a meaning. It is the drama of life, much more than the architecture of organic design that merits the interest of theology. In contrast to the aesthetic or intellectual satisfaction that comes from experiencing a display of elaborate engineering, a drama, as Teilhard understood, requires that one *wait* until it has played itself out before deciding whether it makes any sense or what sense to make of it. And it is just this posture of waiting in patient expectation that characterizes the biblical disposition that we call "faith." Obsession with design, on the part of both ID proponents and evolutionary materialists, is a state of mind governed not by faith but by impatience and perfectionism. Evolutionary atheists and ID advocates alike, despite their obvious differences, share an impetuous demand that God, if God exists, *must* exhibit the divine creative wisdom here and now in the form of exquisitely engineered patterns of design. Otherwise the existence of a divine creator is in doubt.

If life is fundamentally a drama rather than an exhibit of elegant designs, however, one may approach it with the mentality of waiting and anticipation, habits we must put on if we are trying to make sense of any dramatic production. The genre of drama requires putting up with present uncertainty. As a drama works its way toward a climax or conclusion, we need to allow that its passage will be circuitous, indeterminate, and even inelegant. No single episode in a staged drama can deliver the full coherence spectators are looking for prior to the final act. Likewise, to take in the panoramic drama of life, we must be willing to wait. Indeed, the whole drama of cosmic awakening requires that we view life presently not as perfection but as promise. The posture of restrained expectation required by a drama, it so happens, is a requirement also of biblical faith and hope: only those who wait upon the Lord will not be put to shame (cf. Isa 49:23).

TEILHARD'S DRAMATIC PATIENCE

No one was more tuned in to the narrative, dramatic character of life, and indeed the history of the entire universe, than Teilhard, a figure who intrigues Raymo, but whose connecting the drama of life to a personal God remains beyond what Raymo, at least for now, can embrace. My point here, however, is that a theology of evolution may take the drama, rather than the fleeting designs in the sphere of life, as its point of departure for reflecting on the religious meaning of the natural world after Darwin. While design is satisfying to those who think statically, spatially, and in the short term, it is the long journey of life and the universe that interests Teilhard.

To find a place for Teilhard's thought in the context of contemporary intellectual and theological inquiries about the nature of life, therefore, we need to look beneath the narrow theme of design and locate the evolution of life inside the larger drama of an awakening universe. A theology of nature may now look for a kind of intelligibility—a narrative coherence—that lies far beneath the "shallow coherence" of design. Perfect design would freeze life in its tracks anyway, preventing any potential narrative flow toward either tragic or hopeful outcomes. Since the human way of expressing our sense of tragedy and hope is characteristically by way of telling stories, it is not insignificant theologically that scientists are now presenting the universe to us in the form of a dramatic narrative course of events.

Teilhard, as I mentioned previously, was one of the first scientists in the twentieth century to notice and echo the fact that the universe unfolds as a story. For him, the story of life is seamlessly woven into the long cosmic drama that has shown itself to us only after Einstein, especially through the mathematical physics of Georges Lemaître and the astronomy of Edwin Hubble. Theology after Einstein is interested in why the whole universe has a narrative disposition. Why does the physical universe exhibit itself to us in the form of a story?

To be a story, a series of events has to be a combination of unpredictability, consistency, and temporal duration. First, without a degree of unpredictability, any series of events would be completely deterministic, allowing no room for the uncertainty and surprise essential to every good story. Second, without a backbone of lawful physical habits, there would be no steady loom on which to weave the many twists and turns in the story of life. In other words, without the regularities of nature that we refer to as "laws," there would be no "grammatical" grid to hold the story of life together. Third, to sponsor the story of life, the cosmos must provide a span of time sufficiently drawn out for significant things to take place.

My point, then, is that the properties of a story—contingency, regularity, and temporal duration—are already waiting on the cosmic "stove" long before life begins to stew. Evolutionary biology by itself cannot account for this cosmic narrative framework since life presupposes it. A preexisting narrative matrix—inherent in the cosmos from the very start—renders life, along with the whole universe, horizontally dramatic rather than vertically hierarchical. As noted earlier, the theological significance of focusing on the drama rather than the design of life is that a drama can be the carrier of a meaning, one that—at any present moment—still lies hidden from complete human understanding. Until the drama is complete, we cannot properly claim to understand what it is all about or what it means. We can only hope.

OBSTACLES TO HOPE

Consequently, since focusing only on life's designs is a dead end, what dramatic meaning could possibly be fermenting in the story of life? Since the drama is still unfolding, of course, we must wait until it has played itself out to answer the question. Since we live in a far-from-finished universe, according to Teilhard, the only "place" we can look for its meaning is in the future. It is only in the arena of the not-yet that coherence may begin to appear on the horizon. If there is meaning to the drama of life, it can be captured, at present, only obscurely—and not without the virtue of hope.

Today, however, most people continue to live beneath the shadow of two conflicting worldviews that protect us from the bright sun of the dawning future. They both "clip the wings of hope."[7] The first of these future-suppressing perspectives looks for complete intelligibility in the trail of events that make up the cosmic past. Its way of understanding the world is to interpret present reality as simply the inevitable uncoiling of earlier sets of physical elements and conditions. It fosters a style of inquiry and, in the academic world, research programs that look primarily to the past to understand present reality. Or, what amounts to the same thing, it tries to understand the world by resolving present complexity into simpler, subordinate elements and physical regulations with the expectation that by doing so human thought will draw increasingly nearer to full intelligibility and foundational truth.[8]

As outlined in Chapter 2, this first way of looking at the universe is a *metaphysics of the past*. It forms the basis of the evolutionary materialism exemplified above by Barash—a way of thinking espoused by Richard Dawkins, Daniel Dennett, and a host of their disciples.[9] It is a worldview based on the assumption that a right understanding of life can be reached only by starting in the remote past and retracing the series of efficient physical causes that have led to the emergence of life and then to its unplanned evolutionary outcomes. By accounting for all events in terms of inviolable, deterministic physical laws, a metaphysics of the past denies, in effect, that anything *truly* new and surprising could ever arise in the natural world. Whatever happens up ahead in the future—even if it may seem new at first—cannot really be new. It is only pre-atomic simplicity "masquerading as complexity."[10]

The second worldview opposed to Teilhard's dramatic vision of life suppresses the future by looking toward a sphere of eternal being beyond space and time. This view of reality receives its classical expression in the hierarchical picture of the universe with which we began this chapter. According to the "perennial philosophy" that clings to the vertical hierarchical cosmology summarized earlier, all things "here below" are relatively deficient in being and value compared to what is eternal. This second worldview is a *metaphysics of the eternal present.* Its idealizing of timelessness has had great appeal to Christians for centuries. Even today, it remains attractive for the simple reason that it responds directly to human anxiety about perishing. By offering an eternal refuge from the erosion of time and the terrors of history, and by providing tidy answers to the questions raised by death, evil, and suffering, a metaphysics of the eternal present still dominates Christian religious and ethical life. As expected, it cares little or nothing about evolution, the destiny of the universe, or the long-range accomplishments of human history. Theologically, it is more inclined to withdraw from the world than to prepare the world for the coming of God.

Teilhard's alternative to the two approaches just summarized is a *metaphysics of the future.* Although Teilhard does not use this expression himself, he clearly offers us a comprehensive vision of reality, one that in its emphasis on the future is distinct from both classical theology and evolutionary materialism. When he exclaims that "the world rests on the future as its sole support,"[11] for example, Teilhard is in fact making a metaphysical claim.

What holds everything together is not the past or the present but something not-yet, something that has future as its very essence. As we follow the development of his thought from youth to death, we notice that he increasingly sees the world coming together—becoming coherent and intelligible—not from the past or from up above, but from up-ahead.

Materialist interpretations of nature absolutize the deadness of the pre-vitalized past, and this is why they are not equipped to tell us much about life. Breaking things down analytically, Teilhard points out, is equivalent to going back in time to a stage in cosmic history when nature consisted of a multiplicity of dispersed, lifeless atomic units. This was a stage of physical incoherence. The farther back we dig into the temporal past, the more everything, including life, falls to pieces. It is only by locking our gaze on the cosmic future that we may at last dimly sense increasing coherence. In Teilhard's worldview, therefore, it is hope rather than tragic resignation or religious escapism that can give our inquiring minds access to what is going on in the drama of life.

A deep affinity exists, therefore, between Teilhard's understanding of the cosmos and the biblical themes of promise and hope. Although he did not think of himself as doing metaphysics in the old-fashioned (Scholastic) sense of the term, Teilhard was clearly shifting our entire sense of the *real* and the *intelligible* away from the past and eternal present. To discover the full meaning of creation, he wanted us to look forward to a future in which *the whole cosmic story* will be taken, through the mediation of the cosmic Christ, into the everlasting compassion and care of God. To encounter the universe's dramatic meaning and intelligibility, it is not enough to peer intently into the world's past. Nor is it enough for us to "hang around" until it is time for our souls to be swept up into a timeless heaven. Rather, we approach meaning by waiting in faith and working patiently in hope for the whole universe—and we along with it—to be taken into the burgeoning beauty and compassion of God.

Unfortunately, Teilhard's futurist way of looking for meaning has failed to take root in intellectual and religious life, primarily because of the persistence of the first two metaphysical alternatives. It is hard for devotees of the cosmic past or those of the eternal present to imagine how the future can function as the *foundation* of the universe and the purpose of our lives. How can the future be the "sole support," as Teilhard called it, of the universe? Doesn't it make more sense to look to the fixed past or a timeless present for unshakable ground on which to base our existence and satisfy our longing for meaning? How can the temporal future, which never fully arrives, be foundational?

In answering this question, we may look no further than Teilhard's own life journey. Like many other visionaries, Teilhard struggled throughout his lifetime to find a reliable anchor not only for his inquisitive mind but also for his anxious temperament. In early childhood he clung to pieces of iron and rocks in search of momentary refuge from the terror of impermanence.[12] Later on, while still a young man, he even felt the lure of materialism, with its promise to dissolve the uncertainties of personal existence in the mindless nirvana of undifferentiated matter. What could be more permanently grounding and secure, after all, than the eternal, expansive bosom of lifeless matter?[13] That he chose geology as his life's work is consistent with Teilhard's irrepressible longing for what is durable. Since the past is already fixed and cannot change, no wonder that we look to the inert realm of pure matter to find refuge from change and loss.

With great spiritual insight, however, even while he was still a young scientist, Teilhard became critically aware of his own temperamental disposition to live in the past, a lure that can easily attach itself to a melancholic temperament. The further his mind penetrated into the material cosmic past, however, the more he landed on sand rather than solid rock. The deeper he journeyed scientifically into the cosmic past, the closer he came to the primordial state of physical dispersal. Binding himself to the fixed past would remove him from the splendid emergent realms of life and thought while cutting him off from the future and his zest for living.[14] The pull of pure matter, which is equivalent to the lure of the past, only leads our minds and souls downward (and backward) to a state of decoherence and impersonality.

Materialism, nevertheless, can be a powerful temptation. It is seductive not only because it appeals to the analytically reductive mindset of scientific inquiry, but also because it promises to deliver anxious human beings from the demands of personal existence. It appeals to that undeniable part of ourselves that longs to merge with a purely objective realm of being where no subjects and no persons are around to shock us into life.[15]

All of us, as existentialist philosophers have rightly observed, feel the impulse to shed our freedom by immersion in the sphere of the purely objective. Teilhard, too, was fully aware of the ease with which one can relax into the impersonality of sheer materiality. He also realized, however, that neither intellectual nor spiritual fulfillment, nor lasting happiness, can be found by going down the materialist road to the dissolution of personhood and human dignity. The metaphysics of the past that dominates scientific naturalism was unsatisfying to him not only intellectually but also spiritually. Atomist materialism draws us, he discovered, into a soulless desert where all things, including living organisms, become lost in a cloud of sheer multiplicity. While human beings often experience the lure of the impersonal in the guise of sensuality divorced from personhood, Teilhard knew of a parallel temptation in the realm of the mind. He referred to it as the *analytical illusion*, the fiction that we can arrive at a full and final understanding of reality by dissolving all of it, including persons, into lifeless and mindless elements.[16]

The mysticism of lifeless matter with its corresponding metaphysics of the past appeals to our instinct for simplification but not to our need for real understanding. It is only by looking toward the future, Teilhard came to realize, that we may hope to find what is truly real and to make sense of things. Although he was a geologist who spent much of his life digging into the past, Teilhard came to distrust the past as the final resting point of both the spiritual and the intellectual quest. Even in the 1930s, he already felt an occasional twinge of nausea upon opening drawers of rocks in the museums where he had labored so productively. Eventually, he felt like a "pilgrim of the future" making his way back "from a journey made entirely in the past."[17] His forays into the past, though scientifically essential, were in themselves spiritually and intellectually unsatisfying.

Of course, Teilhard agreed that there is a place for analysis in our understanding of the world, and he was never an opponent of the reductive *method* of the natural sciences, only of the "reductionistic" materialist *metaphysics* that is often alloyed with science. Indeed, he retained an enthusiastic intellectual interest in geology throughout his life, even after it was no longer his central preoccupation. He knew that it was only by looking into the past that science has gifted us with essential pieces of the drama of nature. Nevertheless, wallowing in the past after scientific analysis has brought us there will only distract us from a real understanding of the universe. The more our minds travel into the past, the more the cosmos lapses into indefiniteness and deadness.

THREE WAYS OF UNDERSTANDING
LIFE AFTER DARWIN

For this reason Teilhard always found it more interesting to talk about outcomes rather than origins. Our minds and souls are restless until they look to the horizon up ahead and try to fathom how things might be coming together in new and unpredictable ways. But if we seriously adopted Teilhard's futurist perspective on the life-world, how would we make sense of evolution's various outcomes? How would we understand nine standout features of life: *descent, diversity, design, death, suffering, sex, intelligence, morality*, and *religion*?

Each of our three types of metaphysics accounts for the items on this list in its own way. Let us, therefore, bring out their differences by imagining three adjacent panels, each panel representing one of the three metaphysical frameworks discussed above. To simplify our terminology, let us refer to the metaphysics of the eternal present as *the analogical vision*; the metaphysics of the past as *the analytical vision*; and the metaphysics of the future—as represented by Teilhard—as *the anticipatory vision* of life. To highlight the distinctiveness of Teilhard's anticipatory perspective on life, let us begin by sketching how each of the other two metaphysical frameworks tries to make sense of the nine items on our list.[18]

The Analogical Vision (the classical Christian metaphysics of the eternal present)

1. *Descent.* The many species of primates, felines, insects, and other animals closely resemble one another because there exists in the mind of God an ideal model, a perfect image or analog of each organic type. Then the many earthly versions of the heavenly analog are inexact copies, or imperfect analogies, of the sacred originals.

2. *Diversity.* In a Thomistic (analogical) metaphysical perspective, the many different kinds of life exist so that what is lacking in one organism or species, as far as manifesting the divine generosity is concerned, can be supplied by something else, and what is lacking in the latter can be supplied by something else, and so on. The diversity of life makes sense, in other words, by pointing

us toward the superabundance and pure generosity of God.[19]

3. *Design*. Organisms are exquisitely adapted to their particular environments because, underlying nature, there exists an eternal divine wisdom that is reflected, at least dimly, in created forms of order. Wherever design seems flawed, it must be because of sin (original and actual); so, the imperfection in organisms is not the fault of the Creator but of a prehistoric Fall or original sin. No finite arrangement of things here below can adequately represent the Perfection that exists up above, but it can turn our minds to God's eternal wisdom, at least imperfectly.

4. *Death*. Death came into the world ultimately because of sin. Nevertheless, religions may provide comfort in their shared belief that redemption is possible. For example, at death each person's immortal soul may experience final liberation from the earthly veil of tears and arrive at complete union with God.

5. *Suffering*. Suffering exists because sin requires expiation. The pain we experience is ultimately the result of a primordial fault that disturbed an initially perfect creation. Our personal sins exacerbate the original disturbance of order, calling for more expiation. Only a proportionate amount of suffering, therefore, can compensate for sin. Thus the need for a suffering Savior. Fortunately, even in antiquity, there were other theological ways of interpreting suffering. My point here is simply that, before Darwin, the theme of expiation by suffering was a common way of making suffering intelligible (see Chapter 9).

6. *Sex*. Sexual activity is the way in which human beings and other living creatures implement God's injunction to "be fruitful and multiply." This pre-Darwinian understanding of sexuality still prevails in sexual ethics

dominated by the theme of fertility rather than inter-personal intimacy.

7. *Intelligence.* The experience of our restless longing to understand the world can easily be accounted for on the assumption that a divinely created intelligibility pervades all of being. It is the human mind's fragile participation in the infinite divine Intelligence that lures our minds to seek ever deeper understanding of things.

8. *Morality.* Our experience of moral aspiration makes sufficient sense if there exists an infinite and transcendent Goodness that arouses in human hearts the responsiveness we call conscience. The closer the soul comes to infinite Goodness by way of faith and the practice of virtue, the more liberated human desiring becomes from purely this-worldly attachments. The life of virtue prepares souls in this way for their final communion with God.

9. *Religion.* The restless human heart (*cor inquietum*) exists because a timeless, infinite, transcendent Perfection has already quietly touched each soul, arousing in it a longing for final union with the Divine and a willingness to become detached from the material world in its "journey into God." Thus, religions exist ultimately because our souls are always touched by the Infinite.

The Analytical Vision (the metaphysics of the past as typified by atheistic evolutionary materialism)

1. *Descent.* The family resemblances among species that formerly seemed to be different versions of a perfect archetype existing in the mind of God are nothing more than the outcome of accidental modifications of ancestral organisms preserved by blind natural selection

during an unfathomably deep evolutionary journey out of the remote past.

2. *Diversity.* The millions of different species that exist today constitute only a small percentage of the total number of living experiments brought about by Darwinian evolution during ages past. That there have been so many different experiments means that evolution is essentially blind and that the universe is pointless.

3. *Design.* The appearance of adaptive "design" in living organisms has nothing to do with divine wisdom. In the evolutionary past most attempts at adaptation did not succeed, and the living beings we observe today are only a tiny remnant of the total number of attempts, most of which failed to survive and reproduce. Moreover, countless "design flaws" exist, and no adaptation is perfect. Design in living organisms, therefore, is not the product of an intelligent divine Creator but of blind natural selection.

4. *Death.* Death makes good evolutionary sense. Death occurs not because of sin but because of evolution's need for genetic variety. Since most genetic variations are non-adaptive, there must be a sufficient number of organisms available so that by chance a few of these might survive and reproduce. Death makes sense because if living beings never died, there would not be enough room for the random variations evolution needs for adaptation and reproduction by at least a lucky few. Without death in the biological past, we would not be here in the present. There is nothing divine about either life or death.

5. *Suffering.* The capacity for suffering becomes sufficiently intelligible if we understand it simply as a purely natural evolutionary adaptation. The sensation of pain (or suffering) warns sentient organisms that they are in danger of being injured or eliminated. This warning allows

organisms to move out of harm's way. Thus, the capacity for suffering enhances the organism's opportunity for surviving and reproducing. Even this adaptation, however, is never perfect. The point is that suffering has nothing to do with God or expiation.

6. *Sex*. By allowing not only for reproduction (which in simple organisms can take place asexually) but also for a sufficiently plentiful variety of adaptive genetic combinations, evolution long ago discovered the importance of mating. Humans today invest sex with multiple meanings, of course, but originally sex had no other meaning than that of providing sufficient genetic combinations and diversity for the survival of a select few organisms and species.

7. *Intelligence*. The human mind with its exceptional capacity for understanding and knowing exists today because large complex brains capable of reflection and prediction happened to give our remote ancestors a reproductive advantage over organisms that were not smart enough to escape predators or devise shelter and weapons. Our own capacity for reflective thought today is *ultimately* the result of primate and hominid evolutionary adaptations that took place starting several million years ago. Intelligence was not intended by any deity; it just happened to arrive in natural history accidentally and incrementally. It is still around only because it has enhanced the probability of gene survival for select organisms.

8. *Morality*. The fact that human beings have the capacity to be virtuous, and hence considerate of others, can be accounted for by tracing the evolution of cooperative behavior back into our animal ancestry. Morality first came into the story of life faintly when various ancestral species accidentally developed cooperative instincts that

enhanced groups' or species' probability of survival and reproduction. So, there is no need to explain human morality or conscience by bringing in the superfluous idea of divine commandments as the cause of good be- havior. We can adequately understand morality by tracing its origin back to "altruistic" behavior that evolved by accident and proved advantageous in favoring certain lines of descent, starting in the remote evolutionary past.

9. *Religion.* People are religious only because, in the distant human past, some of our ancestors found life more endurable in a harsh universe when their genes tricked them into believing in supernatural powers that made their lives and the exercise of moral behavior seem worthwhile. So, the origin and persistence of the idea of gods, or God, among so many people has a purely natural explanation. The persistence of religion, even today, is due to genes rather than any divine self-revelation.

The Anticipatory Vision (the metaphysics of the future as exemplified especially by Teilhard)

Since the drama of life is not yet complete, the nine items on our list of living traits cannot be fully explained presently, and they may have meanings that an excavation of the past cannot uncover by itself. In a universe that is still coming into being, nothing makes complete sense except in the long term. If the universe is a work in progress, nothing in it can yet be fully intelligible. The following, then, is a highly abbreviated exem- plification of what our nine items look like from a Teilhardian (anticipatory) perspective. Teilhard looks for life's meaning not in the temporal past or eternal present, but in the future opened up by hope. The anticipatory perspective leaves plenty of room for evolutionary understanding of life, but it rejects evolutionary materialism and defends a biblical understanding of God as creating the world from out of the future.

1. *Descent.* At one level of explanation the resemblance of one species to another has a genetic explanation. Scientifically, descent is the result of gradual modifications of shared ancestral genomes. Without denying any of this, an anticipatory interpretation of descent notices that each organism, including each human person, is born into a dramatic and creative cosmic history, made irreversible by the laws of thermodynamics. Ours is a universe that is still coming into being as it moves from past to future. Instead of looking only upstream (*the analytical approach*), or leaping outside the stream altogether (*the analogical approach*), the anticipatory vision looks downstream toward the estuary of life that is presently around the bend and out of sight. Acknowledging our kinship with other species in the wide stream of living experiments, we are impressed not only by life's grandeur (as was Darwin) but even more by a sense that the whole river of life is still flowing toward something significant downstream—something still hidden in the not-yet. The phenomenon of descent, therefore, points our thoughts not only to the past or eternal present, but also to the future, reminding us that the drama of life and cosmogenesis are still in play. Descent is not only a sign that significant things happened in the past but also a promise of "more being" or "fuller being" up-ahead.

2. *Diversity.* Without denying Darwin's three-part recipe—chance, lawfulness, and time—in accounting for diversity in the biosphere, an anticipatory perspective views organic plurality on earth cosmically, that is, as an expression of the universe's dramatic groping toward *differentiation* along with its overall dramatic advance toward

more intense unity in the future. Beauty is a good name for the synthesis of diversity and unity. I believe that Teilhard would agree with Alfred North Whitehead, then, that what gives meaning and purpose to life and to the whole drama of cosmic awakening is the universe's aim toward the intensification of beauty.[20] Such a universe is dramatic also because it includes the possibility of tragedy. The fact of tragedy, however, calls for redemption, and this is why Teilhard understands God not only as the creator but also the redeemer of the universe, as we shall see later.

3. *Design.* From an anticipatory perspective the important theological question is not whether complex adaptive design points to deity, but whether the drama of life carries a lasting meaning. Instances of "design" are essential steps, or "landings," in the cosmic emergence of increasing complexity and consciousness, but we do not grasp their meaning if we view them apart from the larger drama of the universe. The imperfection of present organic design is indispensable to the dramatic flowing of life and the cosmic drama into the future. In other words, if life's designs were fixed, organisms would be so rigidly frozen that life and the universe could not flow in the direction of fuller and deeper dramatic coherence. Moreover, the cosmic drama requires of humans the posture of waiting in hope, not passively but actively. It is only in hope that we can presently begin to sense the ultimately dramatic design of the universe.

4. *Death.* Scientifically, death makes good sense as a prerequisite for genetic diversity in life's evolution. From the perspective of an anticipatory metaphysics, however, the death of individual organisms must be situated within the drama of a universe still coming into being. In a fully finished and completely intelligible universe, death has

no legitimate place: "Death will be no more" (Rev 21:4). But the universe is not yet fully created, hence not yet ready to be declared fully coherent, intelligible, or good. Perishing and death find a foothold in the dark side of a universe that is still unfinished, that is, not yet "perfected."[21] Yet, unless there is something that *everlastingly* "garners" and preserves each episode and each chapter in the cosmic drama, something that delivers it from "absolute death," we should all, as Teilhard says, "go on strike."[22] The reason for our hope is that, in Christ the incarnate Word, every event in the story of life and the universe is saved and transformed in the heart of God. In the drama of our universe, there is no absolute loss, and death does not have the final word.

5. *Suffering.* Darwin observed rightly that suffering is an evolutionary adaptation, but it is much more than that. It is part of the *drama* of life's struggle toward more-being. Like death, suffering has no intelligible place in a fully finished creation. But in a still-emerging universe, suffering arises along with the increase of sentience, subjectivity, and creativity. Suffering is not primarily expiation or pedagogy; it is an inevitable aspect of a universe awakening to more consciousness and more-being.

6. *Sex.* Sexual activity can easily be understood naturalistically as a reproductive necessity and a rich source of genetic diversity. Traditionally, theology has interpreted sexual fertility as a sacrament of divine love and creativity. To suppress fertility has seemed to be equivalent to turning our back on the divine commandment to "be fruitful and multiply." An anticipatory metaphysics, however, moves the discussion of sexuality away from preoccupation with issues of fertility and away from matter-despising versions of the analogical vision of existence. An anticipatory vision is aware of the

omnipresent temptation to depersonalize sex, but an anticipatory understanding of nature redeems sexuality from the dualism of classical, otherworldly theology, as well as from the impersonality that accompanies a materialist metaphysics of the past. Mating, for example, is not simply a biological act, nor is it simply one of the Catholic sacraments. It is also a *promise* of the ultimate union of the universe with God.

7. *Intelligence.* To the Darwinian naturalist, human intelligence is an evolutionary adaptation. In the analogical vision the human mind is an imperfect reflection of divine intelligence. What then does intelligence mean from the point of view of a metaphysics of the future? The emergence of intelligence is a crucial chapter in the drama of a universe opening itself to a future of more-being. As Teilhard states it: "To be" is good. "To be more" is even better. To be conscious is good. To be more conscious is even better.[23] Furthermore, by way of human intelligence, with its quest for understanding and truth, the universe *anticipates* a final coherence or meaning. As long as this coherence eludes us, our minds remain restless. An anticipatory worldview, therefore, takes the human mind to be more than just an adaptation. Our individual cognitive striving is also, at a deeper level than we usually notice, a function of the whole cosmos groping toward increasing coherence, intelligibility, and more-being.

8. *Morality.* To the evolutionary naturalist, human morality is simply an extension into the human species of the tendency of living beings to *cooperate.* Cooperation has enhanced reproductive opportunities in life's evolutionary past, for example, in social insects. In an analogical metaphysics, human moral aspiration is a response to the perfect goodness from which we have been estranged but to which we are still mysteriously tied here below.

An anticipatory perspective, however, locates the source of our moral obligation in the stream of cosmic becoming into which each of us is born (see Chapter 4). The ethical life consists not of spinning our moral wheels in a squirrel cage of ethical challenges in order to prove we are virtuous enough to inherit eternal life; nor is the moral life merely a set of ascetic practices devised to improve our personal character. The moral life, more fundamentally, is one that contributes, even in the simplest and most monotonous ways, to the great work of creation and becoming *more* in a still unfinished universe.

9. *Religion.* To the evolutionary naturalist, religion, like morality, is an adaptation. In the pre-Darwinian hierarchical vision, however, our religious restlessness is the human heart's response to the quiet presence of the Infinite. An anticipatory metaphysics, without denying the insights of either biology or traditional theology, understands religion to be one of the ways in which the cosmos, having now become conscious of itself, opens itself through acts of faith and worship to climactic union with God through Christ-Omega in whom all things hold together (cf. Col 1:17).

9

SUFFERING

Many evolutionists today claim that all aspects of life, including suffering, can be explained in purely biological terms. No room is left, they believe, for religious and theological illumination of why suffering exists in our world and how to deal with it. From the perspective of Darwinian biology, suffering (which I take to be inclusive of the sensation of pain by nonhuman sentient life[1]), is nothing more than an adaptation that enhances the probability of survival and reproductive success in complex organisms. The question we address in this chapter, therefore, is whether Christian theology, when informed by Teilhard's cosmic vision, can add anything of substance to the Darwinian "explanation" of suffering.

Darwin, himself, was skeptical of theology. He came to doubt that the idea of God can shed light on the suffering of living beings. He suspected that suffering is a purely natural phenomenon "well adapted to make a creature guard against any great or sudden evil."[2] Suffering, in other words, is life's warning system, and if at times the torment it brings to individual organisms seems exorbitant, this tragic excess is consistent with a purely naturalistic understanding of life.[3]

Today, according to many of Darwin's followers, religious and theological attempts to explain suffering are meaningless and unnecessary. Contemporary neo-Darwinians consider the suffering of sentient life intelligible enough simply because it helps genes make their way into subsequent generations. Genes somehow sense that they cannot expect to survive unless they fashion organic "vehicles" endowed with sensory feedback equipment that can send messages warning them when their existence is in jeopardy. From a contemporary biological perspective, genes cunningly weave delicate nervous systems into complex organisms to let them know when their potential immortality is being threatened. It may seem that performing such tricks makes genes ingenious, but to most biologists today, the whole show is essentially blind and impersonal.[4]

After writing *On the Origin of Species* and reflecting on its theological implications, Darwin gradually gave up his earlier belief in divine providential governance of the universe. His new picture of life made the natural world seem godless. He was tormented, for example, that ichneumon wasps lay their eggs inside living caterpillars so that newly hatched larvae will have fresh meat on which to nourish themselves. Satisfying as this snapshot of the life-story may appear when viewed from the wasp's perspective, it is difficult, Darwin concluded, to attribute such cruelty to the creative will of a benign divine agent.

Going beyond Darwin, the renowned ethologist Richard Dawkins claims that the suffering caused by the genetic activity of living beings is reason enough for atheism. "So long as DNA is passed on," he says, "it does not matter who or what gets hurt in the process. It is better for the genes of Darwin's ichneumon wasp that the caterpillar should be alive, and therefore fresh, when it is eaten, no matter what the cost in suffering. Genes don't care about suffering, because they don't care about anything."[5] And any universe that puts up with such insensitive behavior is purposeless, blind, and indifferent.[6]

After Darwin, any honest theological response to the brute fact of life's suffering cannot fail to take notice of ichneumon wasps and similar instances of nature's indifference to suffering.

Clearly, life on earth was no picnic even prior to the appearance of human beings, who have added their own accumulation of evil to the wrongness already present in nature. It even seems to the Darwinian evolutionist that suffering, death, and periodic extinctions have been essential, not just incidental, to the ongoing creation and diversifying of life, starting long before humans came along.

Christian hope encourages us to anticipate that in God's good time all tears will be wiped away and death will be no more. So, for those who are moved by faith in the biblical promises, it should not be too much to expect that in Christ God's gift of salvation will finally heal *all* of life's suffering. Nevertheless, religions and theologies still generally avoid the issue of why evolution has to involve so much struggle, travail, and death in the prehuman chapters of the life-story. Theology, today, needs to consider more deeply what evolution entails regarding the meaning of God, sin, suffering, hope, and redemption.[7] Let us consider how theology's encounter with Teilhard's writings can be a proper stimulus to such reflection.

EVOLUTIONARY NATURALISM
AND THE SUFFERING OF SENTIENT LIFE

Darwin, many evolutionists now claim, has provided a fully satisfying "naturalistic" answer to the question of why sentient organisms are subject to suffering. Those like Dawkins, who believe that nature is all there is and that the universe is devoid of purpose, are satisfied with a purely evolutionary justification of suffering.[8] The fact that suffering is so intimately tied to the existence of life is tragic, but naturalists see no need to complicate our attempts to deal with suffering by introducing religious or theological explanations. Moreover, religious myths about suffering and redemption, along with the theologies they inspire, seem hopelessly complicated in comparison with the elegant simplicity of Darwin's recognition of suffering as an evolutionary adaptation.

Evolutionary naturalists theorize that religious answers to the problem of suffering—"theodicies"—still have an adaptive function.[9] Religious illusions, according to the "Darwinian debunkers," trick people into believing that life is worthwhile, and this belief makes them and their children live moral lives so that after death they may be admitted into paradise. The illusory promises of religion give the naive human masses an incentive to run their social lives in accordance with ideals such as "love one another." By controlling our asocial instincts, religious teachings keep on serving the goal of gene survival. The real reason why people still worship, pray, and sing hymns is not because God exists and stirs up a spiritual response in human hearts. Rather, it is simply because religious illusions contribute to the survival of our genes.[10]

Recently, a slightly less simplistic version of Darwinian naturalism has been proposed. It concedes that religions may not be adaptive per se. Rather, religions are "parasitic" complexes that attach themselves to brain functions or cerebral modules that originally proved adaptive for reasons having nothing directly to do with the content of religious indoctrination. Religions, in this latter interpretation, simply affixed themselves unknowingly to natural physiological adaptations that had become essential to hominid survival starting several million years before modern humans appeared. For example, religions easily invaded human brains because these brains had already become especially good at "agent detection."[11] That is, to prepare for potential destructive attacks by dangerous unseen predators, our hominid ancestors had to be endowed with brains that alerted them to the impending danger of hidden agents of destruction. This capacity for agent detection was the primary adaptation, and the habit of thinking about hidden deities later attached itself to those parts of our brains that natural selection had earlier sculpted to be on the lookout for dangerous hidden agents.[12]

IS DARWINISM SUFFICIENT?

What can Christian theologians say in response to this evolutionist debunking of countless myths of redemption that have given religious meaning to suffering? Here, the cosmic vision of Teilhard has considerable relevance. In agreement with Teilhard's metaphysics of the future, the key to understanding suffering theologically is to interpret it in the context of our new awareness of an awakening universe.

First, though, we need not throw away the biological truism that life's suffering is adaptive. From an evolutionary perspective, having the capacity for suffering gives organisms an adaptive advantage over those less generously endowed with sentience. So, the capacity for suffering does indeed serve the cause of gene survival and reproduction. If complex organisms were unable to feel pain or sense the presence of danger, they would risk extinction. At the very least, then, suffering has the meaning of contributing to the long story of life by helping genes survive long enough to be passed on from one generation to the next.

Here, however, an important contribution that Teilhard makes is that suffering cannot occur at all unless there are *subjects*, centers of experience, capable of registering and remembering the sensation of pain or suffering.[13] The question of the meaning of suffering, therefore, is not the only concern. Cosmically, the main mystery is why and how subjectivity—the capacity to be awakened—has made its way into the universe in the first place.

Without subjects, of course, there would be no suffering. But the natural sciences have offered not an iota of insight as to why subjects exist at all. Nor has science told us why the universe is a drama of awakening, one to which, incidentally, science itself is now contributing. Apart from the existence of sentient and conscious subjects there can be no suffering, nor the dramatic *cosmic* awakening that is ferrying the minds of all of us to ports unknown. So, without denying that suffering is biologically adaptive, the sheer existence of subjectivity remains a mystery that transcends any purely Darwinian understanding.

From the Teilhardian perspective that I have been developing, however, the main drama going on is that of a *universe* giving birth not only to life but also to sentience and thought. In light of this stupendous cosmic development, it is hardly illuminating to reduce the last 3.8 billion years of earth's history to a mere matter of gene survival. Ironically, the gene-fixated evolutionary naturalists are themselves issuing their "explanations" of life and suffering from within the newly emergent world of thought. So, if they really believed that the thought world is just one more product of gene survival, then their own thoughts deserve to be debunked as mere adaptation rather than truth telling.

As we have observed, the experiential world of living subjects, both human and nonhuman, is hidden from the objectifying approach of science. Each living subject experiences the world in an "inside" way, beyond the range of scientific scrutiny. We may assume that bats, for example, have experiences. They react in specific ways to environmental stimuli, such as the sun setting and the changing of their world from light to night each day. We shall never know what it is like to be a bat, as the philosopher Thomas Nagel has famously pronounced, but their subjectivity, their memories, their enjoyments, pain, and anticipations are all part of the universe. They participate in the larger cosmic awakening. Scientists, as such, cannot get inside a bat's subjectivity. They are more at home in the world of measurable objects. But it seems silly to deny that the chain of experiences that make up their own life-stories, as well as those of bats and other sentient organisms, is not part of the universe.

Subjectivity, by definition, cannot exhibit itself as one object among others. Since subjectivity is the universe's inner side, we can notice it at all only because each of us also participates in that "insideness" where the universe is awakening in unrepeatable ways. It is only in the inside domain of individual subjects that the awakening and the drama can be registered. Consequently, if we really want to understand the universe and what is going on in it, we cannot ignore the fact that for millions of years it has been a generous manufacturer of subjective experiences. Maybe the whole point of the universe is to bring forth increasingly richer versions of subjectivity.

Ironically, science itself requires the existence of a community of intelligent subjects in search of understanding and truth. For science to happen at all, moreover, the inquisitive human subjects who do science have to *believe* that nature is intelligible. They have to trust that truth is worth seeking. They have to have powerful feelings that the virtue of honesty is necessary to prevent cheating, and of course they have to believe that the human mind can be trusted to arrive at right understanding. For science to be successful, in other words, the inside world of the scientist's own intelligent and moral subjectivity must first be awakened to the transcendental horizon of intelligibility, truth—and goodness.

Even contemporary gene-centered Darwinians cannot cleanse from their thoughts at least tacit references to the reality of subjectivity. In neo-Darwinian writings the tacit acknowledgment of subjectivity remains obvious despite desperate attempts to exorcise it completely from an enlightened view of nature. Science writer Matt Ridley, for example, assumes the existence of subjectivity when he says we must "think of genes as analogous to *active and cunning individuals*" (emphasis added).[14] Ridley knows that science, including biology, is supposed to avoid all reference to subjective agency, but he cannot help endowing genes with intentionality, vision, and even personality. "A gene," he says, "has only one criterion by which posterity judges it: whether it becomes an ancestor of other genes. To a large extent, it must *achieve* that at the expense of other genes" (emphasis added).[15] Genes, Ridley continues, form *strategies* to ensure their survival.[16] Here the ghost of subjectivity asserts itself in what is supposed to be purely objective explanation. Science cannot completely dissociate its discourse from the notion of subjectivity. My main point here, however, is that science cannot tell us *why subjects* that are able to sense, struggle, and suffer came into the universe at all.

Religious subjects, for example, strive to find pathways beyond evil, suffering, and death.[17] Indeed, religion, in its passionate longing for salvation from suffering and death, may very well be the most concentrated instance of life's subjective striving. But, since all striving arises from within the hidden world of subjects, one must conclude that Darwinian biology cannot carry us inside the world of religion any more than it can take us inside any other kind of subjective experience. Evolutionary accounts rightly note that suffering and religion are adaptive, but the actual subjective content of religion is no more reducible to adaptation than the words on this page are reducible to ink and paper. To reiterate, evolutionary science cannot get *inside* the world of religious subjectivity, suffering, and the striving for meaning.[18] Even psychology, to the extent that it calls itself a science, has no access to the "inwardness" or "interiority" of sentient and conscious beings.

Following Teilhard, however, let us ask what suffering looks like cosmologically, not so much biologically. After Darwin we learned that life no longer looks the way it did before. Likewise, after Einstein—and the discovery that the *universe* is a long story of awakening—our perspective on suffering shifts to a wider horizon of meaning, namely, that of the universe itself. If we look at suffering through the wide-angled lens of cosmology, we notice a possible meaning that evades the narrower visions of biology, anthropology, psychology, and other scientific disciplines. Since our Teilhardian reading of the cosmic story in previous chapters has concluded that nature is one long—and unfinished—drama of awakening, we may now ask what suffering possibly contributes to that long adventure. The theory of natural selection may help explain why nervous systems become more complex and hence why sentience and suffering can become more intense in the course of natural history. But scientific method, as such, cannot take us inside the world of subjects or explain why subjectivity has found its way into nature in the first place.[19] We must look for the meaning of suffering, therefore, not simply by learning how it serves the survival of genes, but also by how it contributes to the full awakening of the universe.

THE MEANING OF SUFFERING AFTER DARWIN

Teilhard's thought is especially relevant to this project because it views suffering in the context of an *unfinished creation* rather than in terms of biology alone. In the wake of Darwin and contemporary cosmology it is difficult, Teilhard often notes, to conceive of any time in the past when the cosmos had existed in the state of completion or perfection.[20] Logically, an unfinished universe is imperfect from the outset. In other words, there is always a dark side to the cosmic story.[21] Excessive suffering may seep into the entrails of any universe that is still capable of becoming *more*. Since imperfection is built into an unfinished universe, there is no reason to posit an initial transgression to explain why suffering exists, nor is there a good reason to interpret suffering as expiation or as the penalty for an imagined initial transgression.

Theodicies that center on the idea of expiation have, of course, been influenced especially by the biblical story of Adam and Eve—by the account of their transgression and the penalty of expulsion from paradise. This myth is an expression of what philosopher Paul Ricoeur calls the "ethical vision of existence." It entails a worldview that, as it has been interpreted throughout the centuries, attributes the existence of suffering mostly to human guilt.[22] The ethical vision assumes that, wherever suffering exists, it must have been caused by human acts of disobedience. Guilt, therefore, must be paid for in the sterling of suffering and punishment in order to balance the books. Consequently, a tendency toward scapegoating has come into human history—and still exists—as the tragic underside of the expiatory strain of biblical theology.[23] One of the sad consequences of expiatory religious thought is that it may lead people to look for culprits and to engage in violent acts of retribution wherever suffering shows up.[24] The expiatory vision is intended to provide an answer to the problem of life's suffering, but it ends up contributing even more misery—especially in the form of self-hatred—to the cumulative history of suffering on earth.

Teilhard is deeply disturbed by the narrowness of such a perspective.[25] He is not denying that life is sacrificial. What he is questioning is the entrenched religious habit of associating suffering with expiation. This association only compounds the fact of suffering in the universe. For Teilhard, suffering is real, but it is not rendered intelligible by being interpreted solely as punishment. At a cosmic level of understanding, suffering is a form of information—negative feedback—picked up especially by sentient subjects. Suffering informs us humans that the universe is unfinished and is still coming into being. It can be redeemed only if the universe has a future in which all tears are dried and death is no more. Consequently, what needs explaining theologically—even more than the fact of suffering—is why God would create an unfinished universe to begin with.

Teilhard's answer is that, if God is love, an initially completed universe is theologically inconceivable. This is because an initially finished or perfect creation, if one could imagine it, would be frozen everlastingly into a finalized block. It would have no room for more-being, that is, for a *future*. A finished universe would be dead on arrival, for in its primal completeness it would leave no room for freedom, for human creativity, or even for life. An initially finished universe would have no room for suffering, but it would not be truly *other* than God. It would not be a distinct world at all, but instead an appendage to God's being.[26] An initially finished or perfected creation would be incompatible with God's need for something *other* than God to love. This is why the new post-Einsteinian cosmology, contrary to those who dismiss its theological importance, is significant for implying that the universe is still coming into being. Such a universe, logically speaking, does away in principle with the expiatory explanation of suffering as punishment for a culprit's spoiling of an initial perfection.

Einstein himself, incidentally, did not take to the idea of an imperfect universe. In his eyes, its exquisite underlying geometry was enough to make the universe perfect forever. I believe this is partly why Einstein never conceived of the universe as a drama of awakening. Most cosmologists, contrary to Einstein, have now concluded that the universe's original state was one of simplicity, not perfection, and that it will eventually die by energy exhaustion. The idea of a static, originally "finished" creation had previously allowed theologians to assume that evil and suffering exist because the imagined paradisal perfection must have been violated by an initial transgression. So, if a completed creation existed in the beginning and afterward became defiled by human guilt, then we would automatically look for someone or something to blame for such a breach. Then suffering could easily be interpreted as a penalty for the original transgression, and we would be inclined to picture redemption as a *return* to paradise. If one assumes an originally perfect creation followed by an initial transgression, this would seem to justify a proportionate penalty being imposed on the culprits in the currency of suffering. Before geology, evolutionary biology, and Big Bang cosmology came along, it was far simpler for theology and Christian spirituality to interpret suffering as essentially punishment than it is in the light of contemporary cosmology.

No matter how tidy and appealing the classical expiatory theology of redemption may initially appear to be as an answer to the question of suffering, it has fostered a history of self-righteous blaming, witch-hunting, and revenge. The inner logic of an expiatory worldview, after all, is to demand that things be made right once again, and if suffering is the way to pay for the return to an original perfection, then it seems to be religiously justified. Suffering, in that case, easily becomes tolerated as an essential part of a penal drama of restitution. In a pre-evolutionary universe, to set things right meant *restoring* the perfection that once was and is now no more. Redemption, in that case, is a matter of going *back* to the original perfection rather than *forward* toward a radically new creation.

My point is that an evolving, and hence unfinished, universe alters dramatically the cosmic landscape in which theology may now function if it is to be truly healing. If the universe, as Teilhard emphasizes, is *still* coming into being, and if, even now, it is being drawn toward a new future distinct from its original simplicity, then it could never have existed in a state of original perfection. In the absence of any past state of completed creation, the idea of restoration is no longer applicable. Neither is a theology of expiatory suffering.

The logic of cosmogenesis and evolution has now permanently closed off the path of restoration by expiation. Teilhard offers us an alternative cosmological framework for reconstructing Christian theology, one that is fully compatible with contemporary science, the promises of Jesus, and the goodness of God. In a universe that is still unfinished—one that is even today emerging only gradually from the "nothingness" of original multiplicity—the attribute of perfection can be applied only to a final future cosmic coherence not yet actualized but for which we may hope. Evolution and contemporary cosmology now allow us to question the relevance of theologies that have nourished themselves on nostalgia for a lost paradise. The idea of an unfinished universe, cosmologically, leaves no room for the idea that paradise has been lost, since it belongs to the not-yet. Both the biblical sense of promise and the scientific understanding of evolution may now jointly bar the gate to any return to Eden. Henceforth, explaining suffering as expiation must give way to the fact that the suffering of life is an inevitable part of the drawn-out drama of cosmic awakening.

CONCLUSION

To sum up, Darwinian naturalism cannot fully illuminate the fact of suffering of life since it has no good answer to the question of why the universe gave rise to subjectivity or inwardness—and hence to awakening—in the first place. Even more fundamentally, science has never told us why the universe exists at all. Science, furthermore, cannot say why the universe is a drama of awakening, even though science itself is part of that awakening. Science dwells on objects but tells us nothing about the interior content of subjective experience, including that of religious subjects.

Teilhard's great synthesis invites theologians to think about suffering, not in terms of Darwinian biology, but in terms of a universe that is still participating in its own creation. Because science rules out any primordial cosmic magic, nostalgia over the imagined loss of paradise may now give way to hope for new creation. The cosmic story tells us that the universe, after billions of years, gave rise to life and then, after more billions of years, to thought, and is now weaving a noosphere at least on planet earth (and possibly elsewhere). In earth's playing host to thought, the whole cosmos is still waking up. Consequently, our religious aspirations need not take the route of longing to restore a lost past. They may now extend themselves irreversibly toward a fuller awakening of the universe. This would allow the biblical themes of promise and hope to thrive comfortably alongside the new

scientific understanding of an unfinished universe. In a universe
that is still being created, we may now stretch our hopes—with
Abraham, the Prophets, Jesus, Paul (and Teilhard)—toward the
horizon of an unprecedented future cosmic fulfillment.

Unfortunately, however, the temptation is strong to enshrine
as final some past epoch of imagined splendor, whether in cosmic or human history. Nostalgia can easily become a substitute
for hope. It can twist human longing for a new future into an
obsession with recovering imagined past idyllic moments in
religious, personal, natural, or national history. An earnest encounter by theology with cosmogenesis, however, forbids such
idolatry. Teilhard's cosmic vision disallows Christians and their
theologians, therefore, to overlook the fact that a great portion
of life's forgotten suffering has been tragic and innocent—thus
making expiatory justifications of suffering inapplicable and obsolete. Most suffering in the history of life on earth has nothing
to do with guilt but instead is a natural part of, and a stimulus
to, a cosmic awakening.

Nonetheless, suffering, whatever its cause, still calls out for
redemption. Teilhard's cosmic vision suggests that the meaning
of suffering—at the very least—is to awaken life irreversibly to
move forward in the direction of a new future, one in which
there is room for hope that all suffering will be healed and all
tears wiped away. Instead of looking for culprits and scapegoats,
or indulging in interminable acts of expiation in our present
existence, hope seeks companionship and communion with all
fellow sufferers—both human and nonhuman—on the long
cosmic journey into God. By participating in a "great hope held
in common"[27] we may numb the nostalgia that gives way to the
violence sparked by our instincts to reconstitute some imagined
past perfection.

In an evolutionary setting we can believe more readily than
ever that the age of expiation, as the Letter to the Hebrews
confesses, is altogether a thing of the past.[28] Consequently,

theology from now on need not force the fact of suffering to fit a cosmography that allows pain to be taken as proportionate punishment for guilt. Instead, theology may now inquire, along with Teilhard, why an all-good and all-powerful God would create an *unfinished*, *imperfect* universe to begin with. After all, an unfinished universe is the one we have, and it is one that still has a future. We are part of a universe in which there is room for more-being and hence hope for what is not-yet. A still-evolving universe turns theology away from nostalgia for an imagined state of cosmic perfection allegedly resident in the remote cosmic past or up above in an eternal present.[29] Theological speculation on the meaning of suffering in terms of Big Bang cosmology may now take advantage of an entirely new setting, one in which, following Teilhard's account, the universe is still emerging into being, rather than having been completed in the beginning. There is no need any longer to think of the universal perfection to which human hearts aspire as though it had to have existed fully on the plane of natural or human history. Instead, we may now hope that the universe, since it is still coming into being may attain a fully actualized state of perfection in the future, and that our own striving, struggling and suffering—along with our joys and creations—will in some way remain forever in the redemptive heart of the God who, without ceasing, faithfully awakens the world to the prospect of more-being.

10

THOUGHT

The cosmos, Teilhard often pointed out, is a genesis, an unfinished process of coming into being. On earth, cosmogenesis has given birth to the spheres of matter (the geosphere) and life (the biosphere), and is now seamlessly weaving around our planet a new kind of "geological" stratum, a sphere of mind—the noosphere. Cosmologists should take note of the noosphere simply because it contains visible clues regarding the nature of the *universe.* Among other outcomes, we are coming to realize that the universe is in the business of creating *thought.*

The noosphere, however, has yet to become a serious datum for scientists.[1] The eyes of geologists, archaeologists, and paleontologists are trained to look for chronologically successive levels in the record of planetary evolution, but they have passed over in silence the most recent layer—that of mind or thought—that is now being deposited on the surface of our planet. The attention of most earth scientists has failed to focus on the gradual intensification and distribution of thought in the human phenomenon, even though it is a fully natural, terrestrial, and cosmic development.

Behind this reserve lies the habitual suspicion that beings endowed with consciousness do not fully belong to the universe. I have already pointed out that reference to subjectivity, the interior capacity to register experiences and have thoughts, has been a scientific taboo for several centuries. Even today the subjective phenomenon of human thought is seldom formally considered to be part of the natural world.[2] Cosmology, the study of the cosmos as a whole, however, cannot be truly illuminating as long as it treats the phenomenon of thought as an accidental accretion destined to be dissolved in the mindless material stuff out of which it arose. Until we realize that thought is the outcome of a long drama of *cosmic* awakening, we shall not have understood either the universe or mind. In this chapter, therefore, we explore with Teilhard what mind or thought looks like once we locate it inside the long drama of cosmic awakening.

I would like to introduce this inquiry by calling to mind a recent philosophical controversy surrounding the publication of a single small book, *Mind and Cosmos*, by the esteemed New York University philosopher Thomas Nagel.[3] Nagel's book, the content of which is summarized below, was unexpected and, to many of his fellow intellectuals, disappointing. Understanding why it caused such a stir in contemporary philosophy will help us also understand why scientists have greeted Teilhard's *Phenomenon* with unreasonable suspicion.

The subtitle of Nagel's book, *Why the Materialist Neo-Darwinian Conception of Nature Is Almost Certainly False*, reveals its provocative main point. What Nagel objects to is not evolution but the conflation of biology with materialist ideology. Most of Nagel's critics have taken *Mind and Cosmos* to be an attack on science, but Nagel has no problem with the standard evolutionary narrative of how living and thinking beings emerged gradually over the past four billion years. He does not reject the new scientific cosmic story. What he cannot accept any longer is the widespread academic assumption that a *materialist* worldview—what I have been calling a metaphysics of the past—can make the cosmic story intelligible.

The problem, Nagel believes, is not science but materialist metaphysics. Materialism is the belief that lifeless and mindless "matter" is the ultimate origin and destiny of all that is. Nagel rightly observes that when materialist belief is alloyed with evolutionary biology, as is usually the case today, it only clouds our understanding of life and mind. "Evolutionary naturalism," as he labels the materialist view of the story of life, is not science at all but a spurious nonscientific interpretation of science. Instead of illuminating evolution, materialism only darkens our understanding of it.

This materialist muddling becomes especially evident, Nagel argues, in the failure of cognitive scientists and other theoreticians to explain satisfactorily how "mind," evolution's most exquisite outcome so far, came into being from an utterly mindless universe. Moreover, if, as materialists believe, minds are reducible to physical stuff that has been blindly shuffled and reshuffled by a long and mindless evolutionary process, how can we trust these minds to give us *right* understanding of anything? If the ultimate explanation of mind is a primordial cosmic state of mindlessness, then why do scientists still trust that their own minds can lead us to right understanding or truth? Science has never answered that question. Charles Darwin was aware of the problem. In a letter to a friend, he wrote: "With me the horrid doubt always arises whether the convictions of man's mind, which has been developed from the mind of the lower animals, are of any value or at all trustworthy. Would any one trust in the convictions of a monkey's mind, if there are any convictions in such a mind?"[4]

Darwin, as far as I know, never followed up on this "horrid doubt," nor have most subsequent scientists and philosophers. What is remarkable is that Nagel, a scientifically informed philosopher, now wants us to do so. He takes for granted that mind and cosmos are inseparable. But if the cosmos is fundamentally mindless, and if evolution is a blind, unintelligent movement of matter, how can human minds, which evolution has brought about, be trustworthy? How can we assume that our minds are part of a blind physical process without dragging them back into the mud of mindlessness? If cosmology now forbids any separation of mind from the universe, how can we avoid reducing our own minds to the mindlessness that is thought to permeate the whole universe?

I do not believe that Nagel answers these questions satisfactorily, but he has done philosophy (and theology) a service simply by raising them. As I see it, we need to keep asking how and why we can justifiably trust our minds if they are reducible to mindlessness. Nagel struggles to answer the question, but he cannot easily shake off the materialist intellectual baggage that has suffocated philosophy for several centuries. Perhaps our minds are sufficiently ennobled, Nagel speculates, if the cosmos from which they evolved is not as aboriginally mindless and meaningless as materialists have always thought. Maybe nature from the start has had the quality of directionality that Aristotle gave it in antiquity but that modern science methodically rules out. Perhaps the making of minds, Nagel speculates, is somehow essential to the definition of our universe. If so, the recent emergence of mind in evolution would be neither a miracle nor a fluke. Mind would be an outcome that was in the cosmic cards from the outset.

Nagel's thoughts, here, are incomplete and not very convincing. Despite accusations by his critics, we can be certain that he is not making room for a theological notion of divine guidance. Rather, he is simply trying to justify the confidence we need to place in our minds if they are to work at all. We cannot trust our minds, he seems to suggest, unless the universe from which our minds have arisen in the course of evolution is much *more* to begin with than a state of mere mindlessness. The impressive phenomenon of scientific thought, for example, relies upon our native cognitive abilities to observe, think, understand, deliberate, judge, and decide. How, though, can we believe that these cognitive acts are all reducible to insensate atomic commotion without destroying the credibility of science itself?

Nagel knows he is stirring up trouble, especially among materialist scientists and philosophers, but he is adamant that a materialist cosmic vision simply cannot adequately explain the human mind or give us any logical reasons to trust it. The main problem Nagel faces, then, is that the majority of scientists and philosophers still think of Darwinism as inseparable from a materialist worldview. This association has been habitual, with few exceptions, since the publication of *On the Origin of Species* in 1859. Darwin himself was attracted to materialism, and in the nineteenth century, both Karl Marx and Ernst Haeckel were among the many who embraced Darwin's theory precisely because it seemed to support their metaphysical materialism. Not surprisingly, Pope Pius IX (1792–1878) and other Catholics generally assumed, in reaction, that evolutionary science is merely a mask for materialism. Even today, a good percentage of Christians in the United States identify evolution as the intellectual spearhead of the rampant rise of secularism.

So, Nagel is correct in noting that materialism is the norm in the world of contemporary Darwinian thought. For that reason, it seems to the philosopher Michael Ruse that Nagel is like a horse that broke into the zebra pen.[5] The British philosopher Simon Blackburn mourns the publication of Nagel's book for bringing "comfort" to creationists and others who cannot accept the atheistic implications of evolution.[6] Materialist philosopher Daniel Dennett, according to Michael Chorost, says that Nagel's book "isn't worth anything—it's cute and it's clever and it's not worth a damn."[7] Jerry Coyne, an outspoken atheist and evolutionist at the University of Chicago, advised Chorost that contributing a piece on Nagel to the *Chronicle* would be like writing "an article on astrology."[8] The list of prominent evolutionists who fuse neo-Darwinian biology with materialism, and who therefore repudiate Nagel's book, is long. Is it any wonder that they have no use for any understanding of the universe that refuses to separate mind from nature—such as we find in Teilhard's cosmic vision?

Even Nagel's more restrained critics find it incomprehensible that any informed scientist could claim to be an evolutionist without being a materialist. According to the new Nagel, however, the hollowness of materialism shows up especially in its failure to illuminate the most impressive chapter that has ever occurred in natural history, namely, the universe's relatively recent awakening into thought. The materialist is content to remark that mind arose from the original cosmic state of mindlessness and unto mindlessness it will return. Nagel's awareness of the amazing things that minds can do, however, leaves him deeply dissatisfied with such reductionist banality.

IS MIND A STRANGER
IN THE COSMOS?

In earlier writings Nagel had already expressed suspicion that scientific analysis has no access to the inner experience of living organisms such as bats, let alone access to human subjectivity. His readers, however, did not take his respect for subjectivity to be a rejection of materialism, especially since other materialist philosophers of mind had also expressed frustration at the failure of science to get inside the world of conscious subjects. Even while admitting that science cannot penetrate the world of subjects, they have repeatedly reverted to materialism as the default philosophical setting for their cognitive philosophies.[9] Nagel's latest book, by comparison, is full-blown heresy. It strikes his opponents as the confession of someone who is losing his mind, or at least his faith. The alarm Nagel's defection has aroused in the community of evolutionary naturalists reminds one of the religious anxiety that often follows in the wake of major new scientific revolutions. "*'Tis all in pieces, all coherence gone!*" (Donne).

What is at issue in the negative reactions to Nagel is not so much the well-being of science as the credibility of a whole epoch of materialist belief. Nagel's most vocal critics complain that he is injuring science by making room for miracles, but the atheist Nagel has no supernaturalist intentions. He is certainly not setting out to make room for theology, for which he has no use whatsoever. Nevertheless, in our attempts to understand the cool reception given to Teilhard's ideas by some scientists, it is important to note that Nagel opposes materialism not for religious reasons but because it is *logically* incoherent—as did Teilhard. In the new Nagel, we witness a renowned contemporary philosopher pointing out that materialist naturalism is simply an unreasonable worldview. Any consistent thinker (religious or not) should acknowledge the fundamental irrationality of trying to squeeze mind into a world from which any logical place for mind has already been removed.

Evolutionist Richard Dawkins would respond with typical annoyance that Nagel lacks a deep enough sense of time, failing to consider all that can be accomplished by innumerable minute organic modifications in deep time. Nagel would reply, however, that evolutionary naturalists like Dawkins are the ones pulling a rabbit out of a hat. True, evolution involves immense amounts of time, innumerable accidents, and the impersonal "laws" of nature, but the materialist belief system fails to show exactly how the interplay of dumbness and darkness can manufacture minds whose main function is to rescue us from dumbness and darkness. Time alone, even deep time, cannot add up to an explanation of mind unless something else is going into its creation.

Nagel's proposal is to change our understanding of the universe if we want to make sense of mind. Such cosmic overhauling is not new. Around the middle of the last century Teilhard was already calling for a "hyper-physics" that would allow us to take seriously the fact that mind is part of the universe. The emergence of thought is not just a topic for psychology but also for earth history and cosmology. Long before Nagel expressed his discontent, Teilhard was insisting that the phenomenon of "thought" is a real part of nature, not something that comes in from outside. He saw much more clearly than Nagel that taking mind into account requires a whole new, nonmaterialist understanding of the universe. He lamented the fact that the materialists of his own day were unable to "see" what is right there in front of them, namely, a universe awakening into reflective self-consciousness. If they could only "see" the eruption of mind as a *cosmic* development, it would have been fatal for materialist naturalism. It would have been an exciting new development in cosmology had they acknowledged that nature has always had an "insideness" that has recently burst out in the phenomenon of "thought." But they have failed to see.[10]

The dust kicked up by Nagel's surprising book, in my opinion, renders Teilhard's *Phenomenon* more significant than ever today. Long before Nagel, Teilhard was demonstrating that materialism only obscures any serious attempts to render the discoveries of Darwin and evolutionary biologists intelligible. But in the intellectual world virtually no one has been paying attention. Disappointingly, materialism (sometimes called physicalism) reigns as triumphantly as ever today in learned circles. Nagel would find considerable support in the works of Teilhard for his complaints about evolutionary materialism. I doubt that he would come across any evolutionary scientist today who has carried out the project of fitting mind properly to the natural world, and vice versa, more brilliantly than Teilhard. Moreover, it is hard to find well-known contemporary scientists or philosophers of mind who are familiar with Teilhard's groundbreaking work.

A TEILHARDIAN VISION OF MIND AND NATURE

The powerful instrument of thought that we call the human mind could have arisen in life's evolution only if the universe

from the start was already an awakening. And it could have begun to awaken in the beginning only if it had already been lit
up by the gentle dawning of infinite being, unity, intelligibility,
goodness, truth, and beauty on the eastward horizon of cosmic
becoming. It is because the cosmos has always been prompted
by these invisible but indestructible "transcendentals" that it has
been able to awaken at all.

Teilhard adds to the classical transcendentals (being, unity,
goodness, truth, and beauty) the additional mark of *futurity*. In
his worldview the universe has always been greeted silently by
the coming of the future. That is why it has evolved. In response to
the invisible dawning of the Absolute Future—as theologian Karl
Rahner names the God of Abraham—the universe has taken on
the posture of *anticipation*. When mind arrived full-blown in terrestrial and human evolution, a strain of anticipation had already
graced the cosmos, bestowing on it the quality of being a drama
of awakening. The world has always been leaning on the future
as the ultimate source of its being and becoming. Each human
mind, therefore, instantiates in a concentrated form the entire
universe's unrelenting anticipation of an indestructible future
that empowers our capacity to raise questions.

Long before Nagel, Teilhard was insisting that the phenomenon of "thought" is a real part of nature, not something apart
from it. And he realized much more clearly than Nagel that
accounting for the wondrous attributes of mind or thought
requires a new understanding of the cosmos. Teilhard lamented
the fact that the materialists of his own day were unwilling to
see what was right there in front of their eyes, namely, a universe
awakening into reflective self-consciousness. If only they would
practice a wider empiricism than that of conventional science,
they could literally "see" our planet's blossoming into thought,
and this vision would be fatal for materialist naturalism.

For Teilhard, it is undeniable that, if one steps back and takes
a sweeping view of natural process, there has been a net increase

in organized physical complexity and a corresponding intensification of what he calls "consciousness," at least over the long haul. Why, then, have so many scientists, those who are supposed to know something about "factual nature," missed the cosmic drama of awakening altogether? It is because they have been led astray by the *analytical illusion*, a consequence of looking at things "under too great a magnification."[11] He writes:

> Many biologists, baffled by [the] singular capacity that life displays of dissolving into non-life, believe that they are now forced to jettison it, as a pseudo-reality and a mirage. Surely, however, this is simply because their eyes are still closed to the fundamental and mutually opposed operation of synthesis and analysis in the general structure of the universe. In every field, the mere organic combination of a number of elements inevitably brings about the *emergence* in nature of something completely new (something "higher").[12]

A one-sided atomistic picture of nature abstracts from the inside story of the universe wherein new and increasingly more centered and conscious entities have been emerging in evolution. This is not only a failure of vision—but also of logic. It is the consequence of mistaking atomist abstractions for concrete reality. Teilhard observes that modern thought is still under the spell of a set of abstractions that leave out the inside story of nature. This is not only a failure of sight—but also of reason.

The real problem, as he would say to Nagel, is that conventional science is not empirical enough to capture what is really going on in the universe. In its addiction to objectifying the world, it fails to see the whole picture. Consequently, in evaluating Teilhard's thought, we should not be asking how well his thought holds up *scientifically*, but how well it holds up *empirically*. That is, we should ask how consistently contemporary scientific thinkers follow the cognitional imperative to open all of their senses fully to the world around them.

Specifically, materialists fail to see or notice even their own subjectivity, so they fail to incorporate the most important aspect of human existence and cosmic awakening into their portraits of the universe. As a result, they leave the phenomenon of thought outside of what they take to be the real world. Along with attempts to make sense of the emergence of mind, therefore, we need to ask the more sweeping question of how to tell the *whole* cosmic story from both inside and outside, simultaneously. I believe that only an earthquake in method and metaphysics, as implied in Teilhard's *Phenomenon*, can bring the inside and outside cosmic stories together into the richer synthesis needed to satisfy our drive to understand.[13] Teilhard's way of *seeing* nature is not only a more richly empirical approach to the universe than that of conventional science, but it also points us toward a metaphysics of the future as a reasonable alternative to both the materialist monism of contemporary intellectual culture and the otherworldly dualism of classical theology.

Today an unquestioned materialism still buffers intellectual culture from undertaking the search for a worldview that includes the reality of mind. Some of the most celebrated studies of mind continue to claim that subjectivity is a fluke of natural history.[14] Nagel would be disappointed, of course, that Teilhard's quest for a worldview that liberates the human mind and scientific inquiry from materialist ideology is consonant with a theological understanding of nature. A lifelong atheist, Nagel wants nothing to do with theology. He would be the first to admit that he knows little about it, even though he has lately shown more interest than before. He should be reassured, though, that reasonable theology encourages science to push natural explanations—including the evolutionary and cognitive sciences—as far as they can possibly take us. If there is a place for theology in the human quest for understanding and truth, it is not as a gap-filler or science-stopper but as the grounding dimension of a worldview that justifies trust in our own minds.

I would gently suggest—and I believe Teilhard would agree—that theology may enter the discussion of mind and cosmos most unobtrusively and disarmingly not by providing scientific information, but by addressing the big "worldview" question that Nagel seems on the verge of asking but from which he finally backs off. That question is: Why is the universe intelligible at all? Nagel has to admit that the ultimate adaptive condition for the emergence of mind is that the universe must be intelligible, but like Albert Einstein, he shows no interest in asking why this is so.

Is the world's intelligibility gratuitous, as the materialist claims? Or is it gracious, as Christian theology would assume? Materialists, on the one hand, usually answer that the world's intelligibility, like the universe itself, has no explanation. It "simply is." This response, however, lets the universe drift back into darkness. On the other hand, a theological worldview, as Teilhard again would agree, seeks to ground the world's intelligibility in an infinite wisdom, truth, and love. Such a vision of the world not only makes it a favorable place for scientific inquiry but also provides good reasons for trusting our minds as we look for intelligibility and truth.

It is the assumption of most contemporary evolutionists that the real world is essentially mindless. For Teilhard, however, matter and mind are terms that properly refer not to distinct substances, but to two fundamental tendencies in the evolution of the universe. "Matter" is the inclination of entities to slide back entropically toward the condition of multiplicity and dispersal that constitute the primordial stages of evolution, whereas "mind," "thought," or "spirit" is the propensity of beings to converge toward complex, differentiated unity around a center or goal. What we need today, Teilhard argues, is a "generalized physics, where the internal face of things as well as the external face of the world will be taken into account. Otherwise . . . it would be impossible to cover the totality of the cosmic phenomenon with a coherent explanation, as science must aim to do."[15]

To the evolutionary naturalist it seems obvious that life and mind are unintended accidents simply because in cosmic history their emergence seems both late and local. However, as Teilhard rightly remarked in 1931, "Even if life was, and had to remain, peculiar to the earth, it would not follow that it was 'accidental' to the world. . . . Life and thought might then be peculiar to the earth; but they would still be the life and thought of the [whole] world."[16] Long before astrophysics had theoretically tightened the connection between the existence of "mind" and fundamental physical features of the Big Bang universe, Teilhard had written:

> Man "the thinker," generally regarded as an "irregularity" in the universe, is precisely one of those special phenomena by which one of the most basic aspects of the cosmos is revealed to us with a degree of intensity that renders it immediately recognizable. . . . With man something new, which science had hitherto been able to contain by violent means, burst forth irresistibly. . . . We must make up our minds, by virtue of the general perspectives of evolution themselves, to make a special place in the physics of the universe for the powers of consciousness.[17]

There is nothing noxiously anthropocentric about this perspective. Teilhard's objective is simply to understand what the *universe* really is. To do this, it would be most unreasonable to ignore the phenomenon of thought as though it were not part of the universe. Thought is seamlessly connected to the process of sidereal and biological evolution, and yet scientific materialism denies it. In answering why this is the case, Teilhard writes:

> Because matter can be touched, and because it *appears* historically to have existed first, it is accepted without

examination as the primordial stuff and most intelligible portion of the cosmos. But *this road leads nowhere.* Not only does matter, the symbol for multiplicity and transience, escape the direct grasp of thought, but, more disadvantageously still, this matter shows itself incapable by its very nature of giving rise to the world that surrounds us and gives us substance. . . . Anyone who accepts this starting point blocks all roads that would bring him back to the present state of the universe.[18]

CONCLUSION

So, thought is fully part of the natural world. Hence, any survey of nature that methodically avoids a truly close encounter with this most astounding outcome of evolution cannot be considered truly empirical. Empirical inquiry cannot grasp what "nature" really is unless it looks very closely at the phenomenon of mind no less studiously than any other product of natural history. Since the only universe of which we know, or ever will know, is the one that has *in fact* given birth to beings endowed with minds, it seems extremely shortsighted to draw portraits of nature that leave out this most arresting of all emergent phenomena, or that treat subjectivity only as a cosmic afterthought.

Cognitive scientists will no doubt reply that science is now looking more closely at thought or mind than ever, but they are still missing the point. Science looks at "mind" by turning it into one object among others. It invariably ignores the subjectivity without which even their own cognition would not exist. Ordinary science fails not only to encompass the defining attributes of mental phenomena, but it also presents a picture of nature that is impoverished to the point of desertification by leaving the subjective aspects of cognition off the map of natural phenomena altogether.

Our own intelligent subjectivity, which is just as much part of nature as the blowing of wind and the rushing of water, typically gets left out of representations of nature by "objective science." To be sure, scientists cannot help being tacitly aware of mind, subjectivity, and mental processes. But the actual *experience* of being an intelligent *subject* is seldom examined thoughtfully by most scientists. Consequently, the natural world has seemed to be essentially mindless, and the sciences that allegedly deal with mind are compelled to explain mind by leaving out the irreducibly interior or subjective aspect of sentient and intelligent life that allows us to take note of our mind's existence in the first place. As Teilhard observes, our own mental activity falls among the constituents of nature, so a wide empiricism must take this activity into account. It may be appropriate for scientific method, strictly speaking, to limit itself to studying what is objectifiable, but a wider empiricism, one that attends to *every* aspect of nature, must be called upon to retrieve what science leaves out. To deny that human subjectivity and cognitive activity are inherent in the cosmos, as eliminative materialists believe, is a self-subverting proposition that logically eviscerates every claim their minds make.

It should now be clear, therefore, that mind or thought is the blossoming of a potentiality that has been latent in matter from the very beginning of the cosmic story. This means that there never could have been any moment in natural history where the stuff of the universe was closed off to mind, spirit—or God. Divine action and divine incarnation in the world would be hard to envisage if matter were essentially mindless, but the idea of mindless matter is the product of logical error and the failure to "see" nature's insideness. And it is just this insideness that allows a supreme Subject—the Spirit of God—to interact intimately with nature.[19] It is also the insideness of nature that allows the incarnate and now risen Christ to gather the entire universe—really and not just figuratively—into the crowning majesty of his eucharistic body.[20]

Inwardness, including human reflective self-awareness, is clearly part of the natural world. Thus, it seems deeply ironic that scientific naturalism has systematically turned its focus away from the phenomenon of thought, the most palpably *real* phenomenon each of us has experienced. Instead of looking at the universe in light of the fact that it has become conscious, scientific naturalism assumes that the universe is essentially unconscious. Then it tries—not without the aura of sorcery—to "explain" the emergent fact of mind solely in terms of what it takes to be mindless matter.

To make the impossible project of explaining mind fully in terms of mindless molecules seem feasible, some scientists and philosophers these days have even gone to the extreme of denying that conscious subjectivity has any reality at all. Hence, there is no need to explain it. However, Teilhard insists that a wide empiricism cannot plausibly leave the fact of thought and subjectivity off any realistic map of nature.[21] Thought and spirit are too luminous to be captured by a science accustomed to looking only at the mindless material abstractions that stem from the analytical illusion. To make room for mind in nature, therefore, anyone who professes to see things as they really are must interpret the prehuman evolutionary world in explanatory terms that are large enough to allow for the eventual emergence of human subjectivity from within the bowels of nature itself.

Modern thought has not been open to such an inclusion. Its picture of the natural world has typically been one in which there is no room for subjects of any sort, let alone human persons. Teilhard, however, places humans and other living subjects in complete continuity with our still emerging cosmos. As far as a theology of nature is concerned, the universe's tendency to give rise to subjects suffuses the whole story of nature with promise, thus revealing the universe itself as a very good reason for our hope.

11

RELIGION

Science has now given theology a cosmos that is unmistakably in a state of flux and, in principle, open to surprising new outcomes in the future. We have been asking what this recently discovered cosmic narrative means for our understanding of nature, time, humanity, hope, moral life, spirituality, God, life, suffering, and thought. In this chapter we explore what Teilhard's cosmic vision implies for our understanding of the fascinating phenomenon of religion.

Religion, whatever else it may be, is an especially interesting development in the drama of cosmic awakening. As far as individual persons are concerned, of course, religiousness entails a unique kind of consciousness—a distinct state of human "subjectivity." Religion, though expressed outwardly in rituals and moral actions, is something that goes on "inside" human beings and shapes their feelings and thoughts in fascinating ways. At the same time, however, religion is part of the larger adventure of cosmic awakening. Here we explore, with Teilhard, the connection of religion to cosmic history.

Today, a few scholars, most of whom are unfamiliar with Teilhard, are trying, like him, to connect human history to the longer scientific story of the universe. They call their project Big History. Big History (BH) is new because the scientific story of the universe is new. Only during the last two centuries have scientists slowly pieced together a cosmic narrative that began eons before the human journey commenced on planet earth. Geology, biology, paleontology, archaeology, astrophysics, and other sciences are now connecting the brief human chapter of cosmic history to the scientifically informed story of a whole universe still aborning. Because of recent developments in scientific cosmology, historians are now emboldened to envisage human history as an extension of the cosmic story.[1]

BH intends to tell a continuous story about *everything* that has ever happened in the past. It seeks to attach the relatively recent era of human existence to the earlier and longer cosmic journey. It wants to cover the cosmic historical record prior to life's evolution and link it to human history. In most of its versions so far, however, BH has connected the various chapters in the story only loosely. A sense of "narrative coherence" linking religious subjectivity to the history of the universe, for example, is still missing in most versions of BH. Teilhard, however, situated the phenomenon of religious faith into his cosmic vision long before the idea of BH was ever invented.

The fullest development of BH in print so far is David Christian's *Maps of Time*. The book starts out with several chapters summarizing current scientific cosmology and the evolutionary understanding of the life story. Then Christian adds a series of chapters setting forth what many other summaries of early human history have already provided.[2] The author then links the story of our species to its natural prehistory. In the attempt to tell a continuous story, however, Christian fails to look "inside" the story, hardly noticing the drama of awakening that has been going on in the universe for 13.8 billion years. This oversight leads him, along with other BH scholars, to ignore the cosmic significance of the arrival of religion in the history of consciousness.[3]

Together with Teilhard, therefore, I propose that we tell not only the outside but also the inside story of the universe. In doing so, we may arrive at a whole new way of understanding religion. Instead of treating religion as a purely personal or social phenomenon, or as an illusory means for human persons to escape *from* the universe, as modern critics of religion such as Freud, Marx, and Nietzsche have theorized, I suggest that religious subjectivity is central to the awakening *of* the universe.

Long before the recent arrival of BH in academic life, Teilhard was already telling us the inside story of the universe.[4] His way of reading the cosmic story was "big," but it was also "thick." That is, he told the inside story of the universe along with the outside. In my opinion, drawing the connection between the outside (scientific) story and the inside story of the cosmos has never been undertaken so skillfully as in Teilhard's masterpiece, *The Human Phenomenon*. A truly *big* history, Teilhard has argued, includes both sides of the story. The inside story comes out into the open dramatically in the eruption of human consciousness and moral aspiration. But it breaks out even more dramatically in the terrestrial eruption of religion in human history.

There has always been at least a faint filament of "insideness" with at least some degree of "thickness" in the cosmic story from the very start. But the natural sciences, as we have noted, do not illuminate or even notice the interior cosmic dimension of "subjectivity." An increasingly sensitive vein of interiority has been throbbing in the cosmos from the start, but conventional science is not wired to take its pulse.

Nor should we expect science to do so, since its approach is one of looking only for physical causes of events. Teilhard wanted to expand the meaning of the word *science* to include looking inside as well as outside, but personally I do not consider it necessary to burden conventional science with having to survey the vast field of interiority beneath the surface of cosmic history. It would be enough for scientists to admit that their method of objectifying and measuring aspects of the natural world simply leaves out the deeper dimension of subjectivity and the inside story of cosmic awakening. Then they could admit modestly that it is not within the competency of scientific method to see the inside story. Instead of allowing for the existence of subjects and insideness, however, scientific thinkers have often denied that subjectivity has any real existence at all.

Teilhard was shocked at the unreasonableness of this exclusion, and this is why in the *Phenomenon* he expanded the scope of scientific understanding so that nothing in the universe, including the inside story, would slip out of scientists' sight altogether. Unfortunately, the inside cosmic story has been slipping out of their sight for four centuries. As a result, not only the phenomenon of thought, but also the earth's religious awakening to infinite being, meaning, goodness, truth, and beauty, has been covered up and rendered irrelevant throughout the modern period.

Teilhard was baffled by this refusal to "see" inside the cosmic story. At the same time, however, he loved science and praised its enormous success in uncovering the outside story. He wondered, then, why we have failed to develop a stereoscopic vision, one that allows us to see both sides simultaneously. My own suggestion is that it is not necessary to stretch the meaning of science, as Teilhard tried to do, to include an inside look at what's going on in the universe. Let conventional science stick with the outside, but let those who want to see the whole cosmic story practice a *wider empiricism*. This wider empiricism acknowledges the limitations of normal scientific method and that there are dimensions of the cosmic story that it inevitably leaves out. This includes what Teilhard calls "insideness," or what I am calling "subjectivity."

Ever since Galileo and Newton, science has decided not to talk about subjectivity or, for that matter, about meaning, values, purpose, and God. The success of the outside approach by science, however, does not exclude a look inside. The "outside" aspect of the cosmos, furthermore, is also not fully obvious. It includes physical phenomena that are presently invisible but whose existence can be confirmed at least indirectly by scientific instruments of observation or by mathematical inference. Dark matter and dark energy, for example, have not been obvious in the past, and they are still "seen" only vaguely. But these phenomena fall into what I am calling the outside version of the cosmic story because they are detectable at least in principle by conventional scientific methods of inquiry.

The "inside" story, however, cannot be detected by science, but only by centers of experience known as subjects. It includes all the events that have taken place in the world of sentient human and nonhuman subjects alike. The inside story of the universe is made up of all the sensations, moods, cognitions, desires, enjoyments, and sufferings that have accumulated beneath the outer crust of cosmic history since the origin of life 3.8 billion years ago. The inside story also includes human intellectual, moral, and aesthetic awareness, and it covers our species' religious longing for deliverance from suffering, death, and meaninglessness. Over the course of cosmic history, the "thickness" of subjectivity has widened and its temperature has been elevated.

Subjective experience also underlies artistic creations that have been deposited in outside history. The trail of artifacts visible in the outside story can serve as a "text" that allows us to read what is going on inside. The religious subjectivity of humans is made concrete in works of art, written texts, and liturgical performances whose inner meaning can be grasped only by human subjects who have undergone personal transformations that allow for a sympathetic entry into the mysterious world of religious awakening. Teilhard is a rare example of a great scientist who has developed such a unique sensitivity to the "insideness" of things.

Religious awakening has probably been part of human subjectivity from the beginning of our species' history on earth. I suspect that by the time our human ancestors were migrating out of Africa 200,000 years ago, a stream of religious sensations and thoughts was already flowing from one generation to the next. Linguistic, mythic, symbolic, ritualistic, musical, and other cultural forms of expression were among the vehicles of this transmission. No matter where or when it began, however, the story of religious awakening on earth is just as much part of the cosmic story as the formation of galaxies and the forging of carbon atoms essential to the existence of living subjects. Yet, most contemporary versions of BH, emulating science's focus solely on publicly accessible information, characteristically avoid looking closely at the dramatic transformations going on *inside* the cosmic story.

Following Teilhard, therefore, I recommend that any BH that professes to take into account the *whole* story of the universe must tell the inside story without ignoring the outside. Yet most versions of BH are influenced by materialist philosophical beliefs that have led them to adopt an exclusively outside perspective.[5] Taking for granted the intellectual primacy of objectivist understanding, materialist historians think of religion as a set of illusory human constructs that tell us nothing about what the cosmos really is. To those who believe that everything real is reducible, in the end, to lifeless and mindless matter, religions are childish illusions that distract us from the quest for "objective" truth, a goal that scientific method alone is able to retrieve, at least according to most devotees of BH.

Materialists claim that the new scientific versions of the cosmic story are true, or at least approximately so, and that all prescientific religious myths are "false." E. O. Wilson and Loyal Rue, for example, claim that all religious narratives in human history are obsolete pseudoscientific attempts to understand the world.[6] They allow that religious myths can be biologically adaptive, but they claim that all religious accounts of creation and salvation emanating from the subjectivity of religious people throughout the ages have now been superseded by outside, scientific depictions of what is going on in the observable world. Daniel Dennett, to cite another proponent of scientific materialism's addiction to outside understanding of the universe, tells us that Darwin's scientific account of life has rendered all religious myths, including the entire Book of Genesis, irrelevant to educated people.[7]

The materialist thought-world, in its zeal to arrive at an exclusively objectivist understanding of the world, has virtually denied that subjectivity even exists, let alone that it is a fundamental ingredient of nature as such.[8] Western modernity will be spoken about in future historical studies, I believe, as a brief chapter in the cosmic story during which the universe refused to face its inner side. Ours will stand out as an epoch in which reference to subjectivity became, in effect, taboo.[9] Late modern intellectual history will be looked upon as a dark episode during which the insideness of life, consciousness, morality, and religion was not only ignored but also assumed to be virtually nonexistent. In thicker and more empirical versions of BH yet to be written, cosmic storytellers will point out that the elimination of subjectivity from the natural world gave rise for a brief time to a strange myth in which lifeless and mindless matter alone was accorded the status of true being. Our own period, I predict, will be remembered as a curious interval in cosmic history during which insensate matter was taken to be the ground of all being, and conscious subjectivity was taken to be pure fiction.

A more circumspect BH in the future will record the catastrophic ethical, political, and ecological effects of the modern erasure of subjectivity from authoritative portrayals of the universe. It will recall that the exiling of subjectivity from nature by academic institutions everywhere promoted the elimination of human subjects—in other words, *persons*—from the world of true being. Future "inside" historians may add a footnote expressing horror at how cavalierly scientific materialists such as Steven Pinker, in the early twenty-first century, were referring to human dignity as a "stupid idea."[10] Trustworthy historians will be startled that the modern theoretical elimination of subjectivity from portraits of the cosmos helped turn millions of human persons into objects for the engineering and extermination projects that took place, especially during the twentieth century. Finally, a truly *big* history, one that has yet to be written, will highlight the irony that scientific materialists denied that human subjectivity really exists while at the same time trusting that their own intelligent subjectivity, though allegedly nonexistent, is solely qualified to discover meaning and truth![11]

The virtual elimination of subjectivity from the cosmos by modern and contemporary thought is the main reason why scientists and other academics still ignore and sometimes belittle Teilhard's thought. Teilhard claims—quite against the grain of current academic assumptions—that the universe carries an insideness continuous with the anticipatory orientation of an entire cosmos. This anticipatory aspect is not an illusion, but a dimension essential to the very identity of the physical universe. Future cosmic historians will observe that anticipation has intensified gradually over time, reaching perhaps its high point not in the arrival of thought but in the emergence of religion.

Interpreting religion as a newly emergent development in cosmic history adds an entirely new twist to our understanding of it. From the narrower perspective of biology, religion is merely an adaptation that facilitates the migration of populations of human genes from one generation to the next. From the point of view of cosmology, however, religion is a new chapter in an awakening universe. In hosting the phenomenon of religious subjectivity, the cosmos has now arrived at a point where it reaches out consciously, gratefully, and imploringly toward its indestructible goal. From a cosmological perspective religion is not a symptom of being lost in the cosmos or a means of escaping reality. Rather, religion is a concentration of the anticipatory drift of the whole emerging universe. The feeling of being "lost in the cosmos" that sometimes accompanies religious subjectivity is not necessarily a signal that the physical cosmos is alien to us—as Platonism, gnostic piety, and materialist psychology take it to be. Rather, our subjective religious restlessness is a signal that the whole cosmos is still far from having reached its destiny. From a cosmic perspective, religion, despite its ambiguity and fallibility, is a reminder that the anticipatory "insideness" of an entire universe has yet to reach its goal.

Religion, in this vision, is a refusal on the part of an awakening cosmos to reconcile itself to absolute death. Religion means many things besides, of course, and no doubt its participants are often blind to its cosmic function. Teilhard's cosmic vision, however, leads us to look for the cosmic significance of religion. Religion, among other effects, leads to the intuition that an *indestructible rightness* lies beneath, above, beyond, or within "the passing flux of immediate things," as Alfred North Whitehead puts it.[12] Religions, as Whitehead also emphasizes, have come into history mixed with the crudest kinds of barbarism, and, as we all know, they have been mixed up with unimaginable violence and monstrous atrocities, as Teilhard would agree. Here, however, we are focusing on the cosmic significance of the wide religious consensus that perishing is not final and that a dimension of indestructible rightness permeates, grounds, encompasses, and transcends all transient things. From the point of view of a thickly layered BH, it is especially in religion that the cosmos becomes aware not only of its own precarious perch over the abyss of nonbeing, but also of the possibility of its redemption from absolute perishing.

In religious subjectivity, starting as far back in human history as we can see, countless images, narratives, rituals, and (more recently) theologies have pointed, either directly or indirectly, to an *essential* state of indestructible being wherein life conquers death, light banishes darkness, and the cosmos finds its everlasting fulfillment. If we understand religion cosmologically, as does Teilhard, this expectation is not childish escapism. Rather, religious longing is the way in which an unfinished universe is now embarking unsteadily on a new stage of its own long journey into mystery.

In terms of the whole cosmic drama, subjectivity is what keeps the cosmos open to the future. And religious subjectivity, instead of being reducible to biological adaptation, is the characteristic way in which the cosmos opens itself to the mystery of God. Religious subjectivity, in Teilhard's cosmic setting, is not adaptive fiction devising ways of escaping from a cosmic prison. Rather, religion is an intense mode of anticipation—its roots reaching deep down into cosmic history—that now keeps the cosmos from folding in on itself and collapsing into the inertness depicted by modern materialism and cosmic pessimism.

GOD AS GOAL

What does it add to a Christian sense of God, then, that the universe is still coming into being and that religion, cosmologically considered, is how the universe allows itself to be taken into the indestructibility of a divine mystery? Theological reflection has yet to probe deeply into this question. After Galileo, Darwin, Einstein, Hubble, and Hawking, however, there is no going back to a "fixist" cosmology with its assumption that "the heavens and the earth" came into being perfectly complete in an opening display of divine magic.

Most educated Christians today, of course, have at least a notional sense that the universe is still in process, but how *real* is this awareness? Nearly a century after the rise of Big Bang cosmology, and a century and a half after Darwin's *On the Origin of Species*, the news of an unfinished universe has yet to singe the ears of most Christian theologians and spiritual masters. As far as the idea of God is concerned, I believe the discovery of an unfinished universe has revolutionary potential, but Christian thought and spiritual instruction so far have mostly ignored it.

Teilhard, however, sought to show that our new scientific understanding of the cosmos has, in principle, opened up a whole new space for the exploration of religion and the meaning of the word *God*. Although Teilhard sprinkled new thoughts about God throughout his works, especially in his letters to friends, the intellectually suffocating ecclesiastical atmosphere in which he thought and wrote placed severe constraints on the expression of his "dangerous" new intuitions. So, his ideas about God and the universe deserve more attention in the less restrictive religious environment brought about, in principle at least, by the Second Vatican Council. Since Teilhard's own writings did much to shape the general mood of renewal at the council itself, theologians these days rightly feel emboldened to ask where his sense of God was heading.

Teilhard could not suppress his longing for a theological renewal that would link our prayers, hopes, and moral actions to a universe that is now coming into being. At the same time, he wanted our search for a "new God" to remain completely loyal to the church's main teachings from of old. Fidelity to tradition, however, did not mean for him that we must still cling to the fixist cosmology of traditional theology as though it were part of the deposit of faith.

Science, Teilhard emphasized, has now given us a universe that was never completely finished in the beginning. Furthermore, despite current pessimism about the future of life on earth, science does not rule out the possibility of new and unpredictable outcomes in future epochs of cosmogenesis. Most generations of Christians and other religious believers, however, have had little if any interest in the long-range future of the physical universe. Christians have always looked forward to a new creation, but they have seen little connection between their own final destinies and the present state of things. Even today, many Christians expect an apocalyptic catastrophe to destroy the cosmos and abolish time and physical reality as we know it.

A general indifference to the question of the universe's destiny was understandable as long as the physical world did not seem to be going anywhere. Moreover, living in the physical universe presented so many hardships that people understandably sought to escape it altogether. Even after Copernicus, Darwin, and Einstein, most Christians have continued to picture God as the creator of an essentially immobile universe from which virtuous souls may expect eventually to retire altogether. Not until the last two centuries, especially because of developments in geology, biology, and cosmology, did an awareness gradually begin to dawn in the minds of a relatively few individuals that the cosmos itself is still emerging from simpler stages of being, and that it may have an indefinitely prolonged future of creativity up ahead. Religion, I am proposing here, has a role in shaping the ongoing unfolding of cosmic creativity.

In his search for a "new God," Teilhard did not mean an Absolute that would be discontinuous with Christian tradition. There must be a way, however, of connecting evolution and cosmogenesis to our worship of the God of Abraham, Moses, the Prophets, and Jesus. To his joy, Teilhard discovered such a connection by merging the new cosmic story with the Johannine and Pauline belief that the whole of creation is coming to a head, and that it is being brought to ultimate unity in the resurrected person of Christ. Teilhard's professional research in geology, paleontology, and biology, embroidered with a nonspecialist's reading of physics and cosmology, convinced him that the biblical themes of new creation, promise, and hope are not at all out of tune with what's going on in the physical universe.

Science itself over the past few centuries has been providing reasons for an expectation that something of great consequence is going on in the cosmos, albeit too slowly for most people including the majority of scientists to "see." For Teilhard, the biblical portraits of a God who opens up a future for the finite world, who makes all things new and even becomes incarnate in matter and struggles along with creation, provides the widest and most intelligible metaphysical setting so far for making sense of what science has been digging up. A biblically inspired vision of hope for the whole universe would in principle keep all the incoming paleontological and geological data from looking like curiosities for museum displays.

Teilhard was trained in Scholastic philosophy and, like most Catholic thinkers of his time, he was not an expert interpreter of scripture. Still, it is hard to find anything written by Catholics of his day that, at least in the light of recent theologies of hope, is more biblical in its basic outlook than Teilhard's theology of nature. His lifelong search for something indestructible on which to base his own religious life led him eventually toward an increasingly firm conviction that the universe itself leans on the *future* as its true foundation. A "metaphysics of the past" can situate the world only on a marsh of atomic incoherence. And the prescientific cult of an eternal present does not allow the cosmos to *move*. A "metaphysics of the eternal present," as Friedrich Nietzsche suspected, may even be a symptom of the will to abolish the world of becoming. However, what *can* give consistence to our lives as well as to an unstable universe is the future faithfully arriving from up ahead.

In this cosmic vision things hang together by virtue of their being drawn toward a future that cannot become fully present right now without extinguishing life, freedom, and hope. It is our present *anticipation* of a divine future *up-ahead* rather than a passive participation in a timelessly finished perfection that gives the world its present consistency and simultaneously opens it toward *more-being*. It is in this context that Teilhard calls for a "new God," one who would be the center of convergence for an unfinished universe rather than a governor overseeing a creation that had once been perfect but is now spoiled by sin and the ravages of time.

In summary, and in full agreement with Teilhard, we need a whole new worldview—a "metaphysics of the future"—in which to fashion a truly big and thick history. We need a kind of survey of events that would simultaneously take into account the inside story along with the outside. What makes it possible in the age of science to link religion tightly to the cosmic story is that the universe itself can now be understood as having a dramatic makeup. As long as the universe was thought of as a stage for the human drama, and not as inherently dramatic itself, religion could be interpreted as a desperate maneuver of souls trying to get out of a prison. The newly discovered fact of a universe still coming into being, however, provides a refreshing framework for understanding the age of religion as an essential new episode in the drama of a cosmos awakening to the Absolute Future that we call God.

12

TRANSHUMANISM

Not all directions are good for our advance: one alone leads upward, that which through increasing organization leads to greater synthesis and unity. Here we part company with the wholehearted individualists, the egoists who seek to grow by excluding or diminishing their fellows, individually, nationally or racially. Life moves towards unification. Our hope can only be realized if it finds its expression in greater cohesion and greater human solidarity.

—Pierre Teilhard de Chardin,
The Future of Man

Technological expertise is on the brink of reshaping the human world and its environment more dramatically than ever before. The complexity of earth's noosphere is increasing almost daily. Current scientific developments and expectations in the fields of genetics, robotics, nanotechnology, information science, artificial intelligence, evolutionary biology, and neuroscience are raising unprecedented scientific, ethical, and theological questions about the world's future.[1] How far may those who have control of the emerging technologies go in transforming human beings, and indeed the whole of terrestrial life? How far may they go, both practically and morally, in altering what Christians have for centuries understood to be God's creation?

New scientific ideas and techniques are opening up the prospect of radically tailoring not only what it means to be human, but also what it means to be part of the natural world. Will new technologies eventually take us to a point where clearly defined human nature, at least as known by earlier generations, no longer exists? In evolutionary terms, will there be a time when a sharply delineated "human species" will be supplanted by something quite different?

After Darwin, the notion of *any* clearly distinct "species" has already become suspect, especially now that evolution has come to be understood as the flow of populations of genes from one generation to the next. New discoveries related to the human genome have already apparently made it possible to reconfigure radically our inherited bodily forms and behavioral inclinations, perhaps eventually transforming the human organism and the entire species into shapes now unpredictable. Sensitive artists, scientists, philosophers, ethicists, and theologians are now envisaging a wide spectrum of possible outcomes, many of them intriguing, many others potentially monstrous.

In this chapter, with the help of Teilhard's cosmic perspective, we explore the contribution that Christian theology might make to the building of a worldview appropriate to any future application of the emerging new technologies. Since Christians make up a large percentage of the world's population, it is important to ask whether their visions of the future accommodate or instruct the purveyors of *transhumanism* significantly. I argue that Christian faith and its rich traditions, but especially the biblical motifs of divine promise and liberation, can provide fertile constraints within which any future technological transformation of human persons and our planetary habitat may be carried out. A continually more nuanced scientific understanding of the subatomic world, the manipulability of genes, the plasticity of brains, the rules of evolutionary change, and a host of other scientific insights now provide *Homo faber* with a nearly irresistible opportunity to revamp *everything* in our world radically, including ourselves. But should we do so, and, if so, how far may we go?

To ignore this concern would be irresponsible theologically since the future of human existence and creation itself is now at stake. Theologically, how can people of faith informed by Christian tradition interpret transhumanism within the context of a biblically based worldview? Obviously, we cannot expect from the Bible a detailed set of ethical directives by which to orient future technological experiments. However, Teilhard's Christian hope for the ultimate fulfillment of the entire universe may enlighten theological attempts to understand and respond to transhumanist adventures.

THE NEED FOR A COSMIC PERSPECTIVE

It is essential to ask what the implications of transhumanism are, not just for the earth, but also for the future of the whole cosmos. As a result of developments in science, Teilhard realized that the human drama on planet earth is a recent epoch in a much larger cosmic journey. New scientific awareness of evolution, geology, and cosmology suggests that the human story is one of many emergent chapters in the larger journey of the universe. Consequently, questions about the human future are inseparable from a concern about the entire universe and its destiny.

A circumspect treatment of the possible outcomes of transhumanist adventures, therefore, needs to keep in view the ongoing story of life and the still uncertain future of the cosmos itself. Unlike our religious ancestors, we now realize that we live in a world that is still coming into being. The nearly fourteen-billion-year-old cosmic drama recently presented by astronomy, astrophysics, geology, biology, and other sciences is almost certainly far from finished. Christian thought, it bears repeating, needs to place its questions about transhumanist projects within the unfolding of this as yet unfinished universe.

The enormous amount of time that has transpired since the Big Bang may, for all we know, turn out in the long run to have been only the dawn of the universe's coming into being. Teilhard's cosmic vision implies that Christian theology, therefore, must ask what specific role humans may now have in the process of bringing the world to the fulfillment promised by biblical tradition. Christians, as Teilhard lamented, are not accustomed to thinking about the long-range future of the universe. Early Christians expected an imminent end to terrestrial existence, and our subsequent theologies and eschatologies have usually been so otherworldly and escapist that the physical universe has seemed to be superfluous in the final scheme of divine creation. However, we can still follow the New Testament's imperative to make *this world* ready for the coming of God.[2] What Christianity is about, when viewed in terms of the New Testament vision of reality, is not the forsaking of earth and the universe but preparing our habitat for the coming of God. This process of cosmic transformation begins with our own self-transformation, along with that of our ecclesial, social, and political communities, in expectation of the coming of God.

Because of our ties to life's evolution and the universe's dramatic awakening, our own human transformation involves the liberation of matter and all life along with us. The authentic life of faith consists of expecting that God's promises for the world will be fulfilled, as entailed for example in the Gospel of Luke's portrait of Mary as the paradigm of faith. In the light of science, however, we realize more fully than ever that Christian expectation applies to the entire scheme of things, and not just to humanity and its future. Ever since Darwin and Einstein the linkage of humanity to the long struggle of life and to the even longer drama of cosmic process has become so fully substantiated that it no longer makes sense for theology to separate God's promise of renewal and final human liberation from questions about cosmic destiny.

The inclusive Christian call to personal, terrestrial, and cosmic transformation in anticipation of God's coming must be the starting point of any truly contemporary theology of transhumanism. Now that science itself has demonstrated our seamless connection to the whole cosmic story, any transhumanist project must be subjected to a critical investigation of what it might mean for the earth's future along with that of the cosmos. Is it not the case that the newly emergent opportunities for technological change on earth are now placing the *universe* itself on the verge of undergoing an explosive new chapter in its own dramatic unfolding?

We have noted that, for Teilhard and other scientifically educated people, human history is not the whole show. In the distant cosmic future we must ask whether human history will turn out to be anything more than an ephemeral crossing over to more fascinating episodes in an enormously inventive cosmic drama whose final outcome is currently unknown. It is not wild imagination, but the spirit of Christian hope and love that awakens this question. What role will impending technological adventures have for what we now realize to be the long cosmic epic—one that occurs perhaps alongside a large plurality of invisible physical worlds other than our own Big Bang universe? As we wait "in joyful hope" for the coming of God's kingdom, in what specific ways should Christian thought understand and evaluate current and future attempts on this earth to shape or redirect the evolution of life and nature as we now know them? Let us look at three possible theological responses to these questions.

THEOLOGICAL OPTIONS

One reaction by theology to transhumanism is to demonize, from the very outset, any dramatic changes to the natural status quo. Knowing how to change humanity and nature technologically is not enough to justify doing so morally. The risks of incalculably horrid outcomes are too great. This first approach's reluctance to implement transhumanist dreams arises from a laudable sense of the intrinsic value of nature, life, and persons. Many devout Christians and members of other religious traditions—including especially those of native peoples—are opposed to any radical disturbance of nature. Altering natural processes is permitted only when required for human survival and when ecological sustainability is guaranteed. At its best, this approach could be called *sacramental*. It values "creation" for the simple reason that nature's most precious items—clean water, fresh air, bright sunshine, the fertility of soil, and the extravagance of life—are revelatory of God. It is because of nature's transparency to the Divine that Christian sacramentalism may rely on various facets of matter and life to reveal how God influences and energizes human lives. So, religiously, why would we want to make major adjustments to the natural world at all, especially if such alteration risks the destruction or the impairment of a universe that, despite our lack of gratitude, has already been so extravagantly generous a gift?

If we lose nature, says the Catholic environmentalist Thomas Berry, we also lose God.[3] Sacramentalists such as Berry are especially aware of the environmental disasters that have accompanied the Industrial Revolution, nuclear technology, the deployment of complex and expensive modern weaponry, energy-wasting transportation, and countless other modern inventions. Science has made technology possible, but with such inventiveness comes enormous environmental waste and other calamitous results. Consequently, sacramentalists will be extremely wary of transhumanist projects.

Scientific knowledge, at least as it has been applied so far in modern times, has had many positive outcomes, but it has also made possible the engineering and extermination of millions of human beings and the ruination of immense swaths of our planet's ecosystems. Space technology is now spreading its waste over the heavens as well. The sacramentalists, therefore, wonder whether the gains of scientific technology really outweigh the horrors, such as nuclear holocausts, that technology also makes possible. Wouldn't it be especially naive on our part, therefore, to suppose that transhumanist technology would be able to avoid an unprecedented abuse of persons and their natural settings?

At the present time in human and cosmic history, is it pragmatically prudent, religiously fitting, or morally appropriate to undertake dramatic changes to what generations have referred to as God's creation? Ethically, doesn't a sacramental sense of nature require conservation rather than transformation? And religiously, wouldn't a radical alteration of life and humanity make nature more opaque to transcendent mystery than ever before? Wouldn't transhumanism eventually obscure rather than reveal the sacred mystery that religions take to be the ultimate environment of all finite being?

A second theological response to transhumanist proposals would claim that the sacramental alternative is unnecessarily cautious. It seems insufficiently open to the full liberation of life and too indifferent to the inherent openness of our unfinished universe to new creation.[4] Despite its claim to cherish and revere the natural world in the face of scientifically enabled technologies, the sacramentalists' reserve is ironically unnatural itself. Isn't transforming our environments along with ourselves essential to the very definition of being human? Are we so unlike other animals that we are obliged to keep our hands off the physical universe altogether? How softly must we tread upon the earth without diminishing our human potential? After all, even most nonhuman species have to transform their environments to make them livable. Spiders weave webs, and beavers build dams. Environmental habitats are not just "out there" to be filled in or adapted to, but they are, in some measure, products of their inhabitants' co-creativity with nature. If it is natural for animals to alter their natural settings, shouldn't it be all the more so for ourselves? Humans, quite naturally, survive and thrive only because of their capacity to change their environments artificially. Who then is to say where a transhumanist extension of our creative instincts must start or stop? Who is authorized to lay down fixed boundaries where human inventiveness must cease and people must settle passively into eternally established routines. Must we be so fearful of the future, and so suppressive of what seems to be our native tendency to change ourselves and bring new things into existence?

Let us refer to this second theological approach as *activism*. An activist theology seeks to take advantage of our new understanding of the fact that life is a still unfolding drama—the cosmos is a work in progress—and that humanity's vocation is one of extending the creative process into an indeterminate future. Is it necessarily the case that this more aggressive approach, when applied to the topic of transhumanism, will be contrary to religious reverence for nature and incompatible with a coherent Christian theological vision of creation? Wouldn't it be a violation of human nature and dignity, as well as an irresponsible abandonment of our vocation before God, to suppress our creative capacities to the extent that a pure sacramentalism seems to prefer?

A theological activist would claim that the technologies of late modernity are not unambiguously evil. Rather, they are essential to bringing more-being into the evolving drama of cosmic awakening.[5] Realistically, we must expect new experiments occasionally to go awry. Even though offshore oil rigs may sometimes blow up, kill workers, and contaminate our seas, does this mean we have to stop drilling oil offshore altogether? Aren't there *always* tradeoffs when technology tries out new experiments? Isn't that life? In biological history a risk of temporary chaos accompanies every increase in emergent complexity, but does this mean that no experiments and risks should be taken at all?

Despite possible dangers and even disasters, so says our typical activist, Christians should still not remain opposed to new experimentation, including even the transformation of our species into something quite different from its present biological and anthropological status quo. Why should we not assume that the universe has abundant creative potential in reserve and that the natural urge of human beings to create must be allowed to express itself as an essential feature of human dignity? Isn't it conceivable that God's vision of new creation includes the complicity of human beings in renewing the face of the earth— not just by conservation but also by reasonable invention and prudent intervention?

We seem to be torn, then, between a sacramental quietism, on the one hand, and an impiously assertive adventurism, on the other. The specter of transhumanism brings back before us the never fully resolved theological conflict between Pelagians, those who rely on human effort and activism, and Quietists, those who are content simply to receive the world as a gift and leave it at that.

Is there perhaps a third theological alternative, one that avoids the extremes of both proposals just outlined while remaining true to the biblical themes of promise and liberation—including especially the theme of prophetic justice—and to the crucial Christian affirmation of the dignity of human persons? In the spirit of Teilhard's cosmic vision, I propose the following *anticipatory* approach.

According to this third perspective, it is not only possible but also obligatory for Christian theology to support the natural instincts of human beings to participate in the ongoing creation of the universe of which they are a part. However, this involvement must be carried out within the context of constraints that I list below. The anticipatory approach seeks to be faithful to the biblical sense of promise and hope as well as to our new awareness that the cosmos still has the opportunity for more-being. In agreement with Teilhard, I proposed earlier that the universe is not morally neutral and that our sense of obligation may learn from watching what makes for more-being in its own advance.

Above all, this means following and promoting the cosmic convergent trend toward deeper unity, but only if this unity also promotes differentiation. To be responsible in a brave new world means to be concerned that all future creativity adheres—in an analogous way at each new stage—to the general formula by which more-being has *already* been emerging in the drama of an awakening universe. We find in the cosmic story so far at least three inviolable rules or cosmic criteria that any enhancement of creation by human beings must follow as a condition of appropriate future transformation.

First, a concern for an intensification rather than diminishment of *vitality*. Life must increase rather than decrease. If it fails to increase (become more), it stagnates and dies. To understand what true vitality means, however, we need first to ask how living beings differ from the nonliving. Here it is helpful to understand, at least as a starting point, what the philosopher Michael Polanyi calls the "logic of achievement" as the quality that makes life special. Living beings, Polanyi notes, are defined by their capacity to *strive*.[6] Striving is what sets them apart ontologically from lifeless and mindless kinds of being. Intuitively we all experience living beings as distinctly alive primarily because we tacitly recognize their capacity to *strive* and hence the possibility of their either succeeding or failing in their endeavors.

Evolutionists implicitly recognize the conative (striving) nature of life whenever they talk about the "struggle to exist." They would not use such terms as *striving* or *struggling* when referring to inanimate objects or processes. Physical and chemical processes taken alone do not strive but instead adhere to deterministic routines blindly and unfeelingly. However, precisely because living beings are capable of striving (even if only to stay alive), their mode of existence is irreducible to the mechanical determinism operative in subsidiary physical and chemical processes. Whether the striving that goes on in living organisms is that of a parasite searching for nourishment, a reptile seeking its prey, or a human being reading books in quest of the meaning of life, in any of its countless manifestations vitality means, at the very least, the capacity to strive.

So there is clearly a duality (not dualism) of ways of being in the universe, and it is remarkable that living beings, by virtue of their capacity to strive, stand out distinctly from their inanimate backdrop. As far as transhumanism is concerned, therefore, the question is whether the capacity to strive, that is, to follow the logic of achievement, will continue to remain an essential aspect of the universe. Will vitality accompany future transformed modes of terrestrial and cosmic reality or will everything be subject to complete mechanical control, human scheming, or computational algorithms? In other words, will the need to strive, an essential attribute of vitality—as well as of moral and religious existence—survive the possible transformations to come?

The transhumanist project is itself an instance of human striving in accordance with the logic of achievement, but most technologically inspired transhumanist dreams and projects intend to reduce life and intelligence to inanimate mechanical processes. This reduction has already been the goal of much contemporary biology and cognitive science. Transhumanist plans have yet to show how they will prevent the expulsion of vitality from the sphere of being. To the extent that nanotechnology and cognitive sciences realize the goal of artificializing life and intelligence, the more serious becomes the question of whether vitality can survive such a transformation. The more we seek to replace striving beings with entities that do not function according to the logic of achievement—and this includes the whole sphere of artificial life and intelligence—the more urgent becomes our concern about the survival of *life* into the indefinite future. As of now, it is hard to imagine how even the most complex and sophisticated future technologies will possess the anticipatory attribute of centered striving that is essential to living beings as we know them now.

Polanyi rightly insists that it is "personal knowledge" rather than the impersonal methods of science that allows human beings to recognize the domain of vitality in the first place.[7] The very fact that academicians have set departments of biology administratively apart from those of physics and chemistry is ultimately due to a tacit acknowledgment that there is a special body of living beings who share the trait of striving with humans. Only because we humans, as personal organisms, are striving beings—examples of which are our *longing* to understand, our *desiring* to know, and our *struggle* to find out what is good—are we able to recognize intuitively the trait of striving that makes other related beings instances of vitality.

My point, therefore, is that it has not yet been demonstrated how any artifact or technological product could be alive—and hence contribute to the increase of more-being on our planet—even though technologies will probably continue instrumentally to assist and expand our personal struggles for knowledge, power, or whatever. We can imagine various morally acceptable ways in which new technologies may amplify and improve human endeavor (striving), but will robots or other sophisticated inventions ever become *centers* of striving, that is, real subjects themselves? In what way will transhumanists intensify rather than diminish the "insideness" of the cosmos?

As far as I know, there has so far been little if any consideration by transhumanists of the "logic of achievement" that Polanyi considers essential to all instances of vitality. As of now, it is difficult to imagine how the centered striving that defines our own vitality could ever become implanted into devices referred to as artificially intelligent. Since humans share with other living beings the trait of striving and, along with it, the possibility of tragic defeat, will a transhumanist world still allow for the *dramatic* note of tragedy? Will artificially engineered beings ever be capable of anticipation and hope—attributes essential to the enkindling of further striving?

Human and nonhuman modes of life are bound together in a poignant cosmic striving. All living beings are part of an anticipatory universe that has so far, at least when surveyed over the long run, been intent upon bringing about more-being. But if the transhumanist world is one that will have left behind the capacity to strive, exchanging vitality for technologically engineered entities operating only in accordance with mechanically or chemically deterministic processes, will that be an enhancement in the story of life? Or, instead, would it not itself amount to a great terrestrial and cosmic tragedy?

Second, an increase in the intensity of *subjectivity*. Here Teilhard has much to contribute. Reflection on the fact of striving leads us to posit in each living being at least a minimum of centeredness, interiority, or what I have been referring to as subjectivity. An undeniable trend in the evolution of the universe so far has been that of bringing about a gradual increase in sentience, perceptivity, consciousness, and—at least in human beings—self-awareness, moral aspiration, freedom, the longing for love, and other qualities of inner experience. All vital striving must have a *subjective center* in which the experience of trying, succeeding, or failing is registered. Otherwise, living beings would be indistinguishable from physical objects that do not strive or feel in any sense. The center of striving in each living being lies in the ontological domain of subjectivity, an immediately palpable but un-objectifiable reality. Each subjective center, by definition, eludes being captured by the objectifying methods of modern science and engineering. At present, transhumanist idealization of future forms of intelligence ironically leaves out any considerations of the domain of subjectivity whose attentiveness to the data of experience, whose striving for insight, and whose desire to know make up the core of all human cognition.

Since scientific method can deal only with what is impersonal and objectifiable, it has no direct access to interiority, insideness, centeredness, or subjectivity. Nevertheless, every subject and every mental event is no less part of the natural world than trees and lakes, and so we cannot expect to understand what nature really is unless, like Teilhard, we take into account the fact of subjective experience. To take subjectivity adequately into account, however, we need to practice a wider form of attentiveness or empiricism than conventional science utilizes. The intellectual world, however, is still very far from having appropriated, let alone having advanced and intensified instances of subjectivity.[8]

Transhumanist projections, like other dreams of scientists and engineers, are still usually conceived narrowly in terms of the modern picture of a world without subjects—that is, the world as conceived by modernity since Descartes.[9] In contrast to modernity's world without subjects, true empiricists must not push their own or anyone else's subjectivity—nor, for that matter, the subjectivity of any sentient being—out of sight. Unfortunately, however, transhumanist dreams at present are still burdened with the scientistic assumption that nature is inherently mindless and impersonal, that is, devoid of the inestimable reality and value of subjectivity. As long as expectations of a transformed humanity lack an appreciation of subjectivity and how to protect it, they are paving the way for a considerably diminished rather than ontologically enriched universe.

Third, an increase in *creativity*. Creativity means increasing rather than diminishing the vitality, subjectivity, and aesthetic intensity that the universe has already brought into being before us and without us. Human creativity now and in the future must be tutored by an understanding of how creativity has *already* been happening, prior to our own appearance in evolution. Theologically, creativity means participation in the divine task of bringing something *new* into existence. It means not only conservation, which is absolutely essential, but also a realization that the world remains open to new creation up-ahead. It is the function of a biblically based transhumanist praxis not only to conserve life systems on our planet but also to take measures that will foster opportunities for the emergence of unprecedented forms of life and the enhancement of vitality, subjectivity, diversity, relationality, and creativity in the up-ahead. As long as transhumanist projects contribute to this enhancement, they would seem to be justifiable. This is the essence of a Teilhardian evaluation of transhumanism.

Consequently, it would be unwise for an anticipatory cosmic vision to espouse an exclusively sacramentalist or activist approach. I am opposing, here, any transhumanist adventures that fail to consider prayerfully their possible impact on the already realized cosmic values we have been discussing in this book. If we take a purely sacramentalist approach, it is likely to ignore Teilhard's belief that we are entitled by God to bring new and unrepeatable kinds of being into existence. Yet, transhumanist experiments may also fail to respect, protect, and enhance such values as vitality, subjectivity (including consciousness and freedom), and creativity (whose measure is its aesthetic intensity). This would amount to a tragic end to the story of life. Failure to align ourselves faithfully and docilely with the values that have been established in the emergence of the universe up until now could lead the cosmos into an abyss.

I believe that, before participating in any transhumanist trials, Teilhard would want us to take measures to ensure the liberation of life, a respect for persons, and a mutual flourishing of both nonhuman and human communities, as conditions for the ongoing creation of more-being in the cosmos. The theological scheme that frames this proposal is one in which nature is seen not only as sacrament but also as *promise*. Our unfinished universe is not yet fully revelatory of the Divine. It awaits future creativity and development. In light of the theological recovery of eschatology in the twentieth century, I am especially partial to a theology of hope according to which all of Christian theology remains concerned about the future and hence must be bathed in the extravagant flood of covenantal promises that the Bible associates with the God of creation and renewal.

Our God is the God of promise, who opens up an ever-new future—not just for Abraham, Israel, and the church, but also for the whole universe. The divine invitation to move into an open future of new possibilities applies to the nearly fourteen-billion-year-old cosmic process and not just the human future. Hence, I believe that the idea of the "promise of nature" ideally provides the basis for a scientifically informed Christian theological understanding and evaluation of transhumanist projects.

Beginning with the premise that nature is pregnant with promise, we may favor a metaphysics of the future and view the universe, with Teilhard, as *anticipatory*. In the context of biblical hope, let us highlight the fact that from its very beginning the universe has been open to a whole series of dramatic future transformations. Transhumanism reminds us that we may anticipate still more dramatic outcomes in the future. Theology needs to take into account scientific cosmology, planetary science, and evolutionary biology in order to understand and appreciate the inherently restless and adventurous character of cosmogenesis, so as to awaken our own creative restlessness intelligently, responsibly, and reverently. Thus, as I have proposed, from a study of the cosmic process we may glean a baseline set of criteria (vitality, subjectivity, and creativity) that place necessary boundaries around all efforts we make toward future transformations of nature, life, humanity, and the cosmos.

Cosmological, geological, and biological accounts of cosmic events teach us that nature has always had a dramatic character. The storied picture of an awakening universe began to emerge only in the middle of the twentieth century after careful reflection on the scientific theories of Charles Darwin and Albert

Einstein as well as the new discoveries by astronomy and astrophysics. Prior to that time it was primarily the human story that constituted theology's main horizon and focus. However, now that we understand nature as an ongoing creative process, the question is whether it carries a wider meaning than that of simply being a home for the human adventure.

For our purposes here, the context of Teilhard's unfinished universe provides an intellectual setting in which theology may forge an illuminating alliance with scientists and futurists. Teilhard's cosmic vision allows Christian theologians to discern the ways in which nature, emerging over billions of years, has given rise to increasingly sentient, conscious, and creative modes of being. Four billion years ago, in the sudden arrival of life and biogenetic processes on earth, the *universe* underwent an "information" explosion.[10] More recently, with the emergence of complex brains and minds on our planet (and perhaps analogously elsewhere in the universe), the cosmos began to undergo a "thought" explosion. Currently, with the appearance of transhumanist dreams, human beings are at last witnessing what may turn out to be a distinctively new chapter in the unfolding of a far-from-finished universe. Theology must approach the specter of transhumanism with the reverence of the sacramental approach, the spirit of adventure and creativity of the activist dreams of new being, but also with an eye to enhancing rather than diminishing the values of vitality, subjectivity, and creativity so central to the universe as it exists now.

13

CRITICISM

As far as Teilhard's personal life and his interaction with others are concerned, I have found nothing that contradicts the positive impression he left with friends, acquaintances, and fellow scientists. He was exceptionally kind, cultured, brilliant, reliable, and humorous. He was a "perfect gentleman," as a missionary priest who met him in China relayed to me many years ago. He was especially helpful to younger scientists, critiquing their papers and advancing their scholarship and careers. George Barbour, a geologist who lived and worked with Teilhard in the field, wrote a book testifying to Teilhard's nobility, generosity, and scientific brilliance.[1] As a scientist among scientists, Teilhard's penetrating vision, patience, meticulous habits of research, powers of inference, humility, and spirit of collaboration impressed everyone he knew. His carefully composed scientific papers, and his work in the field solidified his reputation as one of the most prominent geologists and paleontologists in the Far East. Most notable, perhaps, were the contributions he made to the discovery of Peking Man.

While his character and professionalism are beyond reproach, however, not all of his writings, especially *The Human Phenomenon*, have escaped criticism. Since his death in 1955, questions have been raised about Teilhard's scientific thought, his qualifications as a Christian thinker, and more recently, the relevance of his thought to the contemporary search for an ecologically responsible Christian approach to the natural world. In this concluding chapter I cannot respond to these three issues at great length, but let me say at least a brief word about each: Teilhard as a scientist, as a Christian thinker, and as an ecologically responsible thinker and writer.

TEILHARD AS A SCIENTIST

During his lifetime Teilhard was held in the highest esteem as a scientist, but since the time of his death and the subsequent publication of the *Phenomenon*, his writings have sometimes been met with criticism from other scientists. This reserve and even distaste are due in great measure to the fact that Teilhard vehemently opposed the predominantly materialist ideology taken for granted by prominent scientists, especially evolutionary biologists. I have concluded that scientific naturalists are ill-disposed toward Teilhard not so much for scientific reasons as for his conviction that evolution must be carefully distinguished from materialist philosophy. Evolution and cosmogenesis make better sense, Teilhard thought, in a nonmaterialist metaphysical setting, one that gives priority to the cosmic future rather than the physical past. He was certain that the data underlying evolution and cosmology have become less, not more, intelligible when they are interpreted materialistically. Trying to explain life and mind exclusively in terms of earlier-and-simpler physical causes lying in the dead past leads eventually to intellectual incoherence.

As I have proposed in previous chapters, Teilhard was seeking to replace the materialist "metaphysics of the past" with a "metaphysics of the future," a worldview consonant not only with evolutionary science but also with the Abrahamic and early Christian intuition that ultimate reality comes into the present as an ever-renewing future. As a matter of principle Teilhard refused to privilege specific scientific ideas over others for religious reasons, and he always distinguished science sharply from theology. But he was aware that scientific discoveries can be given a variety of interpretations, including that of scientific materialism.

He was impressed, as a person of faith, by the consonance or structural congruity he noticed between St. Paul's vision of a universe converging on Christ, on the one hand, and the scientific discovery of cosmogenesis in which the natural world is moving from past multiplicity toward future unity, on the other.[2] Drawing such a connection, however, is not an act of science but of faith. Teilhard's anticipatory cosmic vision is not a conflation of science with faith since he does not present his cosmic Christology as though it were a scientific theory in competition with other scientific theories. He never thought of his religious understanding of life, mind, and the universe as an *alternative* to Darwin's biology or Einstein's cosmology. Instead, he considered his cosmic vision to be an alternative to *materialist interpretations* of biology and cosmology.

Unfortunately, most of the scientists who have repudiated Teilhard's thought have done so because they have mistaken his Christian theology of nature for a set of strictly scientific propositions. Scientists Jacques Monod, Peter Medawar, and Stephen Jay Gould, along with philosophers of science such as Daniel Dennett, have opposed Teilhard not for his scientific research, of which they know almost nothing, but for his espousal of a worldview opposed to their own materialist scientism.[3] The core of this conflict, as I see it, is not an opposition between science and faith but between Teilhard's metaphysics of the future and the modern materialist metaphysics of the past.

The biologist Julian Huxley and the renowned geneticist Theodosius Dobzhansky were enthusiastic supporters of Teilhard because they were able to distinguish between Teilhard as a pure scientist and Teilhard as a cosmic visionary. His professional scientific papers were never written as vehicles to disseminate his cosmic vision, and scientists today would still find them impressive. Rather, it is Teilhard's philosophical and religious reflections on evolution, such as those in the *Phenomenon,* that have raised objections from his fellow scientists—in almost all cases because they assumed Teilhard was presenting his religious reflections as conventional science. This confusion is partly Teilhard's fault, but even so, the biologist Harold Morowitz was able to give a positive assessment of the *Phenomenon* for its scientific originality, even though he did not share Teilhard's Christian worldview.[4] Many other readers of the *Phenomenon* are also able to distinguish clearly between Teilhard as scientist and Teilhard as religious visionary.

Teilhard clearly understood the difference between science and philosophical or theological reflection on science. Unfortunately, however, he did not always make this distinction explicit. In the opening pages of the *Phenomenon* he claimed that his book should be read not "as a metaphysical work, still less as some kind of theological essay, but solely and exclusively as a scientific study."[5] Yet the *Phenomenon* is much more than science, at least as science is ordinarily understood. As Ian Barbour has rightly proposed, the fairest way to read many of Teilhard's major works—books such as the *Phenomenon, The Future of Man,* and *Human Energy*—is to acknowledge that they are not purely scientific treatises but also forays into the theology of nature.

In any case, Teilhard rightly objected to any philosophy or theology of nature that leaves out what is right in front of our eyes, especially the human phenomenon.[6] Unfortunately, when scientists bother to investigate the latter, they almost always resort to impersonal, mindless explanatory categories that cannot illuminate what is distinctively human. Scientists typically bracket out what each of us already knows "from the inside" to be our most distinctive trait, namely, our subjectivity, our capacity for feeling, thought, judgment, and decision. Scientific thinkers who are partial to materialist metaphysics invariably end up trying to explain the human phenomenon, including the human mind, in terms that are too small to clarify its distinctiveness in nature and evolution.

It is important, therefore, to appreciate the broad meaning that Teilhard gave to the word *scientific*. Above all, he thought that science should take into account the full range of "phenomena" that impress themselves upon our senses, including our interior sensibilities. Science, he thought, must not arbitrarily leave out anything that contributes to our "vision" of the world. This means that science must also take into account the fact of our own "consciousness," even though it is invisible, since it surely tells us something about the character of the universe from which it sprang. Since consciousness is not alien to or outside of nature, we should not ignore it but think of it as nature's inner side, inseparable from nature's visible manifestations.

Why, then, has science overlooked such an impressive reality as consciousness? Teilhard responds:

> The apparent restriction of the phenomenon of consciousness to higher forms of life has long served science as a pretext for eliminating it from its construction of the universe. To dismiss it, thought has been classed as a bizarre exception, an aberrant function, an epiphenomenon. . . . "Full evidence of consciousness appears only in the human," we had been tempted to say, "therefore it is an isolated case and of no interest to science."[7]

But, Teilhard goes on, we must now enlarge our vision:

> Evidence of consciousness appears in the human, we must begin again, correcting ourselves; therefore half-seen in this single flash of light, it has cosmic extension and as such takes on an aura of indefinite spatial and temporal prolongations. . . . Indisputably, deep within ourselves, through a

rent or a tear, an "interior" appears at the heart of beings. This is enough to establish the existence of this interior in some degree or other everywhere forever in nature. Since the stuff of the universe has an internal face at one point in itself, its structure is necessarily *bifacial*; that is, in every region of time and space, as well, for example, as being granular, *coextensive with its outside, everything has an inside*.[8]

Teilhard assumed that those who embrace the scientific spirit should, of all people, be willing to open their eyes. Doesn't science, after all, boast an allegiance to the empirical imperative? Then shouldn't it take into account *all* of the data available to our experience, including the experience of ourselves as subjects, as conscious beings? Why, if we intend to be truly scientific, do we post a "no entry" sign at the point where the cosmos exposes an "interior" dimension? Isn't subjectivity an *objective* aspect of the universe, not something floating in from outside? "The time has come," Teilhard writes, "for us to realize that to be satisfactory, any interpretation of the universe, even a positivistic one, must cover the inside as well as the outside of things—spirit as well as matter. True physics is that which will someday succeed in integrating the totality of the human being into a coherent representation of the world."[9]

Interestingly, Teilhard's materialist critics, though pretending to be metaphysical monists (only matter is real), remain implicitly dualists in the clean separation they make between their own mental life and the physical universe.[10] Teilhard, however, rightly claimed that a widely empirical study of the universe would not exclude the fact of consciousness or "thought" from the field of its inquiry. The universe, after all, includes humans, and so it cannot be understood objectively without taking the phenomenon of human consciousness into account as a terrestrial and, by extension, a *cosmic* phenomenon.[11]

Teilhard thought that the true spirit of science should lead us to practice what I have been calling a *wider empiricism*. Science should take into account *all* the data of experience. A thoroughgoing empiricism should extend its sweep to include the impressive phenomenon experienced immediately by each of us, namely, our own consciousness. An adequate empiricism should attend to the "inside" of things and not restrict its gaze to the outside.[12]

Scientists, like everyone else, can be blind to certain realities in the universe until they have had their eyes opened wide. For this reason Teilhard places a special emphasis on "seeing" at the beginning of the *Phenomenon*. He writes, "These pages represent an effort *to see* and *to show* what the human being becomes, what the human being requires, if placed wholly and completely in the context of appearance." In his "Introduction" to the *Phenomenon* he writes:

> *Seeing.* One could say that the whole of life lies in seeing—if not ultimately, at least essentially. To be more is to be more united—and this sums up and is the very conclusion of the work to follow. But unity grows, and we will affirm this again, only if it is supported by an increase of consciousness, of vision. That is why the history of the living world can be reduced to the elaboration of ever more perfect eyes at the heart of a cosmos where it is always possible to discern more. . . . To try to see more and to see better is not, therefore, just a fantasy, curiosity, or a luxury. See or perish. This is the situation imposed on every element of the universe by the mysterious gift of existence.[13]

While I am appreciative of Teilhard's plea for a wider empiricism, I do not wish to burden the natural sciences with the task of opening our eyes widely to the fact of subjectivity. Physics, for example, does not need to do the work of cognitive science or metaphysics, as long as we do not forget that physics, like every other scientific discipline, abstracts from most of the intricacy of the real world. Likewise, we can put up with the fact that science always filters many things out for the sake of a particular focus. Science is not wrong; it is just limited in what it can see. Each scientific discipline rightly excludes certain aspects of nature from its self-limiting way of observing the world, and this narrowing of vision seems permissible as long as finer nets are available to pick up what gets left behind.

I question, then, whether we need to extend conventional scientific inquiry to include attention to our subjective consciousness, as Teilhard seems at times to propose. Would it not be sufficient to make attention to subjectivity a topic for a wider empiricism than that of scientific method? The late physicist and theologian Ian Barbour, for example, has found in Alfred North Whitehead's process philosophy an empirically based complement to the abstractions of physics and other natural sciences.[14] An empirically oriented metaphysics can acknowledge more explicitly than natural science that subjectivity is pervasive in nature. Barbour's Whiteheadian process metaphysics takes into account the "inside" aspect in all of nature. Regarding process thought, Barbour notes:

> [It] envisages two aspects of all events as seen from within and without. Because humanity is continuous with the rest of nature (despite the uniqueness of reflective self-consciousness), human experience can be taken as a clue to interpreting the experience of other beings. Genuinely new phenomena emerge in evolutionary history, but the basic metaphysical categories apply to all events.[15]

Teilhard did not have available an empirically capacious metaphysics such as Barbour found in Whiteheadian process thought. For this reason I believe we should treat somewhat amiably Teilhard's audacious efforts to expand the understanding of *science* in the direction of the more radical empiricism that for Whitehead and his followers is the job of a descriptive metaphysics.[16] For Teilhard, since neither the science of his day nor the Thomistic metaphysics he had absorbed during his theological training were enough to capture the emergent "insideness" of nature, he sought to stretch the boundaries of science so that the quest for right understanding would not pass over in silence what is clearly an aspect of nature. Teilhard shared with Whitehead, for example, the conviction that our own mental activity is an aspect *of* nature, not something that occurs outside of nature. They both agreed that we need to keep our search for understanding open to whatever is empirically available; this includes the experience of our own subjectivity. If science fails to "see" the dimension of interiority in nature, Teilhard is asking, then what other mode of inquiry will do so?

Teilhard used the word *science* too broadly for the tastes of most scientists today, but there can be no doubt that he was simply trying to get truth-seekers to accept as an empirical datum the human phenomenon as it has emerged in the context of an evolving universe. It is not that he was unscientific, but that he thought science should become *more empirical* than it usually is. This, then, is not as grievous a sin as it is often made out to be. We may object to Teilhard's widening the notion of science, but we have no cause for accusing him of being unempirical.

The phenomena that Teilhard wants us to view are available to everyone's immediate experience. This is why he thought that science, which claims to be rooted in experience, should be able to see them. There can be no reasonable objection on the part of scientists, he thought, to having their eyes opened to new phenomena and new ways of seeing. Additionally, Teilhard was trying to turn our attention toward an aspect of the universe that modern science had not *seen* previously, but which the tools of geology and paleontology are now rendering transparent, namely, the human phenomenon as a new *layer* in terrestrial evolution and as a new chapter in the cosmic story. Since it is only artificially that science tears off the "inside" from the outside of nature, it seems to me that it is not an absence, but an abundance, of empirical concern that led Teilhard to envisage the phenomenon of consciousness as part of nature.

TEILHARD AS A CHRISTIAN THINKER

There have always been critics among Teilhard's readers who have denied that he was an orthodox and innocent representative of Christian tradition. Here, I shall limit myself to a single example. In a 2016 article an old accusation by Christian ultra-conservatives, especially those opposed to Darwinian evolution, has resurfaced. It claims that Teilhard is not only wrong but also complicit in the spreading of moral evil. This appears in a couple of publications by a young Catholic theologian and recent graduate of the University of Notre Dame's Department of Theology. Their author, John Slattery, claims that "from the 1920s until his death in 1955, Teilhard de Chardin unequivocally supported racist eugenic practices, praised the possibilities of the Nazi experiments, and looked down upon those who [*sic*] he deemed 'imperfect' humans." Slattery writes that a persistent attraction to racism, fascism, and genocidal ideas "explicitly lay the groundwork for Teilhard's famous cosmological theology." This, he highlights, "is a link which has been largely ignored in Teilhardian research until now."[17]

A more recent article by the same critic appeared online in *Religion Dispatches*.[18] Here Slattery hangs his claims on eight stray citations from Teilhard's letters and other scattered writings. Teilhard did not elaborate systematically on these passing remarks, most of which can be easily taken out of context. Their style is provocative and mostly interrogatory, and their meaning in every case is highly debatable. Slattery offers them to us, however, as undeniable evidence that Teilhard's true "legacy" is one of hostility to Catholic affirmation of human dignity, equality, racial justice, and concern for the disadvantaged. Most important, however, is Slattery's claim that Teilhard's commitment to these evils influenced his mature "cosmological theology."

Slattery's thesis—offered without any real argumentation—will appeal to those on the Catholic and evangelical right who have consistently repudiated Teilhard for trying to reconcile Christian faith with evolutionary biology. And it will draw no objections from atheistic philosophers, like Daniel Dennett, who have denounced Teilhard's thought for the same reason. Above all, however, it will win approval from readers who suspect that there just *has* to be something deeply perverse about Teilhard's radical rethinking of Christian faith for the age of science.

Instead of digging into Teilhard's mountainous body of work, with which he shows little familiarity, Slattery rests his summation of "Teilhard's legacy" on half a thimbleful of quotations taken out of context. Seasoned Teilhard scholars have known about these remarks for decades but have usually measured their significance in terms of what they take to be Teilhard's *true* legacy. This legacy, I must emphasize here, consists of at least four cardinal principles completely ignored in Slattery's desperate debunking. I have covered these principles in previous chapters, but here they are presented in more condensed form.

First principle. The universe is still coming into being. Theologically, this means that creation is not yet "finished" and that humans, who are part of an unfinished universe, may contribute to the ongoing creation of the world. The opportunity to participate, even in the most excruciatingly monotonous ways, in "building the earth" is a cornerstone of human dignity. It is also a teaching of the Second Vatican Council. The fact that our creativity can sometimes lead to monstrous outcomes does not absolve us of the obligation to improve the world and ourselves. Taking advantage of this opportunity is also essential to sustaining hope and a "zest for living." For, according to Teilhard, nothing "clips the wings of hope" and takes us out of life more decisively than the now-obsolete theological idea that the universe has been finished once and for all by God "in the beginning," and that all we can do religiously is wait for its restoration.

Far from being indifferent to the suffering of the disabled and the marginalized, as Slattery accuses Teilhard of being, the Jesuit priest consistently fostered a vision of life that gives dignity to the helpless and those in need. As he reflected with quiet empathy and unvanquished hope on the incessant suffering of his invalid sister, for example, he developed a profound Christian theology of suffering (see Chapter 9). Furthermore, in the quest for what contributes rightly to new creation and the zest for living, Teilhard set forth as morally permissible *only* those actions and creative projects that are in accordance with the following principles.

Second principle. To create means to unify (creare est unire). Scientifically understood, the emerging cosmos becomes real and intelligible only by (gradually) bringing increasingly more complex forms of unity or coherence out of its primordial state of diffusion and subatomic dispersal. As the universe in the course of deep time becomes more intricately unified in its emergent instances of physical complexity, it also becomes more conscious. Theologically, this second principle is realized in Christian hope as summed up in Jesus's prayer that "all may be one" and in the Pauline expectation that everything will be "brought to a head" in Christ "in whom all things hold together." Teilhard's true legacy lies in his rich Christian sense of a universe converging on Christ, a universe whose destiny is that of being brought into final union with and in God. Almost all the many distortions of Teilhard's intentions stem from a failure to understand exactly what he means by *true* union.

Third principle. True union differentiates. True union does not mean uniformity or homogeneity but a rich, complex mode of being built up out of a diversity of components that are permitted to coexist in a relationship of complementarity. Theologically, the principle that true union differentiates is exemplified in a wondrous way in the doctrine of God as three in one. Scientifically, the axiom that true union differentiates is both a good evolutionary and ecological principle as well as a criterion of survivable social organization. Ecologically, true unity maximizes diversity and acknowledges differences. So does the biblical theme of justice. So, when Teilhard acknowledges "inequalities," he is not supporting injustice, racism, classism, or elitism. He is following an ethical and ecological principle that maximizes diversity and differences so as not to detract from individual value and overall unity.

True unity at the human level of cosmic emergence enhances personal freedom, maximizes otherness, and in that way respects personal dignity. So, when Teilhard expresses "interest" in the fascist experiments of the twentieth century, far from approving them, as Slattery implies, he is simply observing that such movements feed parasitically on a natural human passion for union, but in a twisted manner devoid of any concern for differentiation and personalization. Anyone who has actually read Teilhard's works widely and fairly will notice that he deemed fascist and communist experiments evil insofar as they fail to look beyond uniformity, homogeneity, and ideological conformism to the *true* unity that differentiates, liberates, and personalizes.

Finally, Teilhard presents the cosmic Christ as the paradigm of differentiating, personalizing, attracting, and liberating union. Christ is the Center around which humans and all of creation are called to gather in differentiated, dialogical—and hence intimate—communion (as expressed in the Eucharist). The principle that *true* union differentiates is also the basis of an ecologically responsible cosmic vision.

Fourth principle. The world rests on the future as its sole support. As we survey cosmic history with the scientists, we discover a "law of recurrence" in which something new, more complex, and (eventually) more conscious has always been taking shape up ahead. Scientifically, we can now see that subatomic elements were organized around atomic nuclei; atoms were gathered into molecules, molecules into cells, and cells into complex organisms, some of which have recently made the leap into thought. The most important kinds of emergence can occur, however, only if the elements allow themselves to be organized around a new and higher *center* that lifts them up to the state of more elaborately differentiated unity.

In our unfinished universe a unifying Center and fountain of "more-being" is always awaiting the universe from up ahead. The physical cosmos will be unified finally in the body of Christ. In other words, what gives nature its consistency and unity, what holds it together, is not the subatomic past—where everything falls apart into incoherence—but the always fresh future where everything is gathered into the unifying love of God-Omega.

Once again, God is both Alpha and Omega, "but God is more Omega than Alpha." To experience true union, true being, true goodness, and true beauty, therefore, we must allow ourselves—like Abraham, the Prophets, and Jesus—to be grasped by the Future. Teilhard stated explicitly that his whole theology of nature was an attempt to implement the cosmic expectations of St. Paul and the Fourth Evangelist. It is the God incarnate in Christ that gives the world its consistence. Not to notice this deeply Christian motif in his thought is to do him grave injustice.

Slattery thinks that Teilhard promotes evil also because he is too experimentally and theologically reckless. Yet, it is only under the constraints of Christian hope that Teilhard says we must be ready to "try everything." This hope requires a more adventurous moral life than what we find in classical religious patterns of piety, but Teilhard was looking for a morality rooted in hope—not only for humanity but for the whole universe. His attention to the cosmos and its future can cause confusion to theologians of "the eternal present" who have not yet fully awakened to the fact of an unfinished universe.

As he moved to ground his Christian spirituality in a metaphysics of the future, Teilhard was humble enough to acknowledge that his own thoughts were tentative and revisable. Still, since humans are part of nature, and nature is experimental and remains far from finished, it is perfectly legitimate to wonder, as countless other thoughtful people are doing today, whether and to what extent humans can participate in their own and the world's future evolution. At least in the four principles condensed above (and developed throughout this book), Teilhard's deeply Christian cosmic vision, instead of being "genocidal," as Slattery claims, provides a morally rich framework within which to begin dealing with the hard questions that Teilhard was among the first to raise.

TEILHARD AND ECOLOGY

Recently, some critics of Teilhard have taken him to task allegedly for ignoring and even contributing to ecological problems. They have accused him of promoting a doctrine of progress that fails to rein in the contamination of our planet by wasteful and destructive technologies. By supporting technology and promoting the growth of the noosphere (which, so far, has relied heavily on global communications, physical travel, fossil fuels, and other dangerous developments in human inventiveness), hasn't Teilhard condoned rather than curbed the ecological indifference of modern nations and their reliance on dangerous scientific technologies?

No doubt, in his own lifetime, Teilhard was no more explicitly concerned about ecological issues than were most of his contemporaries. Until recently, Christians, like everybody else, knew nothing about evolution, the age of the universe, and other recent scientific discoveries. Likewise, most Christians knew (almost) nothing about how extensively patterns of human existence and ideological assumptions have endangered the rest of life on earth. It was not until after Teilhard's death that the ecological movement became a major topic in Christian thought, and even today such interest is unsteady. This is why Pope Francis's encyclical *Laudato Si'* came as such a surprise, and even a shock, to many Catholics.

Catholic thought, as we have noted throughout this book, was not prepared for Teilhard either. There is a connection, it seems, between institutional Catholicism's initial aversion to Teilhard and the general Catholic indifference nowadays to *Laudato Si'*. For centuries Catholics and most other Christians have been indifferent to nature and its well-being. It is striking, then, that both Teilhard and Pope Francis have refused, as the apostle Paul had done long ago, to separate concern for human salvation from the destiny of the universe. Many Christians are not ready to hear this good news.

More than any other Catholic thinker in the history of the church, in my opinion, Teilhard showed us how to love God without turning our backs on the world, and how to love the world without turning our backs on God. Catholicism and other Christian traditions are puzzled by this dramatic turn to the cosmos. Starting quite early, Christians have been taught to flee from the world into the heavenly bosom of God. For centuries their otherworldly spiritualities have had negative implications for environmental awareness and ethics. It is hard to imagine how Christians can be fully motivated to care for the natural world if their deepest aspiration is to leave the universe behind at death.

During the last century, however, there has been a gradual shift in Catholic attitudes toward the cosmos. This new turn became explicit at Vatican II and even more so in Pope Francis's *Laudato Si'*. After Einstein, the universe, at least in the minds of scientifically informed thinkers, has gradually become not a place to get away from but an unfinished historical process that still has a future. Gradually, Christian theologians—or at least a solid minority of them—began to *see* that the question of human destiny is inseparable from that of the universe. The story of each human life is tied into the whole history of nature. As a result, the preoccupation of Christians with personal immortality can no longer be used as an excuse to wreck, consume, or remain indifferent to the well-being of the terrestrial portion of the universe.

We humans and the universe are a package deal. We cannot love ourselves truly without loving the universe and working for its full awakening. Our souls are the outcome of nearly fourteen billion years of cosmic turbulence. They cannot be saved unless the universe is also saved. Among Catholic thinkers, at least, I cannot recall anyone who has done more to reunite us to the cosmos than Teilhard. Nothing could be more foundational to Christian ecological ethics than rejoicing in the inseparable *connection* among my story, your story, and the story of the universe.

Consider, then, the ecological implications of Teilhard's awareness of our living in a world that is still in the making.[19] Environmental stewardship in such a universe means more than just our caring for what has been present from life's beginning. It means also our taking care that the process of creation will be given ample opportunity to attain a full realization of its inherent, God-given, evolutionary possibilities. Human beings cannot foresee the cosmic future in detail, but they are morally obliged to take care that the full potential of nature's promise will be allowed to blossom in unknown ways as the universe unfolds, possibly in ever new versions of beauty.

As noted earlier, an unfinished, evolving universe, unlike an initially perfected one, is a universe open to the future. A sense of cosmogenesis, I have been arguing, can give new significance and wider sweep to eschatology, that is, to biblical visions of what we may hope for. The evolutionary quality of life, when placed in the context of an unfinished universe, invites us to extend our hopes to include the future creativity of the whole cosmos. Teilhard's writings refuse to separate earthly preoccupations and concern for our personal destinies from a more overarching passion for the fulfillment of the entire universe. Teilhard's cosmic vision, more than any other of which I am aware, gives us good reasons not only for preserving the achievements of nature so far, but also for preparing nature for new creation and wider beauty up-ahead.

Emphasis on beauty as the end of all things is also fundamental to Pope Francis's ecological vision as expressed in *Laudato Si'*. "At the end," he writes, "we will find ourselves face to face with the infinite beauty of God (cf. 1 Cor 13:12), and be able to read with admiration and happiness the mystery of the universe, which *with us* will share in unending plenitude" (no. 243, emphasis added).

ENDNOTES

INTRODUCTION

1. Emphasis on beauty as the end of all things is fundamental to Pope Francis's ecological vision as expressed in his encyclical *Laudato Si'*. "At the end," he writes, "we will find ourselves face to face with the infinite beauty of God (cf. 1 Cor 13:12), and be able to read with admiration and happiness the mystery of the universe, which with us will share in unending plenitude" (no. 243).

2. Jean Lacouture, *Jesuits: A Multibiography* (London: Harvill, 1996), 441. The citation is from David Grumett, *Teilhard: Theology, Humanity, and Cosmos* (Leuven: Peeters, 2005), 273.

CHAPTER 1: COSMOS

1. Jürgen Moltmann, *Theology of Hope*, trans. James W. Leitch (New York: Harper & Row, 1967), 16.

2. Karl Rahner, *Theological Investigations*, vol. 6, trans. Karl and Boniface Kruger (Baltimore: Helicon, 1969), 59–68.

3. Wolfhart Pannenberg, *Faith and Reality* (Louisville, KY: Westminster, 1977); and Wolfhart Pannenberg, *Toward a Theology of Nature*, ed. Ted Peters (Louisville, KY: Westminster/John Knox Press, 1993).

4. Pierre Teilhard de Chardin, *Christianity and Evolution,* trans. René Hague (New York: Harper & Row, 1969), 107–8.

5. For the preceding, see Pierre Teilhard de Chardin, *The Human Phenomenon*, trans. Sarah Appleton-Weber (Portland, OR: Sussex Academic Press, 1999).

6. Teilhard, *The Human Phenomenon*, 17, 153.

7. Teilhard, *The Human Phenomenon*, 216–18.

8. Pierre Teilhard de Chardin, *Activation of Energy*, trans. René Hague (New York: Harcourt Brace Jovanovich, 1970), 239.

9. Although this chapter focuses on the implications of Teilhard's thought for Catholic theology, most of what I have to say here applies to non-Catholic Christian theology as well.

10. When I use the expression *unfinished universe,* I am not assuming that the universe is heading toward some predetermined ending but simply that right now its future is open ended. The cosmos is promised a fulfillment and redemption, but this does not have to mean something terminal.

11. Pierre Teilhard de Chardin, "The Meaning and Constructive Value of Suffering," in *Teilhard de Chardin: Pilgrim of the Future*, ed. Neville Braybrooke (London: Libra, 1964), 23.

12. Pierre Teilhard de Chardin, *The Heart of Matter*, trans. René Hague (San Diego: Harcourt, 1978), 212.

13. Pierre Teilhard de Chardin, *Human Energy*, trans. J. M. Cohen (New York: Harcourt Brace Jovanovich, 1971), 43–47.

14. In previous works I have been trying to rethink Christian faith in an evolutionary way. In this book I focus more explicitly on the theological implications of an unfinished universe. See *God after Einstein* (New Haven, CT: Yale University Press, forthcoming); *The New Cosmic Story: Inside Our Awakening Universe* (New Haven, CT: Yale University Press, 2017); and *Resting on the Future: Catholic Theology for an Unfinished Universe* (New York: Bloomsbury Press, 2015).

2. FUTURE

1. Excerpts from Gerard Manley Hopkins's poems, "Spring" and "God's Grandeur."

2. Pierre Teilhard de Chardin, *The Prayer of the Universe*, trans. René Hague (New York: Harper & Row, 1973), 120–21.

3. Pierre Teilhard de Chardin, *Writings in Time of War,* trans. René Hague (New York: Harper & Row, 1968), 55–56.

4. Pierre Teilhard de Chardin, *The Human Phenomenon*, trans. Sarah Appleton-Weber (Portland, OR: Sussex Academic Press, 1999), 162–63. Here on earth the awakening of thoughtful beings to truth, goodness, faith, hope, love, peace, and beauty is a relatively new chapter in cosmic history that may be just beginning. The future of creation is still open. The point

of our own lives must have something to do with contributing to this awakening of the universe.

5. Strictly speaking, classical scientific *method* is not permitted to characterize the universe as unfinished or dramatic. However, scientific discoveries are open to philosophical and theological reflection. These modes of inquiry may search for the universe's *narrative coherence*, the kind of intelligibility that can be discovered only through telling stories.

6. For examples of Vatican II's instruction for Catholics to take seriously the new evolutionary worldview, and hence the idea of a still unfinished universe, see *Gaudium et Spes,* in *The Documents of Vatican II,* ed. Walter M. Abbott (New York: Vintage, 1966), nos. 5, 36.

7. One of the central points in Teilhard's *The Human Phenomenon.*

8. Pierre Teilhard de Chardin, *Christianity and Evolution,* trans. René Hague (New York: Harcourt Brace Jovanovich, 1971), 79.

9. Pierre Teilhard de Chardin, *Activation of Energy,* trans. René Hague (New York: Harcourt Brace Jovanovich, 1970), 231–43.

10. I am not certain about the origin of the expression "metaphysics of the future." I believe it may have been used first by the German philosopher Ernst Bloch. In any case, I am adopting it as a label for a worldview that best fits an unfinished universe.

11. See Jürgen Moltmann, *Theology of Hope: On the Ground and the Implications of a Christian Eschatology,* trans. James W. Leitch (New York: Harper & Row, 1967), 16.

12. For further development of this point, see John F. Haught, *God after Einstein* (New Haven, CT: Yale University Press, forthcoming).

13. Teilhard, *Christianity and Evolution,* 79–86, 131–32.

14. A handy compendium and endorsement of this worldview is E. O. Wilson, *Consilience: The Unity of Knowledge* (New York: Knopf, 1998).

15. Peter W. Atkins, *The 2nd Law: Energy, Chaos, and Form,* 2nd ed. (New York: Scientific American Books, 1994), 200.

16. Teilhard, *Activation of Energy,* 139.

17. Pierre Teilhard de Chardin, *Human Energy,* trans. J. M. Cohen (New York: Harcourt Brace Jovanovich, 1971), 172–73. For a book-length critique of the materialist assumptions underlying the analytical illusion see John F. Haught, *Is Nature Enough? Meaning and Truth in the Age of Science* (Cambridge: Cambridge University Press, 2006).

18. Teilhard, *Human Energy,* 29; *Christianity and Evolution,* 178–79.

19. Teilhard, *Human Energy*, 79.

20. Pierre Teilhard de Chardin, *The Heart of Matter*, trans. René Hague (San Diego: Harcourt, 1978), 15–79.

21. For a recent example see Alex Rosenberg, "Why I Am a Naturalist," *New York Times*, September 17, 2011.

22. Teilhard, *Christianity and Evolution*, 240.

23. Teilhard, *Christianity and Evolution*, 76–95.

24. Moltmann, *Theology of Hope*, 92.

25. Moltmann, *Theology of Hope*, 92.

26. Teilhard, *Christianity and Evolution*, 79–95.

3. HOPE

1. Pierre Teilhard de Chardin, *Activation of Energy*, trans. René Hague (New York: Harcourt Brace Jovanovich, 1970), 239.

2. Pierre Teilhard de Chardin, *Hymn of the Universe* (New York: HarperCollins, 1969), 77.

3. Pierre Teilhard de Chardin, *The Human Phenomenon*, trans. Sarah Appleton-Weber (Portland, OR: Sussex Academic Press, 1999).

4. To readers interested in pursuing Teilhard's ideas, my own recommendation is to begin with collections of his essays, especially *The Future of Man*, trans. Norman Denny (New York: Harper & Row, 1964); and *Human Energy*, trans. J. M. Cohen (New York: Harcourt Brace Jovanovich, 1971), rather than plunging immediately into *The Human Phenomenon*.

5. "Address of Pope John Paul II to the Pontifical Academy of Sciences" (October 22, 1996), in *Origins,* CNS Documentary Service (December 5, 1996).

6. Commentators sometimes misleadingly interpret Teilhard as anti-Darwinian. However, it was the materialist ideology adopted by many Darwinians that he challenged, not the incontestable empirical data that support evolutionary theory. Like Darwin, Teilhard allowed for the role of chance and natural selection, but he rightly objected to the naturalistic belief, as strong today as in his own lifetime, that evolutionary mechanisms can provide an *ultimate* explanation of living phenomena.

7. David Grumett, *Teilhard: Theology, Humanity, and Cosmos* (Leuven: Peeters, 2005), 269.

8. Following Teilhard, I sometimes use the term *evolution* in referring both to biogenesis and cosmogenesis. In science today the term usually applies only to biological evolution.

9. Ernst Benz, *Evolution and Christian Hope: Man's Concept of the Future from the Early Fathers to Teilhard de Chardin*, trans. Heinz G. Frank (Garden City, NY: Doubleday/Anchor Books, 1966), 226.

10. Benz, *Evolution and Christian Hope*, 226.

11. Benz, *Evolution and Christian Hope*, 227.

12. Jean Danielou, cited in Benz, *Evolution and Christian Hope,* 226–27.

13. See Jürgen Moltmann, *Theology of Hope: On the Ground and the Implications of a Christian Eschatology*, trans. James W. Leitch (New York: Harper & Row, 1967).

14. Moltmann, *Theology of Hope*, 106–12.

15. Pierre Teilhard de Chardin, *How I Believe*, trans. René Hague (New York: Harper & Row, 1969), 42–44.

16. Jacques Monod, *Chance and Necessity: An Essay on the Natural Philosophy of Modern Biology*, trans. Austryn Wainhouse (New York: Knopf, 1971), 32.

17. See Stephen Jay Gould's essays in *Natural History* (March 1979, August 1980, June 1981). For a refutation of Gould's charges against Teilhard, see Thomas King, SJ, "Teilhard and Piltdown," in *Teilhard and the Unity of Knowledge*, ed. Thomas King, SJ, and James Salmon, SJ (New York: Paulist Press, 1983), 159–69.

18. Daniel C. Dennett, *Darwin's Dangerous Idea: Evolution and the Meaning of Life* (New York: Simon & Schuster, 1995), 320.

19. George Gaylord Simpson, *The Meaning of Evolution*, rev. ed. (New York: Bantam Books, 1971), 314–15: "Man is the result of a purposeless and natural process that did not have him in mind. He was not planned. . . . Man plans and has purposes. Plan, purpose, goal, all absent in evolution to this point, enter with the coming of man and are inherent in the new evolution which is confined to him."

20. For an authentication of Teilhard's standing as a scientist, see Bernard Towers, *Concerning Teilhard, and Other Writings on Science and Religion* (London: Collins, 1969).

21. Harold J. Morowitz, *The Kindly Dr. Guillotin and Other Essays on Science and Life* (Washington, DC: Counterpoint, 1997), 21–27.

22. Morowitz, *The Kindly Dr. Guillotin,* 21–27. See also Teilhard's unfortunately neglected work *The Vision of the Past,* trans. J. M. Cohen (New York: Harper & Row, 1966). Reading this important set of essays would help remove many of the caricatures of Teilhard as unscientific. The book also includes brilliant defenses of evolution against the attacks of creationists and other critics of Darwinian biology.

23. Morowitz, *The Kindly Dr. Guillotin,* 21–27.

24. As pointed out especially by B. Alan Wallace, *The Taboo of Subjectivity: Toward a New Science of Consciousness* (New York: Oxford University Press, 2000).

25. Pierre Teilhard de Chardin, *The Divine Milieu: An Essay on the Interior Life* (New York: Harper Torchbooks, 1965), 105–11; Teilhard, *Human Energy,* 57: "In a concrete sense there is not matter and spirit. All that exists [in the created world] is matter becoming spirit."

26. Teilhard, *Human Energy,* 23.

27. Teilhard, *Human Energy,* 23.

28. Teilhard, *Activation of Energy,* 139.

29. Pierre Teilhard de Chardin, "The Mass on the World," in Thomas M. King, *Teilhard's Mass: Approaches to "The Mass on the World"* (New York: Paulist Press, 2005), 145–58.

30. Teilhard, "The Mass on the World," 150.

31. Teilhard, *Human Energy,* 22.

32. Teilhard, *Activation of Energy,* 231–43.

33. Pierre Teilhard de Chardin, *Christianity and Evolution,* trans. René Hague (New York: Collins, 1969), 79.

34. Teilhard, *How I Believe,* 42.

35. Pierre Teilhard de Chardin, *The Future of Man,* trans. Norman Denny (New York: Harper Colophon Books, 1964), 83.

36. Teilhard, *The Future of Man,* 43–44.

4. ACTION

1. H. Richard Niebuhr makes a similar point in *The Responsible Self: An Essay in Christian Moral Philosophy* (Louisville, KY: Westminster John Knox Press, 1999).

2. Pierre Teilhard de Chardin, *Activation of Energy,* trans. René Hague (New York: Harcourt Brace Jovanovich, 1970), 229–44.

3. Pierre Teilhard de Chardin, *Human Energy*, trans. J. M. Cohen (New York: Harvest Books/Harcourt Brace Jovanovich, 1962), 29.

4. Pierre Teilhard de Chardin, *Christianity and Evolution,* trans. René Hague (New York: Collins and Evolution, 1969), 177.

5. Pierre Teilhard de Chardin, *How I Believe*, trans. René Hague (New York: Harper & Row, 1969), 42.

6. Teilhard, *How I Believe*, 43–44.

7. Teilhard, *Christianity and Evolution*, 92–93.

8. Teilhard, *Christianity and Evolution,* 93.

9. John E. Smith, *Reason and God* (New Haven, CT: Yale University Press, 1961); Schubert Ogden, *The Reality of God* (New York: Harper & Row, 1977).

10. Teilhard, *How I Believe*, 35.

11. Teilhard, *How I Believe*, 35.

12. G. C. Williams, *Plan and Purpose in Nature* (New York: Basic Books, 1996), 157.

13. Stephen J. Gould, "Introduction," in Carl Zimmer, *Evolution: The Triumph of an Idea from Darwin to DNA* (London: Arrow Books, 2003), xvi–xvii.

14. Teilhard, *Activation of Energy*, 139.

15. Teilhard, *Activation of Energy*, 132.

16. Teilhard, *Activation of Energy*, 131–32.

17. Alan B. Wallace, *The Taboo of Subjectivity: Toward a New Science of Consciousness* (New York: Oxford University Press, 2000); David Ray Griffin, *Unsnarling the World-Knot: Consciousness, Freedom, and the Mind-Body Problem* (Berkeley, CA: University of California Press, 1998). In Chapter 10, I say more about the modern intellectual denial of the reality of subjectivity and how it leads to a distorted understanding of the universe.

18. Teilhard, *Christianity and Evolution*, 32.

5. SPIRITUALITY

1. Walter M. Abbott, ed., *The Documents of Vatican II* (New York: Guild Press, 1966), 730–71. Closing message "To Men of Thought and Science," read by Paul Emile Cardinal Leger of Montreal, assisted by Antonio Cardinal Caggiano of Buenos Aires and Norman Cardinal Gilroy of Sydney, Australia.

2. Abbott, *The Documents of Vatican II*, 730–31.

3. Pierre Teilhard de Chardin, *The Human Phenomenon,* trans. Sarah Appleton-Weber (Portland, OR: Sussex Academic Press, 1999); Pierre Teilhard de Chardin, *The Divine Milieu* (New York: Harper & Row, 1960).

4. Henri de Lubac, SJ, *The Eternal Feminine: A Study of the Text of Teilhard de Chardin* (London: Collins, 1971), 136, cited in David Lane, *The Phenomenon of Teilhard: Prophet for a New Age* (Macon, GA: Mercer University Press, 1996), 88.

5. Robert Faricy, SJ, *All Things in Christ: Teilhard de Chardin's Spirituality* (London: Fount Paperbacks, 1981), 52, cited in Lane, *The Phenomenon of Teilhard*.

6. Pope Paul VI, cited in R. Wayne Kraft, *The Relevance of Teilhard* (Notre Dame, IN: Fides, 1968), 29.

7. Pierre Teilhard de Chardin, *Activation of Energy*, trans. René Hague (New York: Harcourt Brace Jovanovich, 1971), 239.

8. Teilhard, *Activation of Energy*, 229–44.

9. Fulton J. Sheen, *Footsteps in a Darkened Forest* (New York: Meredith, 1967), 73.

10. Pierre Teilhard de Chardin, *The Prayer of the Universe,* trans. René Hague (New York: Harper & Row, 1973), 121.

11. Teilhard, *The Human Phenomenon*, esp. 122–25.

12. Pierre Teilhard de Chardin, *The Future of Man*, trans. Norman Denny (New York: Harper Colophon Books, 1964), 75.

13. Teilhard, *The Human Phenomenon,* 27, 207.

14. Pierre Teilhard de Chardin, *Christianity and Evolution*, trans. René Hague (New York: Harcourt Brace & Co., 1969), 240.

15. Pierre Teilhard de Chardin, *Human Energy*, trans. J. M. Cohen (New York: Harvest Books/Harcourt Brace Jovanovich, 1962), 82–102.

16. I have continued this quest in *God after Einstein* (New Haven, CT: Yale University Press, forthcoming).

6. GOD

1. Pierre Teilhard de Chardin, *Christianity and Evolution*, trans. René Hague (New York: Harcourt Brace & Co.), 240.

2. Paul Tillich, *The Future of Religions*, ed. Jerald C. Brauer (New York: Harper & Row, 1966), 90–91.

3. Paul Tillich, *Systematic Theology*, 3 vols. (Chicago: University of Chicago Press, 1963), 3:19.

4. Pierre Teilhard de Chardin, *Activation of Energy,* trans. René Hague (New York: Harcourt Brace Jovanovich, 1971), 231–43.

5. Teilhard, *Christianity and Evolution*, 40.

6. Teilhard, *Christianity and Evolution*, 54.

7. Teilhard, *Christianity and Evolution*, 54.

8. Teilhard, *Christianity and Evolution*, 54.

9. Teilhard, *Christianity and Evolution*, 39.

10. See Part II of Tillich, *Systematic Theology*, 1:163–210.

11. See, for example, Reinhold Niebuhr, "Biblical Thought and Ontological Speculation in Tillich's Theology," in *The Theology of Paul Tillich*, ed. Charles W. Kegley and Robert W. Bretall (New York: Macmillan, 1952), 216–29.

12. Teilhard, *Christianity and Evolution*, 81.

13. Teilhard, *Christianity and Evolution*, 83–84.

14. In some of Tillich's sermons the sense of the future seems more alive than in the *Systematic Theology.* Tillich talks about being religiously grasped by the "coming order": "The coming order is always coming, shaking this order, fighting with it, conquering it and conquered by it. The coming order is always at hand. But one can never say: 'It is here! It is there!' One can never grasp it. But one can be grasped by it." Paul Tillich, *The Shaking of the Foundations* (New York: Charles Scribner's Sons, 1948), 27.

15. Tillich, *Systematic Theology*, 2:33–36.

16. Tillich, *Systematic Theology*, 2:118.

17. Teilhard, *Activation of Energy*, 239.

18. Teilhard, *Christianity and Evolution*, 51.

7. DESCENT

1. Peking Man (*Sinanthropus pekinensis*) lived roughly 750,000 years ago. Teilhard participated in excavations and discoveries of this species of *homo* that took place at Zhoukoudian near Beijing, China, 1929–37.

2. Cited in William P. Phipps, *Darwin's Religious Odyssey* (Harrisburg, PA: Trinity Press International, 2000), 89.

3. Holmes Rolston III, *Three Big Bangs: Matter-Energy, Life, Mind* (New York: Columbia University Press, 2010).

4. Michael Polanyi, "Life's Irreducible Structure," in *Knowing and Being*, ed. Marjorie Grene (London: Routledge and Kegan Paul, 1969), 225–39.

5. Polanyi, "Life's Irreducible Structure," 225–39.

6. Polanyi, "Life's Irreducible Structure," 225–39.

7. Francis H. C. Crick, *Of Molecules and Men* (Seattle: University of Washington Press, 1966), 10; J. D. Watson, *The Molecular Biology of the Gene* (New York: W. A. Benjamin, 1965), 67.

8. Martin Rees, *Just Six Numbers: The Deep Forces That Shape the Universe* (New York: Basic, 2000); and idem, *Our Cosmic Habitat* (Princeton, NJ: Princeton University Press, 2001).

9. Pierre Teilhard de Chardin, *The Human Phenomenon*, trans. Sarah Appleton-Weber (Portland, OR: Sussex Academic Press, 1999).

10. Pierre Teilhard de Chardin, *The Future of Man*, trans. Norman Denny (New York: Harper & Row, 1964).

11. See, for example, Richard Dawkins, *The Blind Watchmaker* (New York: W. W. Norton, 1986); and Daniel C. Dennett, *Darwin's Dangerous Idea: Evolution and the Meaning of Life* (New York: Simon & Schuster, 1995).

8. LIFE

1. Some evolutionary naturalists, citing contemporary neo-Darwinian biology, understand all living traits simply as vehicles in which populations of genes migrate from one generation to the next. See especially Richard Dawkins, *River Out of Eden* (New York: Basic Books, 1995).

2. Jerry A. Coyne, *Why Evolution Is True* (New York: Viking, 2009), 81–85.

3. David Barash, "Does God Have Back Problems Too?" *Los Angeles Times*, June 27, 2005.

4. Chet Raymo, "Intelligent Design Happens Naturally," *Boston Globe*, May 14, 2002.

5. Raymo, "Intelligent Design Happens Naturally."

6. Raymo, "Intelligent Design Happens Naturally."

7. Pierre Teilhard de Chardin, *Christianity and Evolution*, trans. René Hague (New York: Harcourt Brace & Co., 1969), 79.

8. Teilhard understood science's reduction of complex phenomena into ever simpler components as equivalent to going back in time to earlier cosmic periods when atoms and subatomic particles were still dispersed rather than linked together in the more complex forms that came later. Pierre Teilhard de Chardin, *Activation of Energy*, trans. René Hague (New York: Harcourt Brace Jovanovich, 1970), 139.

9. Barash, "Does God Have Back Problems Too?"; Richard Dawkins, *The Blind Watchmaker* (New York: W. W. Norton, 1986); Dawkins, *River Out of Eden*; Richard Dawkins, *Climbing Mount Improbable* (New York: W. W. Norton, 1996); Daniel C. Dennett, *Darwin's Dangerous Idea: Evolution and the Meaning of Life* (New York: Simon & Schuster, 1995).

10. Peter W. Atkins, *The 2nd Law: Energy, Chaos, and Form* (New York: Scientific American Books, 1994), 200.

11. Teilhard, *Activation of Energy*, 239.

12. Pierre Teilhard de Chardin, *The Heart of Matter*, trans. René Hague (New York: Harcourt Brace Jovanovich, 1978), 18.

13. Pierre Teilhard de Chardin, *Writings in Time of War*, trans. René Hague (New York: Harper & Row, 1965), 14–71.

14. Teilhard, *The Heart of Matter*, 27.

15. Teilhard, *The Heart of Matter*, 15–79.

16. Teilhard, *Activation of Energy*, 139.

17. Pierre Teilhard de Chardin, *Letters from a Traveler*, trans. René Hague et al. (New York: Harper & Row, 1962), 101.

18. What follows can be no more than the sparest of samplings. For fuller development, see John F. Haught, *The New Cosmic Story: Inside Our Awakening Universe* (New Haven, CT: Yale University Press, 2017); and idem, *Making Sense of Evolution: Darwin, God, and the Drama of Life* (Louisville, KY: Westminster John Knox Press, 2010).

19. See Thomas Berry, *The Dream of the Earth* (San Francisco: Sierra Club Books, 1988), 79.

20. See, for example, Alfred North Whitehead, *Adventures of Ideas* (New York: The Free Press, 1967), 252–96.

21. Pierre Teilhard de Chardin, *Human Energy*, trans. J. M. Cohen (New York: Harvest Books/Harcourt Brace Jovanovich, 1962), 29.

22. Pierre Teilhard de Chardin, *How I Believe*, trans. René Hague (New York: Harper & Row, 1969), 43–44.

23. Teilhard, *How I Believe*, 35.

9. SUFFERING

1. Some writers do not attribute "suffering" to nonhuman animals, but instead attribute to them only "pain." However, I consider the distinction somewhat arbitrary and unnecessarily anthropocentric.

2. Nora Barlow, ed., *The Autobiography of Charles Darwin* (New York: Harcourt, 1958), 88–89.

3. However, as we now realize, viruses and other kinds of disease, such as hypertension, can invade organisms painlessly, so life's warning systems, like other evolutionary adaptations, are not perfect. See John Hick, *Evil and the God of Love* (Norfolk, England: The Fontana Library, 1968), 333–38.

4. See Charles Sherrington, *Man on His Nature* (Cambridge: Cambridge University Press, 1951), 266.

5. Richard Dawkins, *River Out of Eden* (New York: Basic Books, 1995), 131.

6. Dawkins, *River Out of Eden*, 133.

7. Among recent attempts to understand theologically the suffering of sentient life, John Hick's *Evil and the God of Love* is impressive, but his theodicy is not deeply informed by evolutionary biology.

8. Biologists often employ teleological language in their characterization of evolutionary adaptations, but for them this is not indicative of any wider purpose in nature. However, the question of teleology in life is still being debated. See Michael Ruse, *Darwin and Design: Does Evolution Have a Purpose* (Cambridge, MA: Harvard University Press, 2003).

9. See, for example, E. O. Wilson, *Consilience: The Unity of Knowledge* (New York: Knopf, 1998).

10. Loyal Rue, *By the Grace of Guile: The Role of Deception in Natural History and Human Affairs* (New York: Oxford University Press, 1994), 82–107.

11. Pascal Boyer, *Religion Explained: The Evolutionary Origins of Religious Thought* (New York: Basic Books, 2001); Scott Atran, *In Gods We Trust: The Evolutionary Landscape of Religion* (New York: Oxford University Press, 2002); Daniel Dennett, *Breaking the Spell: Religion as a Natural Phenomenon* (New York: Viking, 2006).

12. Atran, *In Gods We Trust*, 15.

13. Teilhard even wanted to expand scientific method beyond its usual focus on objectifiable data, so that it would embrace both the inside and

outside aspects of nature. I believe this was a strategic mistake methodologically, but it is only fair to point out that his reason for doing so was to ensure that empirically minded thinkers should not leave out any aspect of nature, including what cannot be fully objectified. Teilhard cannot be blamed for seeking a wider empiricism than modern science practices.

14. Matt Ridley, *The Red Queen: Sex and the Evolution of Human Nature* (New York: Penguin Books, 1993), 92–93.

15. Ridley, *The Red Queen*, 94.

16. Ridley, *The Red Queen*.

17. See John Bowker, *Is Anybody Out There?* (Westminster, MD: Christian Classics, 1988), 9–18.

18. See Chapter 5 above.

19. One could also ask whether the neo-Darwinian notion of adaptation has *fully* explained why life has had a tendency to *complexify* at all, especially since simple forms of life, like bacteria, have proven to be quite adaptive and persistent in time without ever becoming complex enough to suffer.

20. This point is implied in many of Teilhard's writings, most explicitly in Pierre Teilhard de Chardin, *Christianity and Evolution*, trans. René Hague (New York: Harcourt Brace & Co., 1969).

21. Teilhard, *Christianity and Evolution*, 40.

22. Even in the Adamic myth, however, the figure of the serpent represents the intuition that evil is more than a human product. Paul Ricoeur, *The Conflict of Interpretations: Essays in Hermeneutics*, ed. Don Ihde (Evanston, IL: Northwestern University Press), 294–95.

23. Ricoeur, *The Conflict of Interpretations*.

24. See Teilhard, *Christianity and Evolution*, 81.

25. Teilhard, *Christianity and Evolution*.

26. Here I am summarizing a theme that recurs especially in Teilhard's essays in *Christianity and Evolution*.

27. Pierre Teilhard de Chardin, *The Future of Man*, trans. Norman Denny (New York: Harper Colophon Books, 1964), 72.

28. Gerd Theissen, *The Open Door*, trans. John Bowden (Minneapolis: Fortress Press, 1991), 161–67.

29. John Hick, in a manner similar to Friedrich Schleiermacher, tries to salvage the notion of an original human perfection by redefining perfection to mean having the *possibilities* for development (*Evil and the God of*

Love, 225–41). But the definition of perfection is the "full actualizing of possibilities." And from all that evolutionists can see, humans have always been part of a universe, in which life feeds on life and in which suffering and death are pervasive, one in which the world's possibilities are presently far from fully actualized.

10. THOUGHT

1. Pierre Teilhard de Chardin, *The Human Phenomenon*, trans. Sarah Appleton-Weber (Portland, OR: Sussex Academic Press, 1999), 3–7.

2. See B. Alan Wallace, *The Taboo of Subjectivity: Toward a New Science of Consciousness* (New York: Oxford University Press, 2000).

3. Thomas Nagel, *Mind and Cosmos: Why the Materialist Neo-Darwinian Conception of Nature Is Almost Certainly False* (New York: Oxford University Press, 2012).

4. "Letter to W. Graham, July 3, 1881," in *The Life and Letters of Charles Darwin*, ed. Francis Darwin (New York: Basic Books, 1959), 285.

5. In Michael Chorost, "Where Thomas Nagel Went Wrong," *Chronicle of Higher Education*, May 13, 2013.

6. Simon Blackburn, "Thomas Nagel: A Philosopher Who Confesses to Finding Things Bewildering," *The New Statesman,* November 8, 2012.

7. In Chorost, "Where Thomas Nagel Went Wrong."

8. In Chorost, "Where Thomas Nagel Went Wrong."

9. I am referring here, for example, to John R. Searle, *Mind: A Brief Introduction* (Oxford: Oxford University Press, 2004), 135–36; Steven Pinker, *The Blank Slate: The Modern Denial of Human Nature* (New York: Penguin Books, 2002); Owen Flanagan, *The Problem of the Soul: Two Visions of Mind and How to Reconcile Them* (New York: Basic Books, 2002); and Daniel C. Dennett, *Consciousness Explained* (New York: Little Brown, 1991).

10. Teilhard, *The Human Phenomenon*, 3–7.

11. Pierre Teilhard de Chardin, *Activation of Energy*, trans. René Hague (New York: Harcourt Brace Jovanovich, 1970), 132.

12. Teilhard, *Activation of Energy*, 131–32.

13. For an extended attempt to do so, see John F. Haught, *Resting on the Future: Catholic Theology for an Unfinished Universe* (New York: Bloomsbury Press, 2015).

14. For example, Pinker, *The Blank Slate*; Flanagan, *The Problem of the Soul*; and Dennett, *Consciousness Explained*.

15. Teilhard, *The Human Phenomenon*, 22.

16. Pierre Teilhard de Chardin, *Human Energy*, trans. J. M. Cohen (New York: Harcourt Brace Jovanovich, 1969), 25.

17. Teilhard, *Human Energy*, 21.

18. Teilhard, *Human Energy*, 22–23.

19. "If the cosmos were basically material, it would be physically incapable of containing man. Therefore, we may conclude (and this is the first step) that it is in its inner being made *of spiritual stuff*" (Teilhard, *Human Energy*, 119–20).

20. Pierre Teilhard de Chardin, "The Mass on the World," in Thomas M. King, *Teilhard's Mass: Approaches to "The Mass on the World"* (New York: Paulist Press, 2005), 145–58.

21. This point is developed most fully throughout Teilhard's *The Human Phenomenon*.

11. RELIGION

1. Astrophysics, for example, has demonstrated that the Big Bang universe has been physically and mathematically disposed from the start to give rise eventually to what I have been calling subjectivity. A usually ignored outcome of the general emergence of subjectivity in the cosmic story is that of religious awareness.

2. David Christian, *Maps of Time: An Introduction to Big History* (Berkeley and Los Angeles: University of California Press, 2004). See also Cynthia Stokes Brown, *Big History: From the Big Bang to the Present* (New York: New Press, 2007); Eric Chaisson, *Epic of Evolution: Seven Ages of the Cosmos* (New York: Columbia University Press, 2007); Brian Swimme and Thomas Berry, *The Universe Story* (San Francisco: HarperSanFrancisco, 1992); Loyal Rue, *Everybody's Story: Wising Up to the Epic of Evolution* (Albany: State University of New York, 2000); Harold Morowitz, *The Emergence of Everything: How the World Became Complex* (Oxford: Oxford University Press, 2002); and Fred Spier, *Big History and the Future of Humanity* (Oxford: Wiley-Blackwell, 2010).

3. An exception is the work of Brian Swimme and Mary Evelyn Tucker, who are fully informed by the natural sciences but are open to

telling a richer and deeper story than science can provide all by itself. Brian Swimme and Mary Evelyn Tucker, *Journey of the Universe* (New Haven, CT: Yale University Press, 2011).

4. See especially Pierre Teilhard de Chardin, *The Human Phenomenon*, trans. Sarah Appleton-Weber (Portland, OR: Sussex Academic Press, 1999).

5. Brown's *Big History*, for example, is explicitly materialist, as are most other versions, at least implicitly. Materialism cannot say anything meaningful about the inside story of the universe because it officially denies that subjectivity even exists.

6. E. O. Wilson, *Consilience: The Unity of Knowledge* (New York: Knopf, 1998); Loyal Rue, *By the Grace of Guile: The Role of Deception in Natural History and Human Affairs* (New York: Oxford University Press, 1994).

7. Daniel Dennett, as interviewed in John Brockman, *The Third Culture* (New York: Touchstone, 1995), 187.

8. Alfred North Whitehead is one of the few scientifically informed philosophers who allow that every mental event is just as much part of nature as outwardly observable events. See Alfred North Whitehead, *Modes of Thought* (New York: The Free Press, 1966), 148–69.

9. Alan B. Wallace, *The Taboo of Subjectivity: Toward a New Science of Consciousness* (New York: Oxford University Press, 2000).

10. Steven Pinker, "The Stupidity of Dignity," *New Republic* (May 27, 2008).

11. For a book-length development of this point, see John F. Haught, *Is Nature Enough?: Meaning and Truth in the Age of Science* (Cambridge: Cambridge University Press, 2006).

12. Alfred North Whitehead, *Science and the Modern World* (New York: The Free Press, 1925), 191–92.

12. TRANSHUMANISM

1. Joel Garreau, *Radical Evolution: The Promise and Peril of Enhancing Our Minds, Our Bodies—and What It Means to Be Human* (New York: Doubleday), 2005.

2. See, for example, N. T. Wright, *Surprised by Hope* (San Francisco: HarperOne, 2008).

3. This is a constant theme in the writings of Thomas Berry. See especially his *Dream of the Earth* (San Francisco: Sierra Club Books, 1988);

see also my critique of Berry in *The Promise of Nature* (Mahwah, NJ: Paulist Press, 1993), 104–6.

4. Here I have in mind, for example, some tendencies in the writings of Pierre Teilhard de Chardin. However, I do not wish to imply that Teilhard is a perfect exemplar of this second type.

5. Pierre Teilhard de Chardin often talks about evolution as a process of creating "more-being." See *Activation of Energy*, trans. René Hague (New York: Harcourt Brace Jovanovich, 1970), 231–43; and *How I Believe*, trans. René Hague (New York: Harper & Row, 1969), 42.

6. Michael Polanyi, *The Tacit Dimension* (Garden City, NY: Doubleday Anchor Books, 1967); idem, "Life's Irreducible Structure," in *Knowing and Being*, ed. Marjorie Grene (Chicago: University of Chicago Press, 1969), 225–39.

7. Michael Polanyi, *Personal Knowledge* (New York: Harper Torchbooks, 1964).

8. Bernard Lonergan, *Insight: A Study of Human Understanding*, 3rd ed. (New York: Philosophical Library, 1965), 72; John F. Haught, *Is Nature Enough? Meaning and Truth in the Age of Science* (Cambridge: Cambridge University Press, 2008).

9. See Alan B. Wallace, *The Taboo of Subjectivity: Toward a New Science of Consciousness* (New York: Oxford University Press, 2000).

10. Holmes Rolston III, *Three Big Bangs: Matter-Energy, Life, Mind* (New York: Columbia University Press, 2010), 41–88.

13. CRITICISM

1. George Barbour, *In the Field with Teilhard de Chardin* (New York: Herder and Herder, 1965).

2. Pierre Teilhard de Chardin, *The Heart of Matter*, trans. René Hague (New York: Harcourt Brace Jovanovich, 1978), 84–102.

3. Jacques Monod, *Chance and Necessity: An Essay on the Natural Philosophy of Modern Biology*, trans. Austryn Wainhouse (New York: Knopf, 1971), 32; Daniel Dennett, *Darwin's Dangerous Idea: Evolution and the Meaning of Life* (New York: Simon & Schuster, 1995); Peter Medawar, "Review of Teilhard de Chardin's *The Phenomenon of Man*," *Mind* 70 (1961): 99–106.

4. Harold J. Morowitz, *The Kindly Dr. Guillotin: And Other Essays on Science and Life* (Washington, DC: Counterpoint, 1997), 26–27.

5. Pierre Teilhard de Chardin, *The Human Phenomenon*, trans. Sarah Appleton-Weber (Portland, OR: Sussex Academic Press, 1999), 1.

6. Ian Barbour, "Five Ways to Read Teilhard," *The Teilhard Review* 3 (1968): 3–20.

7. Teilhard, *The Human Phenomenon*, 23–24.

8. Teilhard, *The Human Phenomenon*, 23–24.

9. Teilhard, *The Human Phenomenon*, 6.

10. For example, Jacques Monod. His book *Chance and Necessity* combines Cartesian dualism with French existentialism and modern mechanism as the only "objective" way of understanding evolution. Subjectivity has no real existence according to Monod.

11. Teilhard, *The Human Phenomenon*, 109–63.

12. Teilhard, *The Human Phenomenon*, 22–32.

13. Teilhard, *The Human Phenomenon*, 3. If it appears to the reader that I have been employing the verb *to see* excessively throughout this book, it is only because Teilhard has given to *seeing* a richer meaning than it ordinarily has. To substitute other terms might cause us to overlook the epistemological breadth that Teilhard gives to the verb.

14. Ian G. Barbour, *Religion and Science: Historical and Contemporary Issues* (San Francisco: HarperSanFrancisco, 1997), 103.

15. Barbour, *Religion and Science*, 194.

16. Alfred North Whitehead, *Process and Reality*, ed. David Ray Griffin and Donald W. Sherburne (New York: The Free Press, 1978).

17. John P. Slattery, "Dangerous Tendencies of Cosmic Theology: The Untold Legacy of Teilhard de Chardin," *Philosophy and Theology* 29, no. 1 (December 2016).

18. John P. Slattery, "Pierre Teilhard de Chardin's Legacy of Eugenics and Racism Can't Be Ignored," *Religion Dispatches,* May 21, 2018. I encourage readers to look at this shorter article.

19. I have summarized this new eco-theological emphasis in John F. Haught, *The Promise of Nature* (Mahwah, NJ: Paulist Press, 1993).

ACKNOWLEDGMENTS

I want to express my gratitude to Robert Ellsberg and Paul McMahon at Orbis Books for their encouragement and expertise in helping me complete this book. In writing it, I have borrowed, adapted, rearranged, and updated material discussed in previous lectures and essays:

The Introduction draws, in part, on my chapter "Pierre Teilhard de Chardin: Communion with God through the Earth," in *Reclaiming Catholicism: Treasures Old and New*, ed. Thomas Groome and Michael Daley (Maryknoll, NY: Orbis Books, 2010), 93–98.

Chapter 2 is adapted, in part, from my chapter "Teilhard de Chardin: Theology for an Unfinished Universe," in *From Teilhard to Omega: Co-creating an Unfinished Universe*, ed. Ilia Delio (Maryknoll, NY: Orbis Books, 2014), 7–23.

Chapter 3 is adapted, in part, from Chapter 5 of my book *Christianity and Science* (Maryknoll, NY: Orbis Books, 2014), 65–81.

Chapter 4 is adapted, in part, from my article "Teilhard, Science, and the Basis of Obligation," *Grace and Truth: A Journal of Catholic Reflection for Southern Africa* 22 (August 2005): 54–67.

Chapter 5 borrows from my chapter "To Women and Men of Science: Science, Spirituality, and Vatican II," in *Vatican II: A Universal Call to Holiness*, ed. Anthony J. Ciorra and Michael W. Higgins (New York: Paulist Press, 2012), 150–65.

Chapter 6 is based partly on my lecture "In Search of a God for Evolution: Paul Tillich and Pierre Teilhard de Chardin," American Teilhard Association, 2002.

Chapter 7 is adapted and revised liberally in part from my article "Human Specificity after Darwin," in *Darwinismes et spécificité de l'humain*, ed. B. Bourgine, B. Feltz, P-J. Laurent, and P. Van den Bosch de Aguilar (Louvain-la-neuve: Harmaton/ Academia, 2012), 51–66; and in part from "Human Evolution," in *The Blackwell Companion to Science and Christianity*, ed. Alan Padgett (New York: Cambridge University Press, 2012), 295–305 (used with permission).

Chapter 8 is in part adapted and revised from my lecture "Darwin, Teilhard, and the Drama of Life," American Teilhard Association, 2011.

Chapter 9 is adapted and revised in part from "Teilhard and the Question of Life's Suffering," in *Rediscovering Teilhard's Fire,* ed. Kathleen Duffy, SSJ (Philadelphia: St. Joseph University Press, 2010), 53–68.

Chapter 10 adapts and revises portions of "Teilhard de Chardin, Thomas Nagel, and *Journey of the Universe,*" in *Living Cosmology: Christian Responses to Journey of the Universe*, ed. Mary Evelyn Tucker and John Grim (Maryknoll, NY: Orbis Books, 2016), 73–80; and "Darwin's Nagging Doubt," *Commonweal* 140, no. 16 (October 11, 2013): 9–11.

Chapter 11 borrows in part from my lecture "Teilhard, Big History, and Religion: A Look Inside," American Teilhard Association, 2015. An expanded version of this chapter's argument may be found in my book *The New Cosmic Story: Inside Our Awakening Universe* (New Haven, CT: Yale University Press, 2017).

Chapter 12 is in great measure an adaptation and revision of my "Trans-humanism and the Anticipatory Universe," in *Humanity on the Threshold: Religious Perspectives on Trans-humanism*, ed. John C. Haughey and Ilia Delio (Washington DC: Council for Research in Values and Philosophy, 2014).

Chapter 13 borrows in part from "Trashing Teilhard," *Commonweal* 146, no. 3 (February 8, 2019): 7–9; and in part from my essay "Seeing the Universe: Ian Barbour and Teilhard de Chardin," in *Fifty Years in Science and Religion: Ian G. Barbour and His Legacy,* ed. Robert Russell (London: Ashgate, 2005), 301–11.

INDEX

prescientific understanding of, 12
Morowitz, Harold, 43–44, 212

Nagel, Thomas, 164, 169, 171
　animal consciousness, on the inability to share, 150
　materialist metaphysics, on the problem of, 162–63, 165
　Mind and Cosmos, 162, 166
　the universe, on the intelligibility of, 172
natural selection, 105, 149
　in the analytical vision, 136–37
　evolution through, 55, 110
　"gene's eye" perspective, 109
　impersonality of, 54, 70, 108, 118, 122
　incremental changes, working through, 123–24
　scientific vision of nature, Christian thinkers ignoring, 119
　suffering, providing explanation for, 153
naturalism
　atomic explanation for all, reliance on, 36
　Darwinian naturalists, 104, 143, 148, 157
　materialist naturalists, 167, 168, 169
　supra-naturalism as weakening Christianity, 89
　See also scientific naturalism
nature, 71, 85, 112, 151, 164, 214
　atomistic philosophy of nature, 28, 130, 170
　co-creativity with nature, 197
　dispersal, sliding back to condition of, 10

divine wisdom underlying, 135
drama of nature, 50, 133, 152–53
ethics and morality, contribution to, 62, 63, 67
full potential of, being allowed to bloom, 225–26
as future-oriented, 17, 18, 78, 99, 171, 222
hierarchy within, 27, 107
humanity and nature, 120
　human consciousness and nature, 12, 166, 168, 169, 213, 217–18
　subjectivity as part of nature, 43, 66, 153, 175, 183, 204, 216
　wrongness in nature, humans adding to, 147
indifference of nature, 55, 146
laws of nature, 115, 127, 167
in metaphysics of the eternal present, 32
as ongoing/unfinished, 72, 207, 223
philosophies of nature
　materialist philosophies of nature, 25, 47, 114
　neo-Darwinian conception of nature, 162
　new story of nature in nineteenth century, 19
　pre-evolutionary understanding of nature, 22, 76
promise of nature, 206
religious responses to nature, 6, 12
　Christian response, 8, 38, 39, 48, 70, 224
　religious reverence for, 104, 198

the inside story, suffering within,
181
neo-Darwinian understanding of,
145–46
original sin, link to, 91, 135
of sentient life, 147–49
Systematic Theology (Tillich), 88

Teilhard de Chardin, Pierre
Christian perspective
as a Christian evolutionist, 12,
105
as a Christian thinker, 218–23
as a Jesuit, 17–18, 43, 88, 98,
220
consistence, spiritual search for, 2
cosmological perspective, 116
contemporary   Christian
thought and, 117
cosmic pessimism, addressing,
59, 85
cosmic vision, 103, 158, 166,
185
dramatic patience of, 126–27
ecological issues and, 223–26
extraterrestrial intelligence, on
the possibility of, 9
futurity perspective, 40, 79
on the essential as the Future,
99
futurist cosmology, 4, 56, 133–
34
metaphysics of the future, calling
for, 24, 99, 149, 211
spiritual joy in an unfinished
universe, 18, 72
zest for living, on the future
providing, 132
hope, nurturing sense of, 19, 20,
32, 35–38

human subjectivity, acknowledging, 67
materialism, on the analytical illusion of, 26, 28, 47, 63, 132,
170, 176
materialist critics of, 214
moral/ethical perspective
building the earth, on taking
responsibility for, 100, 219
ethical action, calling for,
55–56
morality, mixing with science
and faith, 61–65
nature perspective
fixist understanding of nature,
decrying, 22
mind and nature, vision of,
168–74
as a naturalist, 57
Nietzschean thought as suffocating, 89
as the prophet of the Internet, 7–8
scientific perspective
hyperphysics, calling for, 66
as a paleontologist, 2, 36, 38,
106
as a scientist, 44, 210–18
secular hostility toward, 25
theological perspective
awakening universe, on the
theological role of, 114
on God as Alpha and Omega,
87
"new God," calling for, 29, 189
on original sin, 90–91
theological understanding of
life, 30, 122
on universal redemption, 3
Vatican II, influence of writings
on, 14, 75–78, 187